SELF-FULFILLING PROPHECY

Jacob Neusner

SELF-FULFILLING PROPHECY

PROPHECY

Exile and Return in the History of Judaism

BEACON PRESS / BOSTON

Beacon Press
25 Beacon Street
Boston, Massachusetts 02108

Beacon Press books are published under the auspices
of the Unitarian Universalist Association
of Congregations in North America.

Library of Congress Cataloging-in-Publication Data

Neusner, Jacob, 1932–
Self-fulfilling prophecy.
Includes index.
1. Judaism—History.   2. Jews—Diaspora—History—
Philosophy.   3. Jews—Restoration—History of doctrines.
I. Title.
BM155.2.N46   1987   296'.09   86-47756
ISBN 0-8070-3606-4

FOR

ALAN THOMAS

My editor at
The University of Chicago Press

Guide, teacher, critic, partner, and friend

AND

ornament to his profession and calling
as editor to scholarly discourse

CONTENTS

ACKNOWLEDGMENTS

ix

INTRODUCTION

I

ONE

THE HISTORY OF JUDAISM: AN OVERVIEW

5

TWO

BIBLICAL JUDAISMS FOR
AN ISRAEL AT HOME
FROM 1000 TO 586 B.C.

18

THREE

THE FIRST AGE OF DIVERSITY
JUDAISMS FOR THE UNCERTAIN RESTORATION
FROM 586 B.C. TO A.D. 70

32

FOUR

THE FIRST STAGE IN THE FORMATION OF JUDAISM:
THE MISHNAH
FROM 70 TO 200

62

FIVE

THE SECOND STAGE IN THE FORMATION OF
JUDAISM: THE TALMUD AND MIDRASH-
COMPILATIONS
FROM 200 TO 600

99

SIX

THE CLASSICAL AGE OF JUDAISM
FROM 640 TO 1789

151

SEVEN

THE SECOND AGE OF DIVERSITY
JUDAISMS ON THE MODERN AND CONTEMPORARY
SCENE
FROM 1789 TO THE PRESENT

181

EPILOGUE

"AND THE LORD WAS SORRY THAT THE LORD HAD MADE HUMANITY
ON THE EARTH . . . BUT NOAH FOUND FAVOR IN THE EYES OF
THE LORD"

219

GENERAL INDEX

225

INDEX OF BIBLICAL AND TALMUDIC REFERENCES

229

ACKNOWLEDGMENTS

My field theory of the history of Judaism from the beginning to the present rests on a number of completed works, the following in particular: *Foundations of Judaism: Method, Teleology, Symbol* (Philadelphia: Fortress Press, 1983–1985) I-III, *Judaism in the Matrix of Christianity* (Philadelphia: Fortress Press, 1986), *Judaism and Christianity in the Age of Constantine* (Chicago: University of Chicago Press, 1987) and *Death and Birth of Judaism* (New York: Basic Books, 1987). But, as these opening remarks make clear to readers familiar with the other works, this book makes its own point, which is fresh and sustained on its own lines of exposition and argument.

Let me acknowledge those whose conversation and criticism have stimulated and shaped my imagination: William Scott Green, University of Rochester; Jonathan Z. Smith, University of Chicago; Calvin Goldscheider, Ernest S. Frerichs, and Wendell S. Dietrich, Brown University. Many of my best ideas I owe to them; they know which ones. At Beacon Press I owe thanks to my friend and gracious editor, Wendy Strothman, and her thoroughly professional staff.

Jacob Neusner

Providence, Rhode Island
July 28, 1986. My fifty-fourth birthday.

INTRODUCTION

But the serpent said to the woman, "You will not
die, for God knows that when you eat of it your
eyes will be opened and you will be like God. . . ."

GENESIS 3:5

". . . like God" [means] *creators of worlds.*

RASHI (R. SOLOMON ISAAC, 1040–1105)

A Judaism is a system made up of a world view, a way of life, and a
social group that defines its life through that world view and lives in
accord with the descriptions of that way of life. Through time there
have been many Judaisms, that is, many Judaic systems that have defined for Jews the way they should live and understand their world.
These Judaisms have not unfolded in a linear pattern, one leading to the
next, nor have they stood in a continuous and incremental relationship
to one another, one building on the ruins of the last. Rather each took
shape on its own, identifying a critical question and presenting a self-
evidently valid answer to that question. For justification all referred
back to a remote and continuous past; although none could actually
trace itself back in a linear path to "Sinai," that is, to the moment of
God's revelation.

But all Judaic systems have recapitulated a single experience: the
exile and return suffered by some Jews between 586 and 450 B.C. In
586 B.C. the Judaeans of the land of Israel witnessed the destruction of
their capital, Jerusalem, their government, and their temple. Some of
them—mainly the political classes and some other useful populations—were removed from Jerusalem and brought to the victors' country, Babylonia, in present-day Iraq. At that time the exiles drew together
whatever stories, laws, prophecies, and other writings they had inherited out of their past in the land of Israel and produced the Pentateuch,
that is, the Five Books of Moses: Genesis, Exodus, Leviticus, Numbers,
and Deuteronomy. For what they called "three generations," these Jews
lived in Babylonia. In the mid-sixth century, their Babylonian captors
lost a war with the Iranians under the emperor Cyrus, who came from
Persia, in the southwestern corner of Iran. Cyrus and his successor

reversed the policy of the former empire and permitted the various exile groups to return to their homes. Then around 450 B.C., Ezra, a Jewish viceroy for Jerusalem appointed by the Iranian government, took up his duties and rebuilt the Temple of that city. A small number of the Jews who had settled in Babylonia as exiles went with Ezra and resettled in the Land of Israel. Most of the exiles did not return. That was the entire experience of exile and return that defined the basic structure of every Judaism that would come into being. The way exile and return became the pattern for Judaic systems to which the actual experience was alien tells us much about the power of religion not merely to respond to the world but to define it.

The Torah (together with the prophetic writings) was completed between the destruction of the Temple in 586 B.C. and the conclusion of its reconstruction in 450. The Torah preserved the judgment of the generation that first experienced the pattern that has imparted its outline on every subsequent Judaic system. In particular the Five Books of Moses—promulgated by Ezra in 450 B.C. at the climax of the restoration to Israel of its Temple and its land—made the first authoritative statement that Israel could never take its existence as permanent and unconditional. That statement was expressed in such diverse propositions of the Mosaic narrative as these: the land is not given, but promised; the promise to Israel is conditional; the land may be lost; the people may cease to be. And this all depends on what the people do. The Pentateuch captured, for perpetual restatement, the original point of resentment. As repeated by diverse Israels in various circumstances, the document has recapitulated for all Israels the original experience of alienation and reconciliation. To state the matter in one sentence:

The life of an "Israel" was never to be taken for granted but always to be received as a gift.

Each Judaism made its appearance whole and complete, presenting its own set of self-evidently true answers to ineluctable questions: who are we, where do we come from, and what are the conditions of our sustaining life? Each Judaism invented for itself such past as it found necessary, ordinarily consisting of holy books purporting to tell the story of the Judaism at hand, and therefore also to justify and validate it. We shall investigate a number of Judaisms and try to make sense of their distinct, if interrelated, ways of framing the social world of a group of Jews.

I offer what is a social theory of the history of Judaism, not a theological interpretation of the faith. I address an undifferentiated world of readers interested in what religion teaches us about humanity, not a particular readership of Jews in search of a past and an identity out of that past. Readers may expect to gain understanding of how people have not only appealed to a religious system to sort out and solve the problems of their human situation, but have also encountered in a religious system preserved in holy writ the definition of their human situation and so have become something else than what they really were or had to be. In recapitulating resentment this religion provoked and precipitated it. For there was no given to the experience of exile and restoration and no self-evident truth to the explanation attached to that experience.

The theory of religion offered here is the one first recognized in the fall of humanity, the notion that to be "like God" is to "create worlds." I refer to the statement made by the serpent at the fall of Adam and Eve. Explaining why God said the couple in the state of grace should not eat the fruit of the tree of knowledge, the snake said, it is because God knows that when you do you will become like God. The greatest exegete of Scripture in Judaism, Rashi, explained the matter, and I take his statement to be definitive. My thesis is that Judaisms create Jews' worlds. And there is a very specific Judaism that from the beginning imparted its shape and structure on all Judaisms. This pattern accounts for the character of all Judaisms that have ever flourished and predicts the structure of any Judaism that will ever come into existence:

Because the Mosaic Torah's interpretation of the diverse experiences of the Israelites after the destruction of the Temple in 586 B.C. invoked the categories of exile and return, so constructing a pattern from the experience of only a minority of the families of the Jews, in the formation of the Pentateuch, the events from 586 to 450 B.C. became for all time the definitive pattern of meaning. Consequently, whether or not the pattern agreed with their actual circumstances, Jews in diverse settings constructed their worlds in accord with that model. They have therefore perpetually rehearsed the human experience created by the original authors of the Torah in the time of Ezra. That pattern accordingly was not merely preserved and perpetuated, but itself precipitated and provoked its own replication in each succeeding age.

In so framing my general theory of the history of Judaism, I enter a dissent to a prevailing view of the origin and character of religion. Many maintain that religion is determined by extrinsic factors, for example motives of a psychological, economic, or political character. I counter that in the case of Judaism religion imparted its pattern upon the social world of Jews. The study of Judaism provides a source of interesting cases for the proposition that religion shapes the world, not the world, religion. Specifically, it is the religion of the Jews that has formed their world and framed their realities, and not their society, culture, and politics that have formed their religion.

THE HISTORY OF JUDAISM
An Overview

A Field Theory of the History of Judaism

The history of Judaism began with the destruction of the Temple and the exile of part of the population to Babylonia in 586 B.C., and the return of some of the exiles in 450 B.C. These events can be seen as the beginning of the history of Judsiasm because the experience of those few formed the pattern which Israel chose as its history. This is the lesson they claimed to learn from it: nothing is set and given and all things are a gift, land and life itself. The experience of exile and then restoration marked the group as special, different, and select.

This way of seeing things was not necessary, since the Jews who did not go into exile and those who did not come home had no reason to take the view of matters that characterized the Scripture. The land did not require the vision that imparted to it the personality that it received in Scripture: "The land will vomit you out as it did those who were here before you." Nothing in the system of Scripture—exile for reason, return as redemption—followed necessarily and logically. Everything was invented and interpreted.

But that experience of the uncertainty of the life of the group formed the pattern. With the promulgation of the "Torah of Moses" under the sponsorship of Ezra at about 450 B.C., all future Israels would refer to that formative experience as it had been set down and preserved as the pattern for Israel in the mythic terms of that "original" Israel. In that story we find the statement in which every Judaism, from then to now, found the structure of its social existence and the grammar of its intelligible message.

This brings us to the opening generalizations of the introduction:

1. No Judaism has recapitulated any other, and none has stood in a linear and incremental relationship with any prior one.

2. But all Judaisms have recapitulated that single experience of the Torah of Moses that reflected on the meaning of the events of 586–

450 B.C. selected for the composition of history and therefore its interpretation.

That experience (in theological terms) rehearsed the conditional moral existence of sin and punishment, suffering and atonement and reconciliation, and (in social terms) the uncertain and always conditional national destiny of disintegration and renewal of the group. The moment captured within the Five Books of Moses informed the attitude and viewpoint of all subsequent Israels.

This theory of the history of Judaism accounts for the character of every Judaism that has emerged through time, and, I would aver, predicts the shape of Judaisms that will come into existence in the future. My theory points to a particular selection and interpretation of events of a distinctive sort, the character of which imposed its shape upon all Judaisms that followed it, then to now. These events are understood to stand for exile, identified with everything people find wrong with their life, and return, marking what people hope will happen to set matters right. So each Judaism identified what was wrong with the present and promised to make things tolerable now and perfect in the indeterminate future. A Judaism therefore has stood for a situation to escape, overcome, and survive. The repeated pattern of finding the world out of kilter ("exile"), but then making it possible to live for the interim in that sort of world has perpetuated profound resentment: why here? why us? why now? And, indeed, why not always, everywhere, and forever? By recapitulating this particular resentment, each Judaism has related to all other Judaic systems.[1]

I recognize that the usage, *a Judaism,* or *Judaisms,* violates accepted language rules. When people use the word Judaism, they use it only in the singular and they assume they refer to a single religious tradition extending (if not from creation) from Sinai to the present. Instead in this book I refer not only to *a Judaism,* but, more commonly, to a Judaic *system.* That is to say, I define in categories not broadly understood the genus of which I speak—a religion—as well as the species of that genus—a Judaism. Specifically I understand by a religious system three things that are one:

---

1. That is the argument of my *Death and Birth of Judaism* (New York: Basic Books, 1987). There I argue that no Judaism stood in a linear relationship with any other, none formed an increment on a predecessor, and all constituted systems that, once in existence, selected for themselves an appropriate and useful past—that is, a canon of useful and authoritative texts. And that is the order: the system creates its canon. These issues play no role in the present book, although in chapter 7 I review some of the results of the other work.

1. A world view which by reference to the intersection of the supernatural and natural worlds accounts for how things are and puts them together into a cogent and harmonious picture

2. A way of life which expresses in concrete actions the world view and which is explained by that world view

3. A social group for which the world view accounts, which is defined in concrete terms by the way of life, and which therefore gives expression in the everyday world to the world view and which is defined by that way of life

A Judaic system then comprises not merely a theory—a book—distinct from social reality, but an explanation for the group ("Israel") that gives social form to the system and an account of the distinctive way of life of that group. A Judaism is not a book, and no social group took shape because people read a book and agreed that God had revealed what the book said they should do. Rather, a Judaic system derives from and focuses upon a social entity, a group of Jews who (in their minds at least) constitute not *an* Israel but *Israel.*

I imagine that a Judaic system could treat as not essential a variety of rules for the everyday life. Or it could fail to articulate elements of a world view to answer a range of questions others deem fundamental. Contemporary Judaisms do not treat as urgent philosophical questions found absorbing by earlier system builders. But no Judaic system can omit a clear picture of the meaning and sense of Israel. Without an Israel, a social entity in fact and not only in doctrine, we have not a system but a book. And a book is not a Judaism, it is only a book. My choices of what to treat and what to bypass rest upon this principle of the definition of a religious system: a book is not a Judaism and a Judaism is not a book—except after the fact.[2]

How may we know one Judaism from another? When we identify Judaisms in different periods, we begin by trying to locate, in the larger group of Jews, those social entities that see themselves and are seen by others as distinct and bounded, and that present to themselves a clear account of who they are, what they do, and why they do what they do. Religion is always social, and therefore also political, a matter of what

2. The importance of this principle of selection cannot be missed. We have distinctive books that represent certain social groups, but our knowledge of those social groups is imperfect. Consequently we cannot relate the contents of a system to its context or account for the substance of a system by appeal to its circumstance. We therefore know the answers provided by a system—that is, the contents of the book—but do not have a clear picture of the questions or the political or social forces that made those questions urgent and inescapable in that place and time.

people do together, not just what they believe in the privacy of their hearts. And a Judaism for its part addresses a social group, an Israel, by claiming that the group is not merely an Israel but Israel, Israel in its ideal form, Israel's saving remnant, the state of Israel, the next step in the history ("progress") of Israel, but always Israel. So a Judaism, or a Judaic system, constitutes a clear and precise account of a social group, the way of life and world view of a group of Jews.

The theory denies there is now, or ever was, only one Judaism. But there is a single definitive human experience which each Judaism reworked in its own circumstance and context. In a broader sense, then, my theory of the history of a particular religious tradition that comprises a variety of expressions may be summarized in the propositions that generalize on the case of Judaisms:

1. No religious system (within a given set of related religions) recapitulates any other.

2. But all religious systems (within a given set) recapitulate resentment, that obsessive and troubling point of origin that the group wishes to explain, transcend, and transform.[3]

From Judaisms to Judaism

To be an Israel—the social component of a Judaism—has meant to ask what it means to be Israel. The original pattern meant that an Israel would be a social group whose existence had been called into question and affirmed, and therefore would always be called into question and remained perpetually to be affirmed. Every Judaism made its own distinctive statement of the generative and critical resentment contained within that questioning of the given, that deep understanding of the uncertain character of the existence of the group in its normal location and under circumstances of permanence that seemed to characterize the life of every group other than Israel. What for everyone else was a given, for Israel was a gift. What all the nations knew as how things *must* be, Israel understood as how things *might not be:* exile and loss, alienation and resentment; but instead of annihilation, there was renewal, restoration, reconciliation, and redemption. So the experience beginning in 586 B.C. and ending about 450 B.C., written down in the

3. Since all Christianities share the same books—the Torah—that for Judaisms portray the pattern experience of exile and return, we have to wonder how the pattern of recapitulated resentment made its mark on the other family of biblical religious systems. When the comparative study of religions comes into being, that will be an interesting question for reflection.

Torah of Moses, made its mark. That pattern has defined for all Israels over all time that matter of resentment: leaving home and coming home.

To understand these histories of Judaisms, we should imagine a people that tells its story through dance, as do many peoples of Africa, or through ornately carved works of art, as do many peoples of Polynesia and Melanesia. Taking up our position at the edge of the village, we should see jump-dancers of East Africa, each group leaping in its intricate patterns. To us they all appear to jump alike. But to them each set of dancers establishes its own rhythm—jumping here, swirling there. Now if—to continue the analogy—we grasp what is happening, we realize that the dancers' sets each forms its own dance, that is to say, its own story of who it is. Our eye sees the whole, and, untutored, perceives only the generality. But the educated eye discerns the distinct patterns of steps and movements and grasps the distinctions that make important differences. And that eye grasps that it is no village at all, but a meeting of many villages. So too the ignorant vision understands Maori art as a sequence of abstract patterns, but *te Maori* read the story of their twenty-four peoples and their original canoes, each told in its pattern, through its narrative of art. In the Auckland Museum we see the assembly that forms of the whole *te Maori,* but the Maori know better than that.

Jews preserve the many-times-told stories of their groups not through dance nor through art. They create Judaisms, each for its occasion, and then those to whom *a* Judaism is Judaism uncover the continuity and connection between their Judaism and Judaism. Words, not dance and not wood-working—these form the signs and signals of the story. And the words, read in context, form sentences, paragraphs, messages, and Judaisms, each with its full and complete account of the world and what it means, the way of life and how one lives if, for an Israel. What is the one systematic trait that marks all Judaisms and sets them apart from all the dances of the dancers and all the carvings of the carvers? It is the perpetual asking of the question that other social groups seem to have answered for themselves for all time: who are we? That trait of self-consciousness, that incapacity to accept the group as a given, is the one thing draws together Judaisms from beginning to end. Jews' persistent passion for self-definition has characterized all Judaisms. The jump-rhythms of all the jumpers, the swirl of all the swirling lines, the incisions of the wood carvers and the tattoos on all the faces—these find their counterpart in Jews' obsessive self-consciousness about their group. What others take as the given, the Jews perceive as the received, the special, the extraordinary.

That wonderment about who we are and what we mean presents a puzzle, since it is not clear why Jews should not yet have found their answer. For many the answer lies in the distant past, and the explanation derives from the story of what happened. But that is an evasion, for history answers no questions that we have not identified as questions to be answered by history. Just as in logic an argument based on the reasoning, that because one thing came before the other, therefore one thing caused the other, is self-evidently false, so too in ordinary affairs the correctness of events does not rest on temporal sequence.

If, therefore, a mere narrative of history is meant to serve the purpose of explanation, it is because of an evasion on the one side and a deep misunderstanding of the character of Judaisms on the other. The evasion is the easier side to perceive: people find it easier to recite than to explain. The misunderstanding of Judaisms derives from accepting as fact the claim of a Judaism to constitute Judaism: as it was in the beginning, as it is, and as it will be through time. The story of Judaism constitutes a profound theological judgment. It does not record how things really were. But the selections each system makes from the rubbish heap of history—the holy books, the customs and the ceremonies, have always followed the inner logic of the system, which made its choices and pronounced its canon.

Not Linear History but Singular Systems

Every Judaic system has taken as urgent a set of questions which demanded answers. And, in one way or another, those questions have persisted as the center of system after system. They have turned on the identity of the group, and rested on the premise that the group's existence represented a choice and not a necessity. That obsessive self-awareness has masked a deeper experience that evidently defined for one generation after another and for one group of Jews after another the ineluctable question that, collectively, the group had to answer. The Jews' perplexity about who they are presents a surprise and a puzzle.[4]

Since the formative pattern represented by the destruction of the first Temple of Jerusalem in 586 and the return to Zion, the building of the second Temple of Jerusalem, and the writing down of the Torah im-

---

4. By contrast, the Chinese do not obsessively ask, Who is a Chinese? and I have never heard an Armenian debate on the Armenian identity crisis, but the Government of the State of Israel faces collapse every time it tries to decide who is a Jew.

posed that perpetual self-conscious uncertainty, treating the life of the group as conditional and discontinuous, Jews have asked themselves who they were and have invented Judaisms to answer that question. Accordingly, no circumstances have permitted Jews to take for granted their existence as a group. Looking back on Scripture and its message, Jews have ordinarily treated as special, conditional, and therefore uncertain what other groups enjoyed as unconditional and simply given. Why the paradigm renewed itself is clear: this view of matters generated expectations that could not be met, and hence created resentment—and then it provided the comfort and hope that made possible coping with that resentment. Promising what could not be delivered, then providing solace for the consequent disappointment, the system precipitated in age succeeding age the very conditions necessary for its own replication.

Here I propose to sort out some of the Judaisms that have recapitulated that resentment, and compare them with one another. For there have been many Judaisms, each pronouncing its world view, prescribing its way of life, and identifying the particular Israel that in its view, was Israel, bearer of the original promise of God. At this point therefore the reader must wonder why this book bears the title, "Judaism," and not "Judaisms," and speaks of past, present, future, as though I address the description of a single, linear, and incremental religion (or even continuous religious *tradition*). The reason is that I classify all Judaisms as a single species of the genus religion, for all of them used some materials in common and exhibited some traits that distinguished all of them from other species of the genus religion, making of them a single species. Specifically, and this brings us back to the point at which we began, each Judaism has retold in its own way and with its own distinctive emphases the tale of the Five Books of Moses, the story of a non-people that became a people, that had what it got only conditionally, and that could lose it all through its own sin. That was a terrifying, unsettling story for a social group to tell of itself, because it imposed acute self-consciousness and chronic insecurity upon what should have been the firm foundation of society. That is to say, the collection of diverse materials joined into a single tale on the occasion of the original exile and restoration has always also precipitated the recapitulation of the interior experience of exile and restoration—and always because of sin and atonement.

The Four Periods in the Histories of Judaisms

The histories of Judaisms may be divided into four periods. The first was *the age of diversity,* in which many Judaic systems flourished, from the period of the formation of the Hebrew Scriptures, about 586 B.C., to the destruction of the Second Temple, in A.D. 70. The second was *the formative age,* from A.D. 70 to the completion of the Talmud of Babylonia, about A.D. 600. The third was *the classical age,* from late antiquity to the nineteenth century, in which the original definition dominated the lives of the Jewish people nearly everywhere they lived. Finally came *the modern age,* from the nineteenth century to our own day, when an essentially religious understanding of what it means to be Israel, the Jewish people, came to compete among Jews with other views and other symbolic expressions of those views.

THE AGE OF DIVERSITY (586 B.C. – A.D. 70)

The age of diversity lasted nearly five hundred years, and during that time a number of different kinds of Judaisms came into being. The Judaism of the dual Torah developed and competed with those other Judaisms for Jews' loyalty. We cover this age in chapters 2 and 3.

THE FORMATIVE AGE OF JUDAISM (70–640)

The formative age began with the destruction of the Temple of Jerusalem by the Romans in A.D. 70 and ended in 640 with the Arab conquest of the Near and Middle East at the beginning of the Islamic religion. During this period the canon, or authoritative writings, took shape. The canon consisted of the one whole Torah of Moses, our rabbi, and reached Israel in two forms, that is, through two media. One was the written Torah, which the world knows as the Hebrew Scriptures or the Old Testament. During the formative age, sages selected those particular books of ancient Israel's library that Judaism would accept. During the same period the part of the Torah that came to Israel not in writing but orally, through the memory of Moses, the prophets, and the sages, down to the age at hand, also reached definition. The first of the documents that preserved the memorized and orally transmitted Torah in writing was the Mishnah; the last was the Talmud of Babylonia. In between, writings of two kinds reached authoritative status: first, amplifications and commentaries for the Mishnah, and second, the same sort of writing for Scripture. So the formative age saw the composition of a single, cogent canon that constituted Judaism, the one whole Torah of Moses our Rabbi. We deal with this age in chapters 4 and 5.

THE CLASSICAL PERIOD OF JUDAISM (640–1787)

The classical period began with the rise of Islam. The year 1787 refers to the American Constitution, which inaugurated a world in which the political and cultural setting for the Jews in Europe and America changed from what it had been under Christendom. (European readers will justifiably prefer the date of 1789, the French Revolution, for the same indication.) In the classical period a single Judaism, the one teaching the dual Torah of Sinai, came to full definition and predominated. During that time Jews worked out any important ideas or issues within the categories of the Judaism of the dual Torah. A variety of mystical ideas and practices entered Judaism and were naturalized within the Torah. Another example derived from a philosophical tradition that restated the truths of the Torah in terms of the Greek modes of thought represented by Aristotle and Plato as the Moslem philosophical schools transmitted these modes of thought to the West. In the mystical tradition the great work was the Zohar, written toward the end of the thirteenth century in Spain. In the philosophical tradition the most important figure was Maimonides, 1135–1204, who restated the whole of Judaic law and theology in a systematic and profoundly philosophical way. Both of these encompassing modes of thought, the mystical and the philosophical, transformed the one whole Torah of Moses, our rabbi, from a mythic tradition to an intensely felt and profound doctrine of the true nature of God's being, as well as a rational and intellectually rich statement of the Torah as truth. Both found an ample place within the received canon, to which each made a massive contribution of new and authoritative writings. The power of the one whole Torah, oral and written, to encompass and create its own fresh ways of life and thought testifies to the classical and definitive character of this Judaism. So mysticism and philosophy both made their contribution to the altar of the Judaism of the dual Torah. What is even more interesting is that the same original system possessed the power to define its own heresies. We see this in a rapid encounter with Karaism, the heresy that rejected the myth of the dual Torah, and Sabbateanism, the heresy that rejected the myth of the Messiah as a Torah sage. We address this epoch in chapter 6.

THE MODERN AND CONTEMPORARY SCENE (1789–)

In modern times the diversity characteristic of the period of origins has come once again to prevail. Now the symbolic system and structure of the Judaism of the dual Torah competes for the attention of Jews with other Judaic systems, on the one side, and with a wildly diverse range of symbols of other-than-Jewish origin and meaning, on the other. What of the Judaism of the dual Torah in relationship to the life of Israel, the Jewish people over time (not to be identified only with the contemporary State of Israel)? The Judaism of the dual Torah endured and flourishes today as the religion of a small group of people.

In the nineteenth century a number of other Judaic systems came into being. These included Reform Judaism, the first and most important of the Judaisms of modern times. The changes deemed Reforms involved first matters of liturgy and then important issues of doctrine. Reform took seriously the political changes that accorded to Jews the rights of citizens and demanded that they conform in important ways to the common practices of their countries of citizenship. Reform took shape in the first quarter of the nineteenth century. Later, in the middle of the century, Orthodoxy took the position that one could observe the law and also enter into the civilization of the West. Affirming the divine origin of the Torah, Orthodoxy effected a selective piety, for example affirming secular education in addition to study of the Torah. These are the two modern Judaisms of keenest interest in the unfolding of my theory of the history of Judaism.[5] It follows that the Judaic systems of the nineteenth and twentieth centuries took shape within a span of not much more than a hundred years, from somewhat before 1800 to somewhat after 1900. The weakening of the Judaism of the dual Torah and the development of competing Judaisms find exemplification in two important Judaisms in no way continuous with the received system. Zionism and American Judaism constitute not heresies of the Judaism of the dual Torah but Judaisms not defined within the terms and categories of that Torah. They form the best test of my theory of the history of Judaism, since they derive from experiences not generated by the Torah myth. And yet both Judaisms strikingly recapitulate the original pattern of exile and return—even in America, where that pattern conflicts with the political and social reality confronting the Jewish group. We deal with this period in chapter 7.

Prior to the beginning of Judaism in the pattern that prevailed, ancient Israel contributed its canon of writings to the Judaism that came to full expression after 586 B.C. But where we are heading is to the formation of the Judaism that predominated from late antiquity to

5. A third movement—called in Europe the Historical School and in America Conservative Judaism—some decades later took a middle position, affirming the Orthodox position on keeping the rules of the Torah and the Reform view of the importance of critical scholarhip. It is not critical here since it is derivative of the two modern movements that do make a difference.

modern times: the Judaism described by the canon that encompasses the dual Torah, written (Scripture) and oral (the Mishnah), and their amplifications and applications in the two Talmuds, one created in the Land of Israel and the other in Babylonia, as exegeses of the Mishnah, and the midrash compilations as exegeses of Scripture. This leap ahead will make it clear to the reader that among all Judaisms one predominates and today remains paramount, the Judaism that takes as its principal symbol the Torah in the oral and written media, as its holy figure the rabbi, as its world view the account of Israel as a holy people whom God loves and will save from the troubles of this age, and as its way of life the sanctification of Israel in this world in preparation for the age to come. The Judaism of the dual Torah, oral and written, of Israel sanctified in this world for salvation in the age to come, defined Judaism for most Jews. Everything in chapter 2 is meant to point to the original statement of that Judaic system, described in chapter 3, and to its full and complete amplification described in chapter 4.

How Judaism Began: Six Propositions

Let me conclude this overview by stating in six propositions the story of the formation of the Judaism that was a pattern for all Judaisms from late antiquity to modern times.

1. Definition: The Judaism that emerged from antiquity and thrived in Christian and Moslem lands invoked as its definitive symbol the dual Torah, part formulated and transmitted in writing (Scripture, Pentateuch), part formulated and transmitted in memory or orally (the Mishnah and its exegetical works, as well as the exegetical treatments of Scripture called midrashim).

2. History: That Judaism took shape in two distinct stages, marked by the appearance of indicative documents.

3. 70–200: The first stage was represented by the Mishnah, a philosophical law code, about A.D. 200, in consequence of the destruction of the Second Temple and the defeat of Bar Kokhba three generations later. It emphasized sanctification. The question addressed by the Mishnaic system was where and how Israel could remain holy, even without its holy city and Temple.

4. 200–600: The second stage was marked by the Talmud of the land of Israel, also called the Talmud Yerushalmi. It was an amplification and expansion of the Mishnah, in about A.D. 400, in the aftermath of the rise to political power of Christianity. It presented a dual emphasis on both sanctification and salvation. The question taken up by the

Talmudic system—the dual Torah in its first definitive statement—was when and how holy Israel would be saved, even with the world in the hands of the sibling of Israel, Esau-Christendom (and later in the power of the sibling Ishmael-Islam as well). A second Talmud, also serving to explain the Mishnah, took shape in Babylonia and was completed at about 600. This other Talmud, called the Talmud of Babylonia, or the Bavli, drew into itself a vast range of materials, treating both the Mishnah and Scripture, and presented the still definitive statement of Judaism.

5. The Dual Torah, Scripture and Mishnah, Midrash and Talmud: The Judaism of the dual Torah confronted the chronic and pressing questions of the Jews' circumstances and provided answers deemed self-evidently valid. It asked the question of the ascendancy of Esau and Ishmael and answered that holy Israel would ultimately find salvation at the end of time through its life of sanctification of the here and now. That self-evident answer to the urgent question of existence allowed the system to endure from its origin in the fourth century to the point in the eighteenth and nineteenth centuries when original circumstances addressed by that Judaism had radically changed. Then new questions, out of phase with the old, demanded new answers.

6. Components: In its first stage the Judaism of the dual Torah was an amalgam of two of the three strands of the age of diversity. Among three main choices—the messianic, the priestly, and the scribal—the Judaism of the two Torahs began with the priestly (represented by the Pharisees and their method), and the scribal (in the persons of the scribes, or sages and rabbis, and their Torah teachings). The priestly-Pharisaic strand contributed the method—the emphasis on the sanctification of the everyday. The scribal strand defined the content—Torah study, with stress on the mastery of Scripture and the application of the contents of Scripture to ordinary affairs.

The third strand, the messianic, with its emphasis on history, the nation-society as a whole, and the end of time, became important as the Judaism of the two Torahs developed in its second stage. But at the outset the definitive documents—the Mishnah and its closest relations—paid slight attention to that theme.[6] The messianic theme entered the picture when, after the conversion of Constantine, Christianity became the dominant religion of the West, from the fourth century.

---

6. That is not to suggest that the nation as a whole followed suit. Our interest is in the systemic unfolding of Judaism, and that is portrayed by the document before us. We do not know what people outside of our writings had to say on any subjects at all.

Then the messianic theme demanded attention, since Christianity laid stress on Christ as Messiah.

The vast movements of history, culminating in the enthronement of Christ as king of the world in the Roman empire, demanded a response from Israel's sages. In the Yerushalmi and in Genesis Rabbah and Leviticus Rabbah, sages of the time framed an appropriate doctrine of history and of the Messiah: the Messiah will come to Israel when Israel keeps the Torah as sages teach it. Chapter 5 tells that second chapter in the formative history of Judaism. But now we have gotten well ahead of our story. Let us go back to the starting point. Not surprisingly, it was at the destruction of a Temple,—the first Temple, in 586 B.C.—just as the period of the formation of the Judaism that was the pattern for a long time was marked by the destruction of a Temple—the second Temple, in A.D. 70. The history of Judaic systems marked its turnings at times of catastrophe, which served as occasions for renewal, just as has happened in our own day.

BIBLICAL JUDAISMS FOR AN ISRAEL AT HOME

FROM 1000 TO 586 B.C.

Judaism before Judaism: The Biblical Prelude

The Pentateuch refers to events of a long-ago past, beginning with the creation of the world, the making of man and woman, the fall of humanity through disobedience, the flood that wiped out nearly all of humanity except for Noah—progenitor of all humanity—the decline of humanity from Noah to Abraham, then the rise of humanity through Abraham, Isaac, Jacob also called Israel, and the twelve sons of Jacob, then exile in Egypt, and ultimately Sinai. There, the scriptural narrative continues, God revealed the Torah to Moses, and that revelation contained the terms of the covenant that God made with Israel, the family of Abraham, Isaac, and Jacob. The book of Genesis narrates the story of creation and of the beginnings of the family that Israel would always constitute, the children of Abraham, Isaac, and Jacob. The book of Exodus presents the story of the slavery of the children of Israel in Egypt and how God redeemed them from Egyptian bondage and brought them to Sinai, there to make a covenant with them, by which they would accept the Torah and carry out its rules. The book of Leviticus portrays the founding of the priests' service to God through the sacrifice of the produce of the holy land to which God would bring Israel, and specifies the rules and regulations governing the kingdom of priests and the holy people. The book of Numbers provides an account of the wandering in the wilderness. The book of Deuteronomy then presents a reprise of the story, a long sermon by Moses looking back on the history of Israel from the beginnings through the point of entry into the promised land, and a restatement of the rules of the covenant between Israel and God.

Every Judaism, wherever and whenever created, through the Scriptures of ancient Israel [1] traced its beginnings to the creation of the world. Following the biblical record, each system maintained that God created the world and for ten dismal and declining generations, from Adam to Noah, despaired of creation. Then for ten generations, from Noah to Abraham, God waited for humanity to acknowledge the sovereignty of the one God, creator of heaven and earth. Then came Abraham and Sarah. Abraham obeyed God's commandment to leave his home in Babylonia and to journey to the promised land. Israel therefore began with the experience of alienation: "Go from your country and your kindred and your father's house to the land that I will show you" (Gen. 12:1). Through their children, Sarah and Abraham founded Israel, the people of the Lord, to whom later on at Sinai God revealed the Torah, the complete record of God's will for humanity, starting with Israel, the Jewish people. The biblical record goes on to speak of David, the king of Israel and founder of the ruling household, from which, at the end of time, the Messiah is destined to come forth. So Judaism tells the story of the world from creation in Adam and Eve, through the revelation of the Torah at Sinai, to the redemption of humanity through the Messiah at the end of time—a picture of the world, beginning, middle, and end. That account of the history of humanity and of all creation derived from a people that traces it origins to the beginnings of time and yet thrives in the world today.

Ancient Israel—tribes of various origins—had entered the land of Canaan, which became the land of Israel, some time before 1000 B.C. We need not rehearse the familiar tale of how these diverse groups all were described as having formed the family of a single man, Abraham, and his wife, Sarah, through their son, Isaac, and his wife Rebecca, and their grandson, Jacob, and his wives, Leah and Rachel, and their co-wives. Nor do we have to remind ourselves about the story of how the children of this family went down to Egypt on account of a famine, multiplied

1. In Christianity, the Old Testament; in Judaism, Tanakh, that is Torah, referring to the Five Books of Moses, Nebiim, the Hebrew for the prophets, inclusive of the historical books of Joshua through Kings, and Ketuvim, the Hebrew for writings, referring to Psalms, Prophets, Job, and other books. In general I shall refer to the ancient Israelite scriptures as "the Old Testament," simply because that is familiar to most readers. For the same reason, I shall use B.C. and A.D., because they are common, rather than the theologically neutral B.C.E., before the Common Era, and C.E., Common (=Christian) Era sometimes used in Judaic scholarly writing. I do not mean to give offense to my fellow Jews, but I do wish to make as familiar and common as possible what is, in fact, an unfamiliar religion, and by removing the unfamiliar usages of the faith and replacing them with those nearly universally recognized, I think I ease the burden.

there, became enslaved, and, led by Moses, under God's orders, escaped
to the wilderness of Sinai, there to receive the revelation of God for the
founding of their nation and the ordering of their life. We can dispense
with a recounting, moreover, of the single account of what was in fact a
diverse and various process of conquering the land and settling in it.
None of this has any bearing on the history of Judaism, except as a
statement in linear and incremental terms of a set of fables, each with its
own point of origin, each taken out of its original context and placed
into that larger cogent, linear, and incremental setting in which we now
receive them all.

In fact, in Scripture we deal with a composite of materials, each with
its own viewpoint and traits of mind. It was only after the destruction of
the First Temple of Jerusalem in 586 B.C. that the Torah, that is, the Five
Books of Moses, came into being, a pastiche of received stories, some
old, some new, all revised for the purposes of the final authors. It was in
the aftermath of the destruction of that Temple and the later restoration
of the exiles to the land that that authors wrote of the origins of Israel,
the Jewish people. In light of Israel's ultimate destiny, which the authors
took to be the loss and restoration of the land, the origins of the people
in its land took on their cogent meaning. Israel then began its acquisi-
tion of the land through Abraham, and attained its identity as a people
through the promise of the land in the covenant of Sinai, and the entry
into the land under Joshua. Israel's history then formed the story of how,
because of its conduct on the land, Israel lost its land, first in the north,
then in the south—despite the prophets' persistent warnings. From the
exile in Babylonia in 586 B.C., the authors of the Torah recast Israel's
history into the story of the conditional existence of the people; their
existence was measured in their possession of the land on condition of
God's favor. Everything depended on carrying out a contract: do this,
get that, do not do this, do not get that—and nothing formed a given
and nothing was unconditional. The task of the authors demanded the
interpretation of the conditions of the present, and their message in
response to the uncertainty of Israel's life beyond exile and restoration
underlined the uncertainty of that life.

The record of the Hebrew Scriptures, called in Christianity the Old
Testament and in Judaism the written [part of the] Torah, came together only after the end of the period of which they speak. Most of the
writings in the Hebrew Scriptures describe events of the period before
586 B.C., but they were written afterward in the form in which we have
them. What made that year (treated as a symbol for its century) important was also what made people look backward for an explanation of

events—the destruction of the Temple in Jerusalem. The Temple, a place of sacrifice to God of the natural produce of the land—grain, wine, and meat—on altar fires, had been built four centuries earlier. The writings from pre-586 Israel that were drawn together in the Pentateuch, as well as in important writings of history and prophecy—Joshua, Judges, Samuel, Kings, Isaiah 1–39, Jeremiah, Ezekiel, and some shorter works—all were meant to explain what had ultimately happened: the destruction of the Israelite state, including its Temple, monarchy, and priesthood, in 586 B.C.

The Pentateuchal formation and explanation of history made two important points.

First, the Pentateuchal traditions, now drawn together into a single unitary and (more or less) continuous, if repetitive, account, specified that Israel stood in a contractual relationship with God. God had revealed the Torah to Israel, and the Torah contained God's will for Israel. If Israel kept the Torah, God would bless the people, and if not—as Leviticus 26 and Deuteronomy 28 clearly explained—God would exact punishment for violation of the covenant.

Second, the prophetic writings emphasized that God shaped history—those particular events that made a difference—in a pattern that bore deep meaning. Whatever happened carried out God's will, which the prophets conveyed. Put together in the end so that the prophetic writings appeared to foretell the destruction that would come, the prophets' writings therefore contained a message entirely harmonious with the basic message of the Pentateuchal ones.[2] Judaism began with the formation of the larger part of the Hebrew Scriptures, the Pentateuch and the main constituents of the prophetic books. We may therefore say that while the (genealogical) Israel of the Torah of Moses traces its origins back to Abraham, Isaac, and Jacob, and while historians tell the story of Israel from remote antiquity, the continuous and unfolding religious tradition we know as Judaism begins with Scripture. Scripture as we have it commences with the destruction of the first Temple by the Babylonians in 586 B.C.

If we examine the components of the present composite, we gain our first opportunity to examine whole and complete a single Judaic system. Since all Judaisms begin with the making of the Five Books of Moses as the Torah of God given to Israel in Sinai, we realize that using the word Judaism for a strand of the Pentateuch represents a considerable anach-

2. That is not to ignore the innocence that draws together utterly contradictory messages in detail—the prophetic critique of the cult for instance.

ronism. For a single formative experience stood at the beginning of all Judaisms, and each Judaism in its manner recapitulated that experience. The original definitive experience imposed its outlines on every Judaism, framing the questions that characterized them all, but allowing for the diversity of their respective answers. That is why for the materials that came down from the period before 586 B.C. we cannot invoke the category Judaism except for purposes of exposition. None of the prior systems in its original statement addressed the urgent question of 586–450,[3] that is of exile and return, and none of them recapitulated that pattern of human and national experience.

From the time of the great Jewish philosopher and scholar of ancient Israel, Baruch Spinoza, in the seventeenth century, scholarship has identified in the Pentateuch a number of distinct strands of narrative, each exhibiting its own indicative marks of language and viewpoint and each addressed to the way of life of a particular Israel. Two are visible to the naked eye: the book of Deuteronomy, which scholars call D, which explicitly announces that it will recapitulate everything that has gone before and then resolutely rewrites the whole—history, law, and theology—and the Priestly Code, recognized as "the Torah of the priests" even by the rabbis of the Talmud (though they understood it to be God's Torah for the priests rather than the Torah in God's name written by the priests, as we now know it to be). The priestly code, referred to as P, covers parts of Genesis, Exodus, and the whole of Leviticus and Numbers. Both of these sources themselves join together discrete strands of materials. One among a number of documents now patched together into the Five Books of Moses is called J after the name of the Lord, Yahweh, that is characteristically used in its narratives, and is generally referred to as the Yahwistic account. Another is called E, after the name of God, Elohim, that predominates, and therefore is identified as the Elohist. These two strands are joined together in JE. The fact that the Pentateuch is made up of stands by itself makes no difference in our understanding of the Torah of Moses as it emerged in the time of Ezra, about 450 B.C., and none made a singular impact on any of the Judaisms that flowed from the Torah of Moses. But each in its day made a statement concerning a particular social and political context—an Israel. Each explained the world formed by that Israel—its way of life. And each one also provided a complete picture of the world that came to concrete expression in that way of life—its world view. So while we cannot call J or D or P a Judaism, each allows us to see a whole and

3. Though all of them were made to address that experience in the final statement.

complete system—way of life and world view, addressed to a particular social group—before the formation of Judaism.

The basis for identifying a strand of the Pentateuch as the writing of the Yahwist—specifically, Genesis 2–11, 12–16, 18–22, 24–34, 38, 49, Exodus 1–24, 32, 34, Numbers 11–12, 14, 20–25, Judges 1—is not only use of the name Yahweh for God. It is also the association of other indications with the appearance of that name. For example in the Yahwist system Moses' father is called Reuel; the mountain, Sinai; and the Palestinians, Canaanites. Where God is called Elohim, Moses' father-in-law is Jethro; the mountain, Horeb; and the Palestinians, Amorites. For another example, the creation myth of Gen. 1:1 has God/Elohim create the world. Then Gen. 2:5–25 has Yahweh make the world, and this creation myth differs in fundamental ways, in substance and style, from the former. The biblical narrative covers the same ground two or more times. For example a patriarch fools a foreign king three times about his wife's status (Gen. 12:10–20, 20, 26:1–11), twice with Abraham and Abimelekh. There are two flood stories, with seven animals brought on one ark, but pairs on the other. These and many other indications have persuaded most biblical scholars (outside of circles of believers, who have had no difficulty harmonizing everything into one cogent statement) that there are four strands interwoven in the Pentateuch, the Yahwist, which we consider here, the Elohist, the Deuteronomist, and the Priestly, henceforth J, E, D, and P.[4] We are interested in these materials only as they form systems—complete statements of how things are and why they are the way they are and what "Israel" must do because of that fact. We want to identify the systems—the Yahwist's and the Deuteronomist's and the Priests' in particular—with the circumstances addressed by those systems. That brings us to the Yahwist's account of Israel: who and what is Israel, how Israel should see the world, what Israel should do—J's theory of an Israel, its world view, and its way of life—J's Judaism.

Had the Temple not been destroyed in 586 B.C., and had some other experience imposed its pattern upon all the Israelite systems to follow, these strands, read each on its own, would have been so composed as to provide all together examples of that other pattern. That pattern would have identified a world created by an Israel that had never left home in exile but then returned to its land—that had never confronted extinction and survival—unimaginable though that Israel must be for us.

4. W. Lee Humphreys, *Crisis and Story: Introduction to the Old Testament* (Palo Alto: Mayfield Publishing, 1979), pp. 65–69.

What Judaism might have been had Israel been spared the crucible of exile and return, alienation and reconciliation, God alone knows. But through the Torah as we know it, God has not told us.

The Yahwist's Judaism for an Imperial Israel, 950 B.C.

The Yahwist's Judaism, written in the time of David and Solomon, asked the question of empire: for what? how long? why us? That question in no way intersects with the Pentateuchal one in its final formulation: on what condition? For J is a firm and final statement. In the time of King Solomon, people looked backward to account for the great day at hand. The Yahwist's account, produced at the height of the glory of the Davidic monarchy, in the time of Solomon around 950 B.C., wanted to tell the story of the federation of the federated tribes, now a single kingdom under Solomon, with a focus on Zion and Jerusalem, the metropolis of the federation. The Yahwist told the history—that is to say the theology—of Israel from its origins. He made the point that the hand of Yahweh directed events. The message he derived from that fact was one of grace. What he wanted to know from the past was the present and future of the empire and monarchy at hand.[5] The Yahwist told the story from the creation of the world to the fulfillment of Israel in the conquest of the land. His purpose was to affirm that what had happened to Israel—its move from a federation of tribes to an empire under David and Solomon—was the work of God, whom he called Yahweh.

W. Lee Humphreys summarizes the Yahwist's Judaism, the world view explaining an imperial Israel and the way of life of Israel as empire: "The Israel of the empire was Yahweh's creation for which Yahweh had a mission." Humphreys lays great emphasis on how God chose a particular person to carry out the mission: Abraham and Sarah, Isaac, Jacob, and others—all appeared weak and unworthy, but God chose them anyway. The message, as Humphreys paraphrases it, is this:

> The Yahwist focused attention on just one man, then on twelve sons, then on a band of slaves in Egypt, then on fugitives in Sinai's wastes. Repeatedly endangered, seemingly about to vanish on many occasions, small, weak, and often unworthy, these ancestors of the Israelite empire of David and Solomon were sustained again and again, even in the land of the god-king pharaoh,

---

5. I follow the excellent and clear account of Humphreys, *Crisis and Story*. I take Humphreys, rather than a broader selection of scholarly writings, simply because he seems to me to provide a clear and simple statement of the consensus view.

because they were a chosen people, elected by a god who upheld and preserved them.

That is the message. What is the place of Moses as lawgiver in this picture? It is minor. The Yahwist's picture reduces the covenant at Sinai to modest propositions; the legal stipulations are few, and are focused in Exodus 34.[6]

The Lord said, Here and now I make a covenant . . . You shall not make
  yourselves gods of cast metal.
You shall observe the pilgrim feast of unleavened bread . . .
For every first birth of the womb belongs to me . . .
For six days you shall work but on the seventh day you shall cease work.
You shall observe the pilgrim feast of Weeks . . .
You shall not offer the blood of my sacrifice at the same time as anything
  leavened . . .
You shall bring the choicest first fruits of your soil to the house of the Lord
  your God.
You shall not boil a kid in its mother's milk.

Exodus 34:10–26
(TRANSLATION: THE NEW ENGLISH BIBLE)

The unconditional quality of the promises of God to Abraham—and later to David—dominates throughout.

At issue are the promises to the patriarchs and their children, not the contract between God and Israel. Israel was destined by divine grace for its glory in Solomon's time. So for the Yahwist Moses was a minor figure relative to the patriarchs. And what was important about Moses was not the giving of law but some of the narratives of his leadership—Exodus 1–24, 32, 34. And these we read as testimonies to the mentality of the Davidic monarchy. So when we hear the tale of the golden calf, the breaking of the tablets, and the forgiveness of God as an act of grace, we listen to sublime narratives told in the age of Solomon and to the world of Solomon: God's grace favored Israel in an age knowing grace, a powerful message to a self-confident empire.

Humphreys provides a systematic statement of this Judaism:

Adam and Eve are driven from the garden and must thereafter scratch out a living from the ground by hard labor. In time they must die, for they no longer have access to the tree of life. The disorder intensifies as brother turns against brother . . . then man is set against man in a blood feud . . . The boundary separating the divine and the human is trespassed . . . Because of human perverseness, nature and the deity destroy humankind in a flood . . . Finally

6. Humphreys, *Crisis and Story*, p. 76.

an attempt by humans to overreach themselves with their tower results in a scattering of nations and confusion of tongues. . . . The human family grows ever more alienated from the deity and from one another until the harmonious order has in every way dissolved. The state of blessing found in the garden has become one of curse . . . In the Yahwist's epic, death becomes the human fate because of an act of human disobedience, the flood is just punishment by a deity whose creation has turned against him . . . The range of vision abruptly narrows [with the entry of Abraham]. An alien having only limited contact with the natives and setting but shallow roots, he lives with a promise that alone sustains him . . . In time the deity's blessing and charge were transferred to his son Isaac, then to Jacob, and through Jacob to the Twelve Tribes. . . . By implication the blessing and charge passed from the Twelve Tribes to the Israel of David and Solomon.

Israel then is given a mission: to serve as a blessing for all the families of earth. Yahweh's promise to Abraham, Humphreys notes, "recalls the promise made through Nathan the cost prophet to David in 2 Sam. 7:9: "I will make for you a great name, like the name of the great ones of the earth." The promise to Abraham thus came to fulfillment in the empire of David and Solomon. The monarchy fulfilled Yahweh's promise, and in the promise to Abraham God validated the empire building of David and Solomon. Why did God favor Israel? It was, in Humphreys' summary: "to be the vehicle for life, peace, integrity, and harmony in the created order, to reverse the currents set in motion by the first human act of disobedience."

The Yahwist joined the themes of the formation of the tribes into a federation and those of the building of Jerusalem and the monarchy, using the stories to legitimize the empire. What is important in the Yahwist's picture is the unconditional character of the account. The promise to Abraham was not conditional; it was tied to no strings: "The assurances found in Genesis 23:2 and 2 Samuel 7:9–16 carry the force of certainty, of actions already coming into effect."[7]

I took you from the pastures . . . I have been with you wherever you have gone . . . I will make you a great name among the great ones of the earth. I will assign a place for my people Israel; there I will plant them and they shall dwell in their own land . . . The Lord has told you that he would build up your royal house. When your life ends and you rest with your forefathers, I will set up one of your family, one of your own children, to succeed you and I will establish his kingdom.

2 Samuel 7:8–13
(TRANSLATION: THE NEW ENGLISH BIBLE)

7. Humphreys, *Crisis and Story*, p. 76.

The world view expressed in this Judaism thus addressed an Israel that "would fill their role in the divine plan . . . [The Yahwist] reflects the heady days of the empire when briefly under David and especially under Solomon all things seemed possible. For a time Israel would shine forth like a light, revealing Yahweh's concern for all the nations of the earth."[8] What we do not find is more interesting that what we do find: there is no stress on a covenant, the conditional character of Israel's existence, the uncertain right to the land, or the unclear identification of the people. The traits of a heightened reality—in which possession of the land depended upon the character of the society built upon it, and in which the very existence of the people constantly demanded explanation and justification—those recurrent characteristics of the Judaisms after 586 played a slight role in the Yahwist's serene and confident Judaism, in his view of the world from the height of Jerusalem, and in his account of the way of life of a normal people, living securely in its rightful place. No later Judaism would conform to this view.

The Yahwist's picture—with its beginning and middle, but no end—did not impart its attitude on later Judaisms, because the Yahwist's fundamental conception of Israel in the world in no way corresponded to the experience of Israel in the world. This was a Judaism that did not invent, but was invented by, the ordinary reality of the social world—a Judaism that was created by politics. Only later on shall we uncover Judaisms that created their own politics—those world-defining Judaisms that reproduced in diverse settings that original experience of exile and restoration that the Yahwist could not imagine. So the Yahwist gives us a fragment of one Judaism before Judaism. But it is hardly the only one.[9] We move on to another in search of a religion that imparted *its* pattern upon the social world.

The Deuteronomist's Judaism for a Client-Israel, 620–570 B.C.

The fact that the Yahwist's Moses spoke to the imperial age of Solomon surely made a difference to the two authorships of Deuteronomy, one about 620 B.C., at the end of the long period of Assyrian hegemony in the southern kingdom, Judea, and the other at about 570 B.C., after the destruction of Jerusalem but long before the return to Zion under

8. Humphreys, *Crisis and Story*, p. 77.

9. How should we ignore the fact that the Yahwist's and the Elohist's strands were woven together? That too testifies to its own setting, one not defined by the experience of exile and return. It is not pertinent to my argument, merely a further exemplification of it.

Persian sponsorship. We know that the Yahwist's Moses for an imperial age did not serve the Deuteronomistic authorships, simply because those writers presented another way of life and world view for another Israel (and a very fresh Moses). If we turn to the book of Deuteronomy, we find a very different picture from the one we get in the portions of Genesis and Exodus contributed by the Yahwist.[10] Now Moses stood at the center, and he preached a magnificent sermon before his death as a narrative of Israel's history. That sermon formed the setting for an enormous law code. At the heart of matters was this claim: here is God's law, which you must keep as your side of the contract that God made with you in bringing you out of Egypt and into the promised land. Moses now served to validate the laws of the book at hand, Deuteronomy.

Deuteronomy came into existence in a time of the shaking of the foundations of the politics of the Near East and Israel. The book of Deuteronomy in its earliest phase came to light toward the end of the seventh century, at about 620 B.C., forty years prior to the destruction of the first Temple of Jerusalem. What had happened in the period of the writing of Deuteronomy was that Israel had spent a whole generation under Assyrian influence, and only now, with the waning of Assyrian rule over the Near East, did it emerge from that sphere of cultural influence. It was a time of transition in which the established political system of the Near East gave way. For nearly two thousand years prior to about 600 B.C., Egypt and Mesopotamia had formed the centers of international power. Syria and Palestine had constituted a buffer. One final empire, Babylonia under Nebuchadnezzar, came to center stage at the end of the seventh century B.C. Having conquered Jerusalem and exiled the Jews to Babylonia in 586, it fell by the mid–sixth century B.C. That marked the end of the old order of the Near and Middle East.[11]

Deuteronomy is a brilliant work of fictional autobiography, present-

10. Since we are interested only in examples of Judaisms before Judaism, we do not have to survey the components of J, let alone the Elohist, nor the combination of the Yahwist's and Elohist's Judaism into JE. These matters are enormously interesting, but not relevant to the history of Judaism.

11. Then the first of the three great empires that would take over the entire Near and Middle East, each from outside the region entirely, made its appearance. The empires were the Iranians under Persian rule, then the Greeks under Macedonian rule, then the Romans. The Iranians from the east took power in the mid–sixth century B.C. and held it for two hundred years. Then the Greeks, led by the Macedonians under Alexander, conquered the region in the fourth century B.C. and held sway for about two hundred years. Then the Romans, who first dealt with Israel in 140 B.C., took over the hegemony of the region by the mid–first century B.C. and held it for seven hundred years, down to the Arab conquest under Islam in the seventh century A.D.

ing a long speech by Moses, as an account of the past for the present. The book addressed a fully articulated national state and projected contemporary problems and matters of doubt into what then appeared to be a more secure past.[12] Humphreys provides our account of the message and purpose of Deuteronomy:

> Israel had prospered when it was loyal to the covenant and had suffered when it was disloyal. This pattern is revealed in the framework that was used to bind together the once separate stories about the federation's tribes and judges in the Book of Judges [as well]. . . . Loyalty to Yahweh and his stipulations brings life and security, gifts of the god who first called Israel into being from Egyptian slavery. Disloyalty will result only in death.[13]

2 Kings 22 tells the story of the supernatural discovery of a book of the law, and many maintain that the book corresponds to Deut. 12–26. A point of stress in these chapters of Deuteronomy is that in Jerusalem and only there could Yahweh be worshipped; only the priests of Jerusalem were valid. So the book of Deuteronomy in its earliest layer made two points: first, one could worship only Yahweh, and second, one could worship Yahweh only in Jerusalem. Moses formed the authority for the story but not the leading actor. That was the first part of the story. That message hardly served the needs of Israel after 586, when the people could not get to Jerusalem.

Deuteronomy asked a critical question, the one concerning disaster and destruction, and, when the document reached its final stage it answered that question. Then the book took its part in a much more encompassing and massive history of Israel, the books of Deuteronomy, Joshua, Judges, Samuel and Kings. That great work of historical narrative came into being, in its final composition, after 586, and was assembled in the light of the catastrophe in order to answer a question of life and death: why have these things happened to us? The past had to live again to explain the present and secure the future. This second phase in the unfolding of the tale of the Deuteronomistic historians took place after the destruction of the Temple in 586. Moses then served to provide the authority for an explanation of the entire history of ancient Israel, culminating in the tragedy at hand. Now Moses was lawgiver, and the laws formed the covenant between Israel and God. Israel had violated that covenant and the resulting destruction was at hand. Again Humphreys:[14]

12. Humphreys, *Crisis and Story*, p. 147.
13. Humphreys, *Crisis and Story*, pp. 148–9.
14. Humphreys, *Crisis and Story*, p. 146.

In Judah and Jerusalem some would turn back to Moses, attempting to redeem the crisis of 587 B.C. [when the Temple was destroyed] by placing it in the theological framework of the old federation story of Israel's origins, for only in this way could Israel's tragic end be understood as the harsh but just action of its god Yahweh. In Moses, who had led Israel from Egyptian slavery, who had mediated the covenant on Mount Sinai, and whose death before the promise of land had been fulfilled had given an effective symbol to Israel's tragically unfulfilled promise, they found a mirror in which to view their own experience. This group found their charter in the book of Deuteronomy, which received its final form at their hands. From this base they reviewed Israel's history from the entrance into Canaan to the exile in Babylon after 587 . . . They produced an extended theological survey of Israel's history that now comprises the books of Joshua through 2 Kings. Their book is called the deuteronomistic history because the basis for judgment is found in Deuteronomy.

The Moses of Deuteronomy was a great preacher and gave a sermon on the plains of Moab. He projected out of a secure past an account of the later issues and problems and doubts.[15] In Deuteronomy Moses said a great deal and did much less. In the Yahwist chapters of Exodus Moses did much but gave few laws. The contrast is clear. The single message is that Yahweh worked through the Babylonians because Israel had followed the accomodationist policies of the Israelite kings during the Assyrian hegemony.

The Judaism of Deuteronomy contained many of the motifs that would predominate later on, with its emphasis on convenantal nomism,[16] on keeping the contract that God had made with Israel by carrying out the rules that constituted the conditions of the contract. But the later definitive traits, with their emphasis upon the conditional character of the life of Israel, the insecure hold on the land, the uncertain identification of the nation and its need constantly to affirm its identity—these marks of self-consciousness scarcely broke through. The appeal to Israel's past accounted for the present. But the Deuteronomistic strand of the Torah of Moses contained little instruction on what was required for the future.

15. Humphreys, *Crisis and Story,* p. 147.
16. We owe the phrase to Edward P. Sanders, *Paul and Palestinian Judaism* (Philadelphia: Fortress, 1979), who insists that this is the characteristic theology of the pre-70 Pharisees and of Judaism in general. I see no reason to differ, since that is, after all, the message of the Torah to begin with. See also his excellent *Jesus and Judaism* (Philadelphia: Fortress Press, 1985).

Crisis and Resolution

The small number of Israelite families who remembered the exile, survived in Babylonia, and then toward the end of the sixth and fifth centuries B.C. returned to Zion, knew things that Israel before 586 could never have imagined. The vast majority of the people did not undergo the experiences of exile and return. One part never left and the other never came back. That fact shows us the true character of the Judaism that would predominate: it began by making a selection of facts it deemed consequential, hence historical, and ignored in that selection the experiences of others who had quite a different perception of what had happened—and for all we know a different appreciation of the message. The fact that the ones who came back and many who were taken away were priests made all the difference, as the books of Ezra and Nehemiah indicate. For to the priests, what mattered in 586 was the destruction of the Temple, and what made a difference "three generations later" was the restoration of Zion and the rebuilding of the Temple. To them the cult was the key, and the Temple was the nexus between heaven and earth.

The nation—as seen and defined by the priests—restored to its land could be compared to a person healed from a life-threatening illness or to a poet. To such as these, nothing loses its astonishing quality. Life cannot be taken for granted. Life becomes a gift, each day an unanticipated surprise. Everything then demands explanation, but uncertainty reigns. The comparison fails when we realize that, while the consciousness of life as a gift of grace changes things for the survivor alone, the return to Zion, cast as it was into the encompassing language of the Five Books of Moses, imposed upon the entire nation's imagination and inner consciousness the unsettling encounter with annihilation avoided, extinction postponed, and life renewed—the Temple restored, as portrayed in P's Leviticus and Numbers.

To explain the power of the priests tale, we need hardly invoke the conception of a shared national consciousness, a collective myth of nationhood subject to condition and stipulation, forever threatened with desolation, and always requiring renewal. For the Torah taught that one lesson of the human condition of Israel every Sabbath everywhere to everybody. So to Israel the Torah imparted the picture of society subject to judgment. And it was the priests' judgment in particular that prevailed. All Judaisms to come in some way or other found in the priests' pattern the model to which they would have to respond. The priests' Torah, the Pentateuch in its final statement, constituted the first Judaism.

THREE

THE FIRST AGE OF DIVERSITY

JUDAISMS FOR THE UNCERTAIN RESTORATION

FROM 586 B.C. TO A.D. 70

Event and Pattern

A Judaism asks an urgent question and supplies a self-evident compelling answer. The issue addressed by Judaic systems from the Pentateuch onward was, and would remain, Who is Israel? And what are the rules that define Israel as a social and political entity? In one way or another Israel, the Jewish people wherever they lived, sought ways to declare itself distinct from its neighbors. The stress on exclusion of the neighbors from the group, and of the group from the neighbors, ran contrary to the situation of ancient Israel, with the unmarked frontiers of culture and the constant giving and receiving among diverse groups which were generally characteristic of ancient times. The persistent stress on differentiation and the preoccupation with self-definition also contradicted the facts of the matter. In the time of the formation of the Pentateuch, the people Israel was deeply affected by the shifts and changes in social, cultural, and political life and institutions. When, a century and a half after the formation of the Pentateuch under Ezra and Nehemiah, the Greeks under Alexander the Great conquered the entire Middle East (about 320 B.C.) and incorporated the land of Israel into the international Hellenistic culture, the problem of self-definition came to renewed expression. And when the war of independence fought by the Jews under the leadership of the Maccabees (about 160 B.C.) produced an independent state for a brief period, that state found itself under the government of a court that accommodated itself to the international style of politics and culture. So what was different? What made Israel separate and secure on its land and in its national identity? In that protracted moment of confusion and change the heritage of the Five Books of Moses came to completion. The same situation persisted that had marked the age in which the Pentateuch had delivered its message, answering with compelling responses the urgent question of the nation's existence. That constituted the formative chapter in the history of all Judaisms: exile and return as the history of Judaism. Let us begin from the beginning, with the Pentateuchal reading of events and their meanings framed after 586.

The principles of the Pentateuchal Torah and the historical and prophetic writings of the century after 586, namely Israel's heightened sense of its own social reality, its status as an elected people standing in a covenantal relationship with God, in fact spoke out of the inner structure of the system. They expressed its logic, not a logic intrinsic in events, even in events selected and reworked. They applied its premises, not the data of Israel's common life in either Babylonia or the land of Israel. For the system not only selected the events it deemed consequential, but also spoke of events that had simply never happened. Consider the Jews who remained in the land after 586, or those who remained in Babylonia after Cyrus's decree permitting the return to Zion. For both groups, for different reasons, there was no alienation, also, consequently, no reconciliation, and their lives corresponded to the merely normal, as in any other nation. Treating exile and return as normative imparted to the exile a critical and definitive position. It marked Israel as special, elect, and subject to the rules of the covenant and its stipulations. But to those who stayed put, the urgent question of exile and return, and the response of election and covenant, bore slight relevance. If we want an example of a religious system creating a society, we can find few better instances than the power of the conception of Israel expressed by the Pentateuch and associated writings, of the period after 586 B.C., to tell people not only the meaning of what had happened but also what had happened: to create for Israelite society a picture of what it must be and therefore what it had been. That sense of heightened reality and that intense focus on the identification of the nation as extraordinary represented only one possible meaning of the events from 586 onward. But the system of the Torah and the prophetic and historical writings as framed by the priests and given definitive statement under the auspices of the Iranians' Jewish viceroy in Jerusalem, Nehemiah, with Ezra as counsellor is the only one to have prevailed for all the succeeding centuries.

What happened in 586 and after does not correspond to the myth fabricated out of what happened. In both the Torah and the prophetic-historical books Scripture said that Israel had suffered through exile, atoned, and attained reconciliation, and had renewed the covenant with

God, as signified by the return to Zion and the rebuilding of the Temple. Although only a part of Israel in fact had undergone those experiences, the Judaic system of the Torah made normative that experience of alienation and reconciliation. In this case, religion did more than merely recapitulate resentment; it precipitated it by selecting as events only a narrow sample of what had happened, and by imparting to that selection of events meanings pertinent to only a few.

Thus the paradigm began as a paradigm, not as actual events transformed into a pattern. The conclusions derived from the pattern came not from reflection on events but from the logic of the paradigm itself. The paradigm created expectations that could not be met, and so renewed the resentment captured by the myth of exile. At the same time it resolved the crisis of exile with the promise of return. This self-renewing pattern formed the self-fulfilling prophecy that all Judaisms have offered as the generative tension and critical symbolic structure of their systems.

Since, chief among the propositions of the Torah of Moses is the notion of the election of Israel effected in the covenant, we may say that, systemically speaking, Israel—the Israel of the Torah and the historical-prophetic books of the sixth and fifth centuries—selected itself. The system created the paradigm of the society that had gone into exile and come back home and also the covenant that certified not election but self-selection.

At the very foundations of the original Judaic system, the account of the sequence of events from 586 when the Israelites were exiled to Babylonia to about 450 when they had returned to Zion and rebuilt the Temple, we find history systemically selected, and therefore by definition invented. The same is so for a long list of systemic givens, none of them actually matters of self-evidence. It follows that it is Scripture— and Scripture alone—that says that what happened was that Israel died and was reborn, was punished through exile and then forgiven, and therefore—and this is critical—to be Israel in a genealogical sense is to have gone into exile and returned to Zion.

The Model Judaism: The Priests' System for an Israel in Trauma and the Normative Judaism of Second Temple Times

The way of life of the Judaism that set the norm for the Second Temple period was the holy way of life depicted in the Five Books of Moses. The Pentateuch encompasses four sources, originally distinct, three—J, E, and D, or the Yahwist, the Elohist, and the Deuteronomist—deriving from the period before 586 and one—the Priestly—from the period afterward. But from our perspective, the Judaic system represented by the Pentateuch came into being when the several sources became one—as we now know them. That work was accomplished by priests in the time of Ezra, around 450 B.C. The world view came from the account of heaven and earth and the definition of Israel presented in the Pentateuch. The Israel of that Judaism found its definition in the same Scripture: Israel encompassed the family of an original father, Abraham. Israel now consisted of the genealogical descendants of that original family. Thus the Scripture of the first Judaism was the Five Books of Moses, the setting encompassed Israel after the exile and return to Zion, and the system centered on the explanation of the rules that would keep Israel holy—that is separate for God alone. Central to the life of holiness was the "tabernacle," conceived as the model for the postexilic Temple.

While the Judaism represented by the Pentateuch of about 450 B.C. drew abundant materials from the period before 586 (which is why we have such components of Scripture as the Yahwist's and Deuteronomist's writings), the statement at the end derived from and expressed the viewpoint of the priesthood. That is why a large portion of the Pentateuch devotes time and attention to the matter of the cult—the centrality of sacrifice, the founding of the priesthood and its rules, and the importance of the Temple in Jerusalem. That is why many of the stories of Genesis are aimed at explaining the origin, in the lives and deeds of the patriarchs, of the locations of various cultic centers prior to the centralization of the cult in Jerusalem. They explain the beginnings of the priesthood, the care and feeding of priests, the beginnings and rules of the sacrificial system, the contention between priestly castes—Levites and priests—and diverse other matters. The Pentateuch in these ways laid emphasis upon serving God through sacrifice in the Temple, conducted by the priests, and upon Israel's living a holy way of life as a "kingdom of priests and a holy people,"—all in accord with God's message to Moses at Sinai. But of course "Sinai" stood for Babylonia. In Babylonia the priests drew together the elements of the received picture and reshaped them into the fairly coherent set of rules and narratives we now know as the Pentateuch.

While making ample use of ancient tales, the framers of the Pentateuch as we now have it flourished in Babylonia after 586 and conceived as their systemic teleology the return to Zion and the rebuilding of the temple—hence the centrality in the wilderness narratives of the tabernacle and its cult. So the setting of the Judaism of the priests imparted to the scripture of that first setting its ultimate meaning: response to historical disaster followed by unprecendented triumph. Their vision is characterized as follows:

> In the priests' narrative the chosen people are last seen as pilgrims moving through alien land toward a goal to be fulfilled in another time and place, and this is the vision, drawn from the ancient story of their past, that the priests now hold out to the scattered sons and daughters of old Israel. They too are exiles encamped for a time in an alien land, and they too must focus their hopes on the promise ahead. Like the Israelites in the Sinai wilderness, they must avoid setting roots in the land through which they pass, for diaspora is not to become their permanent condition, and regulations must be adopted to facilitate this. They must resist assimilation into the world into which they are now dispersed, because hope and heart and fundamental identity lay in the future. Thus, the priestly document not only affirms Yahweh's continuing authority and action in the lives of his people but offers them a pattern for life that will ensure them a distinct identity.[1]

The net effect of the Pentateuchal vision of Israel, that is, its world view seen in the aggregate, was to lay stress on the separateness and the holiness of Israel, while pointing to dangers of pollution by the outsider. The way of life corresponded with its stress on the distinguishing traits of an Israel threatened by the outsider. The fate of the nation depended upon the loyalty of the people in their everyday life and to the requirements of the covenant with God. So history formed the barometer of the health of the nation. In these ways the several segments of the earlier traditions of Israel were so drawn together as to make the point peculiarly pertinent to Israel in exile. The center of the system lay in the covenant that told Israel: Keep these rules and you will not again suffer as you have suffered. Violate them and you will. At the heart of the covenant was the call for Israel to form a kingdom of priests and a holy people.

If we ask for a single passage to express the priests' Judaism, we look to the book of Leviticus, which concerns the priesthood above all, and its version of the covenant, in Lev. 19:1–18 (given in the Revised Standard Version):

> And the Lord said to Moses, "Say to all the congregation of the people of Israel, You shall be holy, for I the Lord your God am holy.
> "Every one of you shall revere his mother and father and you shall keep my sabbaths, I am the Lord your God.

---

1. Humphreys, *Crisis and Story*, p. 217.

"Do not turn to idols or make for yourselves molten gods; I am the Lord your God.

"When you offer a sacrifice of peace offerings to the Lord, you shall offer it so that you may be accepted. It shall be eaten the same day you offer it or on the morrow, and anything left over until the third day shall be burned with fire. If it is eaten at all on the third day, it is an abomination, it will not be accepted, and every one who eats it shall bear his iniquity, because he has profaned a holy thing of the Lord; and that person shall be cut off from his people.

"When you reap the harvest of your land, you shall not reap your field to its very border, neither shall you gather the gleanings after your harvest. And you shall not strip your vineyard bare, neither shall you gather the fallen grapes of your vineyard; you shall leave them for the poor and for the sojourner. I am the Lord your God.

"You shall not steal, nor deal falsely, nor lie to one another. And you shall not swear by my name falsely and so profane the name of your God; I am the Lord. You shall not oppress your neighbor or rob him. The wages of a hired servant shall not remain with you all night until the morning. You shall not curse the deaf or put a stumbling block before the blind, but you shall fear your God; I am the Lord.

"You shall do no injustice in judgment; you shall not be partial to the poor or defer to the great, but in righteousness shall you judge your neighbor. You shall not go up and down as a slanderer among your people, and you shall not stand forth against the life of your neighbor; I am the Lord.

"You shall not hate your brother in your heart, but you shall reason with your neighbor, lest you bear sin because of him. You shall not take vengeance or bear any grudge against the sons of your own people, but you shall love your neighbor as yourself; I am the Lord."

The children of Abraham, Isaac, and Jacob would form an extended family, genealogically the people of God, keeping the covenant God sets forth. This mixture of rules we should regard as cultic as to sacrifice, moral as to support of the poor, ethical as to right dealing, and above all religious as to "being holy for I the Lord your God am holy." All together the mixture of rules portrays a complete and whole society: its world view holiness in the likeness of God, its way of life an everyday life of sanctification through the making of distinctions, and its Israel, Israel. But as we know from other writings of the time, it was a very special Israel, an Israel characterized by genealogical purity, meaning, in this context, separation not only from the nations but also from those Israelites who had not undergone the experience of exile and return to Zion. For along with the revelation of the Torah of Moses, Ezra insisted that the Israelites divorce the wives they had taken from the "peoples of the land," who were none other than the descendants of those Jews who had not gone off into exile in Babylonia. The definition of who is Israel lay at the foundation of the system.

Elsewhere the book of Leviticus contains a clear statement of the consequence geared to the events of the recent past: "If you walk in my statutes and observe my commandments and do them, then I will give you your rains in their season" (Lev. 26:3); "But if you will not hearken to me and will not do all these commandments, . . . I will do this to you: I will appoint over you sudden terror . . . and you shall sow your seed in vain for your enemies shall eat it . . . Then the land shall enjoy its sabbaths as long as it lies desolate while you are in your enemies' land." (Lev. 26:34). The Judaism of the priests answered the question of how to prevent the events of the recent past from ever happening again. It gave as its answer the formation of a separate and holy society, an Israel. Israel must obey the rules of holiness. If it does, then by keeping its half of the covenant it could make certain God would honor the other half: "And I will give peace in the land, and you shall lie down and none shall make you afraid" (Lev. 26:6). For the next five hundred years, the Judaic system of the Pentateuch predominated. And this brings us back to the proposition that, in the case of Judaism, religion imparted its pattern upon the social world and polity of Jews.

Why has the original paradigm survived? For it is one thing to explain how a system took shape, but another to account for its long-term effect. One reason covers the near term. Another explains its long-term power of self-evidence.

As to the power of the Pentateuchal system in its original fifth-century context, the Judaism that obtained through the Second Temple period—the priests' system of sanctification, the way of life conforming in its fundamental structure to the priests' points of concern, the world view repeating in mythic-historic language the priests' perspective on what counted—flourished because the priests had the power to make it stick. The reasons are clear. First, framing matters in their terms, the priests were the ones who organized and set forth the Torah as the Jews would receive and revere it. They furthermore controlled the political institutions of the country as the Persian government established them. Consequently their perspective—with its emphasis on the Temple and its holiness, and the cult and its critical role in sustaining the life of the land and the nation—predominated in defining public policy. And the Temple government had the necessary political support to sustain its authority. It laid forth the Torah as its political myth, and did not have to resort to force at all. Since the Torah of Moses at Sinai defined the faith, explained what had happened, and set forth the rules to ensure God's continuing favor to Israel, the final shape and system of the Torah made a deep impact on the consciousness and attitude of the people as a whole.

But why did this particular Judaic system prove definitive long after the political facts had changed? The original Judaism answered the question of exile and restoration. With the continuing authority of the Torah in Israel, the experience to which it was originally a response was recapitulated, in age after age, through the reading and authoritative exegesis of the original Scripture that had preserved and portrayed it: "Your descendants will be aliens living in a land that is not theirs . . . but I will punish that nation whose slaves they are, and after that they shall come out with great possessions" (Gen. 15:13–14). The priests' Judaism persisted because the Scriptures themselves retained their authority. More important was the fact that the Judaic system devised by the priests in the Pentateuch addressed, and also created, a continuing and chronic social fact of Israel's life.

So long as the people perceived the world in a way that made urgent the question that Scripture framed and answered, Scripture enjoyed the power of persuasion that imparted to it the self-evident status of God's will revealed to Israel. The priests' system therefore imposed itself even in situations in which its fundamental premises hardly pertained. When the world imposed upon Jewry questions of a different order, then Jews went in search of more answers—an additional Torah (hence the formation of the Judiasm of the dual Torah)—and even different answers (hence the formation, in modern times, of Judaic systems of a different character altogether).[2] But even then a great many Jews continued to view the world through that original perspective created in the aftermath of destruction and restoration, that is, to see the world as a gift instead of a given, and to see themselves as chosen for a life of special suffering but also special reward.

There were two reasons for the perennial power of the Judaic system of the priests to shape the world view and way of life of the Israel addressed by that Judaism. The first reason is that the tension precipitated by the interpretation of the life of the Jews as exile and return persisted; it persisted and kept renewing the resentment, since the memory of loss and restoration joined with the danger of further loss.

The second reason is more important: the question answered by the Five Books of Moses persisted at the center of national life and re-

2. These matters will be clarified in due course.

mained urgent. It is true that the question persisted because Scripture kept reminding people to ask it. But we have to ask what was at stake and so penetrate into the deepest layers of the structure. For the sacred persistence in the end rested on judgments found valid in circumstances remote from the original world subject to those judgments.

Sacred Perseverance and the Exegesis of the Everyday: Why the Priests' Judaic System of Sanctification Persisted

The Temple and its rites formed the centerpiece of the national life of Israel. Large numbers of people came to Jerusalem for the pilgrim festivals of the autumn and spring: tabernacles in the autumn, Passover and Pentecost in the spring. So it was not only the minor sects or the writings of a small political-theological elite that testified to the centrality of the priests' vision in the life of Israel. The very critical role played by Jerusalem, with stress on the holiness of the Temple and the supernatural importance of its cult, makes us realize the importance of that original Judaism, the Judaism of the Five Books of Moses that took shape after 586. Accordingly we have to wonder why the priestly themes and repertoire of concerns should have so occupied the imagination and fantasy of the people as a whole. What requires explanation is the continuity from the priestly code of the sixth century B.C. to the beginnings of the Mishnaic code of the second century A.D.—a period of seven hundred years, a longer spell than the span of time that separates us from Edward the Confessor and an independent Wales or from the West's Fourth Crusade to the Land of Israel. For as we shall see, the Mishnah—and therefore the Judaism that flowed from that central document—represents the fundamental structure generated by the priestly perspective on the condition of Israel.

The grammar of the sacred belonged to the priesthood from olden times. That is why it becomes urgent to dwell on why the priestly code should have exercised so profound and formative an influence upon the life of the Second Temple and beyond. The reason that the priestly code of the Five Books of Moses that expressed the priestly emphasis on sanctification exercised the formative power it did is the following:

The problems addressed and solved by the Judaism of the Five Books of Moses remained chronic long after the period of its formation, from the seventh century down to its closure in the time of Ezra and Nehemiah. The priestly code states a powerful answer to a pressing and urgent question. Since that question would remain a perplexity continuing to trouble Israelites for a long time, it is not surprising that the categorical structure of the priestly answer, so profound and fundamental in its character, should for its part have continued to define systems that would attract and impress people.

Once more we have to locate ourselves in the time of the completion of the Mosaic Scriptures, that is, in the late sixth and fith centuries B.C., to identify the critical tensions of that period. The same tensions persisted and confronted the thinkers whose reflection led to the conclusion—in resolution of those ongoing points of dissonance—that the Temple's holiness enveloped and surrounded Israel's land and demarcated its people too. What marked ancient Israel as distinctive was preoccupation with defining itself.

The reason for the persistence of the exegesis of the everyday as a sequence of acts of sanctification—was the Torah's encapsulation, as normative and recurrent, of the experience of the loss and recovery of the land and of political sovereignty. Israel because of its (in its mind) amazing experience had attained a self-consciousness that continuous existence in a single place under a long-term government had denied others (and had denied Israel before 586, as the Yahwist and the Deuteronomist testify). There was nothing given, nothing to be merely celebrated (as the Yahwist thought) or taken for granted (as the Deuteronomist thought) in the life of a nation that had ceased to be a nation on its own land and had then once more regained that (once normal, now abnormal) condition. Judaism took shape as the system that accounted for the death and resurrection of Israel, the Jewish people, and pointed for the source of renewed life toward sanctification now and salvation at the end of time.

The result of the codification and closure of the law under Ezra and Nehemiah was to produce the Torah as a law code that laid heavy emphasis on the exclusive character of the Israelite God and cult. "Judaism"—the priestly Judaism of the Pentateuchal composite— gained the character of a cultically centered way of life and world view. Both rite and myth aimed at the continuing self-definition of Israel by separation from the rest of the world and exclusion of the rest of the world. Order against chaos meant holiness over uncleanness and life over death. The purpose was to define Israel against the background of the other peoples of the Near and Middle East, with whom Israel had much in common, and especially to differentiate Israel from its near relations and neighbors—for example, Samaritans—in the same country. The issue of who is the other persisted, extending the definition of the other: the woman, the slave, the minor, the near-Israelite, the Gentile; later on the Christian (sharing common Scriptures) was a special kind of not-Gentile Gentile.

Acute differentiation was required because the social and cultural facts were precisely to the contrary: common traits hardly bespoke clear-cut points of difference, except of idiom. The mode of differentiation taken by the Torah literature in general and the priestly sector of that literature in particular was cultic. The meaning, however, was also social. The power of the Torah composed in this time lay in its control of the Temple. The Torah made the Temple the pivot and focus of all life. The Torah literature, with its concerned God, who cares what people do about rather curious matters, and the Temple cult, with its total exclusion of the non-Israelite from participation and (even more so) from cultic commensality—these raised high the walls of separation and underlined such distinctiveness as already existed. The life of Israel flowed from the altar; what made Israel Israel was the altar.

The differentiation contrasted with the life of Israel before 586. So long as Israel remained essentially within its own land and frame of social reference, the issue of separation from neighbors could be treated casually. When the very heart of what made Israel was penetrated by the doubly desolating and disorienting experiences of both losing the Land and then coming back, the issue of who was Israel came to the fore. Confusion in economic and social relationships, and the fact that the land to which Israelites returned in no way permitted distinct Israelite settlement, made pressing the issue of self-definition. The issue has persisted for the rest of Israelite history, from the return to Zion and the formation of the Torah literature even down to our own day. The reason for this persistence? It is that the social forces which lent urgency to the issue of who is Israel would remain. So long as memory remained, the conflicting claims of exclusivist Torah literature and universalist prophecy, of a people living in utopia, in no particular place, while framing its vision of itself in the deeply locative symbols of cult and center—these conflicting claims would make vivid the abiding issue of self-definition. At issue was life—its source and its sustenance. For if we ask why the Temple with its cult proved enduringly central in the imagination of the Israelites in the country, we have only to repeat the statements which the priests of the Temple and their imitators in the sects were prepared to make. These explain the critical importance of cult and rite. If we reread the priestly viewpoint as it is contained in the books of Leviticus and Numbers, as well as in priestly passages of Genesis and Exodus, this is the picture we derive.

The altar was the center of life, the conduit of life from heaven to earth and from earth to heaven. All things were to be arrayed in relationship to the altar. The movement of the heavens demarcated and celebrated at the cult marked out the divisions of time in relationship to the altar. The spatial dimension of the land was likewise demarcated and celebrated in relationship to the altar. The natural life of Israel's fields and corrals, the social life of its hierarchical caste system, and its political life (not only in theory) centered on the Temple as the locus of ongoing government—all things in order and in place. The natural order of the world corresponded to, reinforced, and was reinforced by the social order of Israel. Both were fully realized in the cult—the nexus between the opposite and corresponding forces, the heavens and the earth.

The lines of social and political structure emanated from the altar. And it was these lines of structure which constituted high and impenetrable frontiers to separate Israel from the Gentiles. Israel, which was holy, ate holy food, reproduced itself in accord with the laws of holiness, and conducted all of its affairs, both affairs of state and the business of the table and the bed, in accord with the demands of holiness. So the cult defined holiness. Holiness meant separateness. Separateness meant life. Why? Because outside the land—the realm of the holy—lay the domain of death. The lands were unclean. The land was holy. For the Scriptural vocabulary, one antonym for *holy* is *unclean,* and one opposite of unclean is holy. The synonym of holy is life. The primary symbol of uncleanness and its highest expression is death. So the Torah stood for life, the covenant with the Lord would guarantee life, and the way of life required sanctification in the here and now of the natural world.

Sorting Out Judaic Categories in the Age of Diversity: Sagacity, Sanctification, and Salvation

My stress on the paramount position of the priests' Judaic system, though justified by the priestly caste's prominence in the design of the Torah of Moses, should not obscure the two other components of Scripture which made their impact both then and later on. For the Pentateuch did encompass Yahwist, Elohist—J, E, the two combined as JE—and the Deuteronomist—D—as much as the priestly code—P—and the later Scriptures put together in the image of P. Even before the definition of the final canon, the canon of the Hebrew Scriptures took in the entirety of the prophetic corpus and important writings of the

Wisdom tradition as well. These historical-prophetic and sapiential writings made their contribution to the system of the priests, which reworked the whole into its own distinctive statement, and also captured in writing fundamental dimensions of national existence. They too would make their impact upon the shape and structure of all Judaisms to come. I refer to the existential dimensions represented in writing by historical and prophetic books, on the one side, and by instruction on how to live such as is given by Ecclesiastes, Proverbs, Job, and equivalent writings, on the other. The earlier component of the Scriptures, in Hebrew *Nebiim* or Prophets, represented by the writings of Isaiah, Jeremiah, Ezekiel, the Twelve Minor Prophets, and—in the Judaic canon—by Joshua, Judges, Samuel, and Kings, laid stress on the course of history as the mode of God's revelation of God's will to Israel. The later element, represented by many of the books of the writings in Hebrew, *Ketubim,* or Writings, encompass such works as Psalms and Proverbs, Job, and Ecclesiastes (in Hebrew: *Qohelet*). These two other strands of the Hebrew Scriptures require specification and description as well, even though, in the history of Judaism in its formative and classical phases, the priestly approach predominated and absorbed the other two on its own terms. Because we cannot account for the character of the priests' Judaism of Temple and Torah without attention to the character of the priests' choices, we must examine what they rejected or treated as subordinate as much as what they chose out of the received writings of ancient Israel before 586.

In fact, as the character of the types of biblical writings testifies, ancient Israel yielded three quite distinct points of emphasis—definitions of what mattered in the life of individual, community, and nation, and what did not. These points covered matters of doctrine and law, history and the meaning of events, and the conduct of the everyday life: the priestly, the prophetic, and the sapiential topics. Among these, only one, the priestly, yielded a fully articulated and ongoing system. The others made their profound impact, to be sure, but none provided a definitive structure for a Judaism or a model for Judaisms. But the Judaisms that did emerge presented successive reworkings of all available points of emphasis. We may gain perspective by noticing how the received materials were reworked in the interests of the systemic composition.

Let me try to describe the Judaisms that focus on the three points of emphasis I have just listed: the one that stressed doctrine, law, and way of life, emerging from the priestly viewpoint; the one that emphasized the meaning and end of history, produced by the prophetic angle of vision; and the one that took a special interest in the wise conduct of everyday affairs, yielded by the wisdom writings. To conduct this description I shall construct an ideal type for each: a Judaism all of a single fabric, expressive of a single point of interest and emphasis. What would a Judaism have looked like if produced solely within the priestly, or prophetic, or sapiential point of emphasis? For that purpose I offer a picture of the symbol of each such Judaism, its ideal human being or hero, its way of life, and its world view.

The definitive symbol, both visual and verbal, tells us what was at the center of a Judaism. We can point to three central symbols, each definitive of a Judaism: (1) a Torah-scroll—ideal of wisdom (2) the victory wreath for the head of the King-Messiah—prophetic ideal, and (3) an altar for an offering—priestly ideal. Again, we look for a visual realization of a Judaism, a concrete representation, the architectural and symbolic center and focus of the system. For the sapiential vision, this can be a building in which people assemble, with the principal object of visual attention being a niche on the eastern wall containing a Torah scroll. The buildings of the community of Jews who built a monastery community at what is now called Qumran, by the Dead Sea, set their visual focus elsewhere. The central rite of the community focused on eating a meal; so the table or altar was their visual center, stressing the priestly viewpoint. Christians familiar with the Lord's Supper will properly expect that in the community of Judaism formed by the disciples of Christ in the early decades of Christianity, during which the disciples all saw themselves as Jews, a table or a baptismal font would have provided the visual center. The biblical books that deal with the ancient Israelite Temple—for example, Leviticus and Numbers, Ezekiel 40–48, various psalms and prophetic passages—imagine yet another visual center of another Judaic system. It is an altar, also a priestly symbol. On it bonfires are kept burning; pieces of meat, loaves of bread, and other agricultural produce are displayed or burned up as offerings to God in heaven, that is gifts delivered by smoke. This Judaism is one of sacrifice by priests in a holy Temple. So its definitive action is not study of the Torah, as for the community of wisdom, but making offerings, and its leaders are not learned persons, called rabbis, but people permitted to carry out the sacrifice, called priests. A concrete representation of the prophetic symbol could be the throne of the Messiah-King, it could be a steed, or tragically it could be a cross on a hill top.

Now that we have seen how symbols may express the whole of a system, we may turn to three Judaic systems in still more concrete terms. I refer to the types represented by a priest, a prophet, and a sage, hence the priestly, prophetic, and sapiential. We can identify an ideal type or hero for each: the priest, the messiah (for the prophetic realization of salvation), and the sage, each with a definitive activity: cult for the priest, battlefield for the messiah, school and government office for the sage. Israel's heritage yielded then the cult with the priesthood, the prophetic and apocalyptic hope for meaning in history and an end of the times which would be embodied in the coming of the messiah, and the torah with its scribes and teachers. Priest, soldier, sage—these figures stand for Israel, or part of the nation. The symbols—Temple altar, sacred scroll, and victory wreath for the head of the King-Messiah—represented Jewish society at large. At the foundations were the organization of the people of Israel and the selection and interpretation of events that constituted its history. The social groups for which these symbols stood were, first, the caste of priests; second, the profession of scribes; third, the calling of general or prophet.

Since a well-defined way of life is a systemic necessity, we come third to examine the way of life of an ideal system. The three Judaic systems we examine in this abstraction yield (again, only for purposes of a mental experiment) three ways of life. The priest viewed society as organized through lines of structure emanating from the Temple. His caste stood at the top of a social scale in which all things were properly organized, each with its correct name and proper place. The inherent sanctity of Israel came through genealogy to its richest embodiment in him, the priest. Food set aside for his rations at God's command possessed that same sanctity; so too did the table at which he ate his food. To the priest, the sacred society of Israel produced history as an account of what happened in—and (alas) on occasion to—the Temple. To the sage, by comparison, the life of society demanded wise regulation. Relationships among people required guidance by the laws embodied in the Torah and interpreted by the sage. Accordingly, the task of Israel was to construct a way of life in accordance with the revealed rules of the Torah. The sage—master of the rules—stood at the head. In our third system, the prophets insisted that the fate of the nation depended upon the faith and moral condition of society, and history testified to the external context and inner condition of Israel, viewed as a whole. Both sage and priest saw Israel from the aspect of eternity. But the nation lived out its life in the history of this world, coveting the very same land as other peoples within the politics of empires. The Messiah's kingship would resolve the issues of Israel's subordinated relationship to other nations and empires, establishing once for all time the correct context for priest and sage alike.

The three modes of human existence expressed in the symbolic systems of cult, Torah, and Messiah demanded choices. The proper conduct of the cult of sacrifice in the Temple determined the course of the seasons and the prosperity of the land, or else it was merely ritual. The Messiah will save Israel, or he will ruin everything. So the way in which symbols are arranged and rearranged settles everything. Symbol change is social change. The particular way the three are bonded in a given system reflects an underlying human and social reality. The three symbols with their associated myths, the world views they project, and the ways of life they define, stand for different views of what really matters. So, to conclude this mental experiment, let us translate the symbols we have surveyed—the three points of emphasis of three Judaisms—into the everyday life of ordinary people. When we lay out the existential foundations of the several symbolic systems available to Jews of antiquity, we penetrate to the bedrock of Israel's everyday reality.

We ask, finally, what was at stake. The points of stress and human concern of the three Judaisms emerge when we ask what made one particular focus—the priestly, the sagacious, or the messianic—appear more compelling and consequential than the others. The answer becomes obvious when we realize that each addressed its singular and distinctive point of concern and spoke about different things to different people. Priests and sages turned inward, toward the concrete everyday life of the community. They addressed the sanctification of Israel. Messianists and their prophetic and apocalyptic counterparts turned outward, toward the affairs of states and nations. They spoke of the salvation of Israel. Priests saw the world as a realm of life in Israel, and death beyond. They knew what happened to Israel—what made Israel die or live—without requiring a theory about the place of Israel among the nations. For priests, the nations formed an undifferentiated realm of death. Sages addressed home and hearth, fathers and sons, husbands and wives, masters and disciples, and the village and enduring patterns of life. What place was there in this domestic scheme for the disruptive realities of history, wars and threats of war, and the rise and fall of empires? The messianic emphasis encompassed the consciousness of a singular society amidst other societies. So at issue for the priest was order, regularity, and "being." For the prophet and Messiah it was, disruption, spontaneity, and "becoming."[3]

We err if we imagine that, in the histories of Judaisms, any Judaic system exhibited in pure form the categorical traits—emphasis, sym-

3. I need hardly specify my debt, in this entire analysis, to Max Weber.

bolic structure, and mode of organizing everyday life and society—of one of the three fundamental divisions that Scripture lays out for us: the Pentateuchal and priestly, the historical and prophetic, and the wisdom writings. I have described them as ideal types. But in the situation of everyday life, every system drew heavily on the three antecedent strands of ancient Israel's writings. And the two sects we take up now teach us how the received categories were reworked to accord with the structural traits of the paramount and dominant system, the priests' Judaic system of the Torah of Moses. We find in the sects the definitive characteristics of the larger and encompassing system of which they constitute distinctive and special expressions. These characteristics emerge in extreme and definitive form, and that is why the sects' systems attract our interest. There are two that matter for our purpose, Essenes and Pharisees.

From Category to System: Prologue to Two Radical Statements of the Common Judaism of the Age of Restoration

Systemic analysis begins in the social group. Without an Israel, a social entity in fact and not only in doctrine, we have not a system but a book. And a book is not a Judaism, it is only a book. Our interest focuses not on the imaginary worlds of theologians, philosophers, or visionaries, but on the social systems—the Judaisms—that Jews have created. We focus on two sects, the Essenes, represented by the commune at Qumran, and the Pharisees. Each realized in sharp and extreme form the ideals of the normative system of the priests' Torah of Moses. The reason is that we have in hand bits and pieces of compositions, most of them not in the context of a sustained and cogent systemic statement, and none of them reaching us in a particular social setting, related to a distinctive social group, expressive of its characteristic way of life.[4]

4. The categories of a literary or a theological character, among which the extant writings are now organized, do not serve for systemic description. That is why for the moment we pay no attention to the bulk of the writings of the Second Temple period conventionally identified as "the apocrypha and pseudepigrapha of the Old Testament," or even those books or passages of the Hebrew Scriptures assigned to the Second Temple period, such as the book of Daniel. They provide important clues as to the perspective of individuals or small circles. That is not to suggest that the writings of an apocalpytic character, such as Enoch, do not speak for a distinctive social entity within ancient Israel, or that they do not attest to a world view. They assuredly do adumbrate a complex and suggestive picture of reality. But we cannot describe that picture in its larger social setting: who held it, where and when, what urgent questions found their

The literary statements of the Essenes of Qumran and the Pharisees make constant reference to issues of the Priestly Code. One encompassing example of that fact is the stress among both groups upon cultic cleanness and uncleanness: the preservation of food and of meals in conditions required only for the Temple and the priests in the Priestly Code of Leviticus and Numbers. Each group—each a sect expressing in an extreme and pure way the value of the society as a whole—laid emphasis upon the holy Temple. In each case the members of the sect wanted to obey the rules of holiness as they applied to the Temple even when they were in their homes. Now those rules involved aspects of everyday life. But one point of emphasis was on the conduct of the priests in their eating of their share of the holy offerings to God. Specifically, the priests had to keep a set of rules of consecration when they ate their meals, which were made up of the priests' portion of the sacrifice.

The Essenes of Qumran observed a set of rules of cultic cleanness when eating their meals. So too the Pharisees were (among other points of definition) people bound by observance of common rules governing the preparation and eating of meals. Both groups imitated the priests and so entered into that state of holiness achieved by them. Each defined itself around the eating of cultic meals in the state of cleanness prescribed by Leviticus for Temple priests in the eating of their share of the Temple sacrifices. We begin with the Essenes.

---

self-evidently valid answers in the world view, and how that world view reached full material expression in the way of life of the social entity. In another book (Jacob Neusner et al, ed., *Judaisms and their Messiahs* [Cambridge: Cambridge University Press, 1987]), we found it difficult to undertake appropriate systemic analysis of the social setting for the messiah doctrine, or the use of the messiah theme, of apocalyptic groups in apocryphal and pseudepigraphic writings. Accordingly, since a book is not a system, we omit reference not only to Philo's philosophy of Judaism, or to the Maccabees' politics and the history that explained their polity, but also to those suggestive and important works of visionaries of space and time that attested in words to social worlds other than those we presently consider. (Similarly in chapter 6 we make no reference to the great philosophical systems of Maimonides and other medieval philosophers of Judaism and in chapter 7 to the counterpart systems of nineteenth- and twentieth-century theologians.) Interesting in their own terms, they do not constitute Judaisms. The writings of apocalypse and vision shine out of an empty part of heaven, stars in a black sky, and part of no galaxy. The system is there, but so far we have too slender knowledge of its society and circumstance. So for the moment we work with what we have and address two sets of writings that do describe Israels.

The Essenes' Judaism of Sanctification and Salvation

The ancient Jewish library discovered in 1947 at Qumran, at the Dead Sea, portrays the way of life and world view of a social group similar in many ways to what had been known about the Essenes from literary descriptions out of antiquity. The Essenes portrayed in the Qumran Library formed a Jewish sect that laid emphasis on purity rules in eating their meals and in conducting their sexual lives. They flourished in the last two centuries B.C. to A.D. 68. The main component of the world view of the Essene Judaism was the conviction that the community formed the final remnant of Israel and that God would shortly annihilate the wicked. These converts to the true faith would be saved, because their founder, the teacher of righteousness, had established a new covenant between the community and God. So this Israel would endure. The task of the community was to remain faithful to the covenant, endure the exile in the wilderness, and prepare for the restoration of the Temple in its correct form. The Essenes recapitulated the history of Israel, seeing themselves as the surviving remnant of some disaster that had destroyed the faith, and preparing for that restoration that they anticipated would soon come, just as it had before. We find in the Essenic system a replication of the Judaic system of the priesthood, with one important qualification. While the Judaic system represented by the Pentateuch laid great stress on the holy way of life, the Essenic system as represented by its library combined the holy way of life with a doctrine of salvation at the end of time. The principal components of the scriptural composite—Torah laws, prophetic-historical interpretation, and sagacious rules on the conduct of everyday life—found counterparts in the library of the Essene community. Essenic Judaism reworked the strands into a distinctive and characteristic statement of its own.

The library contains a variety of documents which in the aggregate portray the viewpoint of the sect that preserved the writings and revered them. Among the more important documents are the Community Rule (also called the Manual of Discipline), a handbook of instruction for the head of the community, which outlines the aims of the group and provides a picture of the rite of entering the covenant of the community.[5] Those who joined the sect lived a holy life, and all others were allies of Satan. The postulates are marked by the spirit of truth or

5. Geza Vermes, *The Dead Sea Scrolls: Qumran in Perspective* (London: Collins, 1977), p. 46.

falsehood, or the spirit of light or darkness, and the master had to know the difference. The code also provided rules for the life of the community, and these rules were meant to govern until the Messiah came. It ended with a hymn of thanksgiving. Vermes compares the Community Rule to the counterpart rules of Christian monasticism which define the life of the community. At the end of time the sect's affairs would be taken over by two Messiahs, one of Israel, and one of Aaron (the priesthood). The messianic rule describes the life of the individual from childhood education to marriage to participation in the everyday life of the group and in its militia.[6] Yet another rule, called the Damascus Rule, provided law on the institutions of the community, vows and oaths, the tribunal, witnesses and judges, purification by water, sabbath observances, cultic cleanness, and the like. Still another, the War Rule, described the conduct of the war to be fought at the end of time. In fact the war represents the struggle between good and evil, in which God will intervene. Vermes described the document as follows:

> The author places the spiritual battle within an imaginary historical context and provides the armies of angels and demons with earthly allies: the Sons of Light are represented by the children of Levi, Judah, and Benjamin; the Sons of Darkness, by the Gentiles headed by the final enemy, the Kittim. Jerusalem is foreseen as reconquered after six years of the war, and the Temple worship restored, and plans for a defeat of all the foreign nations are elaborated in the seventh year.[7]

The Temple Scroll presents rules on purity and impurity, festivals, building the Temple, and the Israelite king and his army. There are in addition writings of hymns, psalms, prayers, and wisdom. In all, if we invoke once more the principal strands of Scriptural writings, we find continuations of all three: Torah writings of doctrine and law, prophetic-historical writings on the meaning and end of history, and sapiential writings on the correct conduct of everyday affairs.

The group—represented by the writings that describe the way of life of a holy community preparing for a war at the end of time and the world view of a struggle between light and darkness—saw itself as Israel, pure and simple: the true Israel. The group divided up into priests and laity, with the priests called the sons of Zadok, recalling the legitimate high priest in the time of David. The lay people divided themselves into twelve tribes. So the whole meant to recapitulate the

6. Vermes, *Dead Sea Scrolls,* p. 48.
7. Vermes, *Dead Sea Scrolls,* pp. 52–3.

true Israel of the scriptural account.[8] A high point in the life of this Israel was its common meal:

> That the common table was of high importance to Qumran daily life is evident from the fact that only the fully professed and the faultless. . . . were allowed to sit at it. There is no explicit mention of a ritual bath preceding the meals, but from various references to purification by water . . . it is likely that the sectaries immersed themselves before eating.[9]

Since in the priests' Torah, the consideration of cultic cleanness concerned the Temple in general, and in connection with eating food it specifically concerned meals made up of the priests' share of the sacrifices to the Lord in the Temple, we may draw one inference. The Israel residing by the Dead Sea saw itself as a holy community bound by rules governing the sanctification of the Temple priesthood in the conduct of the aspects of the life of the priesthood that were pertinent—eating holy meals. Vermes finds in the description of the group two distinct societies, one resident in the desert, and the other in cities. In the former the community lived in seclusion, while in the latter the members were surrounded by outsiders. But both groups claimed to constitute the true Israel.[10] The sect lasted as a social group—a Judaism—from the beginning of the second century B.C. to A.D. 68, when the community was destroyed by the Romans. The end of the world indeed had come, and the Temple was destroyed shortly afterward.

The most characteristic trait of Essenic Judaism was its emphasis on the community as the elect, united here and how with the angels of heaven:

> God has caused his chosen ones to inherit the lot of his holy ones
> He has joined their assembly to the sons of heaven,
> to be a council of the community
> a foundation of the building of holiness
> an eternal plantation throughout all ages to come.[11]

Each one who joined the group entered that remnant of Israel. Then all formed the "sons of light" that would endure to the end:

> Those born of truth spring from a fountain of light, but those born of falsehood spring from a source of darkness. All the children of righteousness

8. Vermes, *Dead Sea Scrolls*, p. 88.
9. Vermes, *Dead Sea Scrolls*, p. 94.
10. Vermes, *Dead Sea Scrolls*, pp. 105–106.
11. Vermes, *Dead Sea Scrolls*, pp. 170, (iQS 11:7–9).

are ruled by the Prince of Light and walk in the ways of light, but all the children of falsehood are ruled by the Angel of Darkness and walk in the ways of darkness.[12]

Reckoning time by its own calendar—by the sun instead of the moon—dividing the year in its own way, the community lived by its own rhythm, as the doctrine outlined here would lead us to expect.

How is the power of the experience of exile and return revealed in the Essenic system of Qumran? The elements of the original paradigm are first, the notion of a saving remnant, a chosen few, which surely originated in the pattern of Israel that endured after 586; second, the conception of a community with a beginning, middle, and end, rather than a community that exists more or less permanently; third, the notion that the Israel at hand replicates in its being the sanctification of the Temple. These are large and encompassing principles, and within them we can find the indicative traits of the Essenic system. All commentators on the Essene library of Qumran have found striking the community's sense of itself as different, separate from the rest of Israel, the clean few among the unclean many, the saved few, the children of light. The fundamental notion that the small group constituted in microcosm the Israel that mattered rested on the premise that the Israel out there, the nation as a whole, lived conditionally. The Israel out there had failed; it was (in the mind of the Essenes) the children of darkness. Making distinctions within the old Israel in favor of the new required the conviction that the life of Israel was not a given, a fact of ordinary reality, but a status to be achieved, a standing to be attained through appropriate regeneration or sanctification. And that basic notion expressed the general pattern of the Pentateuchal structure: Israel is called, formed as something out of nothing, a very particular entity, subject to very special conditions: the children of light as against the rest, the children of darkness. In that conviction of the Essenes I see nothing more than a restatement in fresh terms of the conclusions of the experience of death and resurrection that the nation had endured. The prerequisite for an acutely self-conscious understanding of themselves as the children of light, of the rest as the children of darkness, was the original experience of national death and resurrection.

12. Vermes, *Dead Sea Scrolls,* pp. 171 (1QS 3:13–4:1).

The Pharisees' Judaism of Sanctification

The rich, contemporary documentation of the Essenic Judaism finds no counterpart in the Pharisaic system, about which we do not have a single piece of information deriving from a contemporary, firsthand witness-participant. Several writers claim that they were Pharisees: Josephus, the Jewish general turned historian of the War of 66–73 and of the Jews; and Paul the apostle. But neither one provides a clear picture of what being a Pharisee meant to him in the spell of his life in which he later claimed he belonged to the sect. We know about the shape of the Pharisaic system only from references to it in three disparate writings. Consequently we do not stand on firm ground when we address our agenda of questions to the Pharisaic system. The first body of evidence derives from references in the writings of Josephus. The second body of references appears in the Gospels, especially in Matthew, Mark, and Luke. Brought to completion at more or less the same time as Josephus's work, these documents, like those of Josephus, were written outside of the land of Israel. The third set of references to Pharisees originated in the land, but transmitted whatever its authors knew about the Pharisees only through a long process of revision and reworking into what ultimately became the Mishnah. Since this corpus of references reached completion only about A.D. 200, it is the most difficult to use. And as a further disadvantage, when conceptions in the Mishnah (and related writings) derive from the period before 70, it is not entirely clear that they come from the Pharisees in particular.

While the evidence hardly derives from first hand sources we cannot ignore the Pharisees' statement of a Judaic system. The reason is that, as all sources concur, the group constituted a consequential force, a real social entity, and not merely a body of abstract ideas or viewpoints broadly held. When Josephus and Paul claimed to have been Pharisees, in their minds that claim clearly carried weight and significance. The Gospels' Pharisees were a distinct group, with a strongly held viewpoint. Josephus is even more explicit in his description of the Pharisees as a philosophical school, for he assigns to them indicative positions on a number of issues addressed in common by other schools, such as the Essenes and Sadducees. It must follow, for our purposes, that in the Pharisees we confront a somewhat confused picture. On the one side we see a group somewhat analogous to the Essenes, whose cogent system—way of life, world view, addressed to a clearly defined Israel—has parallels in the Pharisees' clearcut way of life, observing the dietary regulations others thought applied only in special circumstances or not at all, projecting a world-view of lay people pretending to be priests, speaking of all Israel and not only a saving remnant. On the other side, Josephus's picture of a philosophical sect that formed a political party does not quite fit. Then the Gospels' account with its stress on both dietary and related regulations but also on the group's political influence draws the whole together. Josephus, for his part, also alleges in behalf of the Pharisees a political influence that, before the destruction of the Temple, they are not likely to have exercised. On that picture provided by Josephus, the ancient historian, Morton Smith, in a justly famous discovery, comments as follows:

> It is almost impossible not to see in such a rewriting of history a bid to the Roman government. That government must have been faced [after 70] with the problem: which group of Jews shall we support? . . . To this question Josephus is volunteering an answer: The Pharisees . . . have by far the greatest influence with the people. Any government which secures their support is accepted; any government which alienates them has trouble . . . Josephus's discovery of these important political facts (which he ignored when writing the Jewish War) may have been due partly to a change in his personal relationship with the Pharisees . . . The more probable explanation is that in the meanwhile the Pharisees had become the leading candidates for Roman support in Palestine and were already negotiating it.[13]

The later writings of the rabbis, first published after 200, assign to authorities known to have flourished before 70 sayings concerning a variety of matters. But most of them deal with two issues: first, problems of cultic cleanness; second, rules governing the tithing of foods. The same matters formed the center of the polemic against the Pharisees in Mark's and Matthew's accounts of Jesus' life and teachings. The Pharisees tithe mint and cummin and neglect weightier matters of the law. The Pharisees clean the outside of a utensil—a consideration of cultic cleanness—while they neglect the inside. That is part of the evidence in the Gospel accounts of the Pharisees' hypocrisy: outward piety, inward sin.

With the Pharisees, we have a group that stressed keeping laws concerning the correct preparation of food, including reserving a portion of the crops for the support of the priesthood and other scheduled castes. Scripture had specified a variety of rules on the matter, in general holding that God owned a share of the crops and that God's share was to go to the holy castes (Priests, Levites). When Pharisees made sure that

13. Morton Smith, "Palestinian Judaism in the First Century," in *Israel: Its Role in Civilization*, ed. Moshe Davis (New York: Harper and Row, 1956).

everything that was supposed to go to the castes did, they were obeying the rules that linked meals to the altar and its service. Scripture had furthermore laid down rules governing uncleanness: its sources and effects. Such sources, specified in Lev. 11–15, derived from the bodily flux of human beings and certain deceased creatures, for example. The effect of contact with such sources of uncleanness was not only hygienic but mainly cultic: one affected by uncleanness could not enter the Temple (e.g., Lev. 13–14, the leper). Those considered unclean as a result of contact with a corpse and other sources of uncleanness specified at Lev. 11–15, for example, were prohibited from having sexual relations. But one made unclean in that way also could not go to the Temple. For the authors of the priestly code the concern for the cleanness or uncleanness of utensils and persons, was to protect the cult and the Temple from the dangers seen to lurk in the sources of uncleanness. But the rules affecting uncleanness laid out in the Mishnah—many of them going back to the earliest stratum of the Mishnaic system before 70 and probably to Pharisaic origins—deal with domestic matters. The fundamental assumption throughout is that one eats in a state of cultic cleanness not only food deriving from the altar but also meals eaten at home. The more important assumption is that ordinary people, and not only priests, must keep those rules. Put together, the two premises point to a group that was made up of lay people pretending to be priests— much on the order of the Essenes—who treated their homes as temples, and their tables as altars. Once again we recall the model of the Essenes, who evidently held that their commune constituted holy Israel, and their table, an altar.[14]

Both the Pharisees and the Essenes distinguished themselves by their stress on the sanctification of the everyday life of Israel beyond the walls of the temple. This they did, in particular, through keeping the laws of holiness as they applied to the propagation of life—family and sexual matters—and the maintenance of life—meals and preparation of food. The Pharisees held that all Jews—represented by themselves—should enter the status of temple priests and perform actions carried out by

14. I find myself unable to harmonize the picture of the Pharisees in the Maccabean court as a political party with strongly held philosophical convictions and the indications of a quite different sort of group, namely Jews who treated their everyday existence as holy by eating at home as though they were priests in the Temple of Jerusalem. My best guess is that before Herod—who completely changed the political conditions of the Jews in the Land of Israel and ruled much more exclusively than had the Hasmoneans—the Pharisees formed one sort of group and after Herod, a different one. But that is only a guess.

priests on account of their status. The table of every Jew in his or her home was like the table of the Lord in the Jerusalem Temple. A kingdom of priests and a holy people stood in one relationship to God: a relationship of separation from the unclean (including the unclean peoples) and from death. Everyone had to keep the priestly laws. Everyone had to prepare food in accord with the laws of tithing, important as they were to the priesthood's support, and of cultic cleanness. These considerations marked the sectarian character of diverse groups within the normative Judaism of the day, as Morton Smith observes:

> Differences as to the interpretation of the purity laws and especially as to the consequent question of table fellowship were among the principal causes of the separation of Christianity from the rest of Judaism and the early fragmentation of Christianity itself. The same thing holds for the Qumran community, and within Pharisaic tradition the [Pharisaic] *havurah* [fellowship]. They are essentially groups whose members observe the same interpretation of the purity rules and therefore can have table fellowship with each other. It is no accident that the essential act of communion in all these groups is participation in common meals.[15]

Food which had been properly grown and tithed fell into the category of what could become sacred. A person in a state of cultic cleanness fell into that same category. So far as our sources indicate, the table fellowship that expressed the realization of the Pharisaic system took place routinely every day. We have no records of elaborate rites connected with the holy meals, nor do we have sources that explain how, if one kept the body alive through sanctified food, one sustained the soul as holy, too. In that respect, the Pharisees appear to have differed from the Essenes, with their elaborate rules and circumstances of table fellowship.

The way of life of the Pharisees in the first century therefore affected ordinary people living everyday lives. People took as their task the sanctification of the profane. The opportunity for acts of holiness came in kitchens, beds, marketplaces, whenever someone picked up a common nail, which might be unclean, or purchased wheat, which if dry remained cultically clean and when tithed could be prepared and eaten. The perpetual ritualization of everyday life represented for the first century Pharisees the opportunity for the sanctification of the common life of Israel. Israel was to form a kingdom of priests and a holy people, and what that meant above all was that the everyday was to be made

15. Morton Smith, "The Dead Sea Sect in Relation to Ancient Judaism," *New Testament Studies* 7 (1961): 347–360.

sacred. Furthermore, the Pharisees, unlike the Essenes, stressed that the laws were to be kept, in the everyday Israel, by the Jewish people in the everyday world. The Pharisaic quest for wide public knowledge and observance of the purity laws surely accounts for the polemic of the Gospels.

How did the Pharisees' system compare with our paradigm? The congruence between the points of interest within the Pharisaic system and the pattern of the Priestly Torah proves striking indeed. The book of Leviticus represented the cult as the center of the life of the nation. The Pharisaic way of life certainly concurred. Indeed, the Pharisaic stress on the sanctification of the home and the paradigmatic power of the Temple for the home points to a more extreme position than that of the priests themselves. What the priests wanted for the Temple, the Pharisees wanted for the community at large. And in that way the Pharisees carried to more radical extreme the fundamental systemic position of the priests' Torah of Moses. Admittedly, we have slight access to positions taken in the first century by the Pharisaic system on other matters, besides those represented by the Gospels and the later rabbis of the Mishnah. No one can imagine that the group took positions only on the questions at hand, which deal with partial aspects of a complete system. The Essenes at Qumran presented a substantial account of the meaning and end of history, a doctrine of salvation; they spelled out in so many words their doctrine of Israel—or themselves as the final remnant of Israel. We may characterize the Pharisaic system as a Judaism of sanctification. And we are able to identify the pattern of the sixth and early fifth centuries. No wonder, then, that Pharisees, by all accounts, affirmed the eternity of the soul (as Josephus says) or the resurrection of the dead (as Luke's picture of Paul in Acts maintains). For the way of sanctification led past the uncleanness of the grave to the renewed purity of the living person, purification out of the most unclean of all sources of uncleanness, the realm of death itself. The pattern of sanctification of the everyday brought immediacy to the cosmic pattern of death and resurrection.[16]

The Uncertain Restoration and Its Aftermath

The trauma of annihilation and rebirth, as portrayed by the Torah of Moses, brought about yearning for one thing above all: no more. The

16. If we omit reference to the Pharisees' theory of history or ethics, it is not because the group did not have such a theory. We do not know whether its theory proved so

restoration gave Israel a second chance at life, but Israel also could rely on its knowledge of the rules that governed its national life to make certain there would be no more experiences of exile and alienation. That is why the picture of what had happened presented solace, and why people wanted to accept the portrait of their world. The Essenes and Pharisees each knew what was expected. In the case of the Essenes, it was a holy way of life now, leading to salvation in the coming age, which was near at hand. The Pharisees stressed the sanctification of the everyday world, so that Israel at large had to live in accord with the rules of the Temple, even when eating ordinary meals outside of the Temple. In these two groups, we find the common faith of all Israel in the covenanted relationship with God portrayed by the Torah and fulfilled in the requirements of the Torah: convenantal nomism.

The premise of the Torah of Moses, however, never corresponded to the reality of Israelite life in the very period—the sixth century B.C.—in which the fundamentals were stated. The original pattern of exile and return imposed itself upon the social reality of Israel in the Land of Israel and promised that conforming to the covenant would guarantee a long-term future of peace and prosperity. But the terms of the restoration portrayed by the Torah of Moses in the time of Nehemiah and Ezra described a world that no one with clear sight could ever have perceived. The land from the time of Ezra in about 450 for a century and a half was a frontier satrapy of the Persian empire. Alexander's conquest, at the end of the fourth century, left Israel a province in the successor empire of one of his generals, and a century later another successor empire took control of the country. True, both rulers left the Temple intact and under the control of the priesthood. But the Torah had hardly promised a nation governed by outsiders. A brief span of independence—during the period in which one empire, the Seleucid successor empire of Alexander, declined, while the next, that of the Romans, had not yet taken complete control—changed little. For the government of the Maccabees, from the mid–second century to the mid–first century, not to mention that of Herod and his sons, client state of Rome, from the mid–first century B.C. to the war of 70, or even the government of the patriarch and the sages that the Romans put into place after 70—none of these regimes corresponded to the picture presented by the Torah.

---

distinctive as to form part of the definition of what made the group different, an Israel unto itself. We realize that the group shared the "common theology" that consisted of the entirety of Scriptures, and traditions as well.

There was a Temple and the priests ran it. But the ideal government depicted in Leviticus and Deuteronomy and the real regime of the client state had virtually nothing in common. One could not open the Torah and recognize the reality of the contemporary politics or, therefore, explain it. That is why the restoration proved uncertain, disparate with the reality that the Judaic system(s) of the day purported to create. In fact the Judaisms did not shape reality, they contradicted it. And they continued to call into question the givens of the world and to create, in their place, their own social world: their fantasy, a world view expressed in a cogent way of life to an Israel—each component reenforcing the others in a castle built on sand.

To conclude let me refer to my opening proposition: religion constitutes an independent variable that shapes, and is not merely shaped by, the world beyond. It is not merely that the Torah of Moses does *not* describe social reality and does *not* present world experienced. Rather the Torah of Moses generated the system which created the world view and the way of life of the Israel that constituted a Judaism. And that system not only contradicted the facts of Israelite life in the age in which it came to expression, but it also contradicted the prospects of Israel, a small and inconsequential people with an inflated view of itself. The condition for the continuing power of the Judaic system of the Torah not only required the recapitulation of resentment, but also produced what was required. That was the constant renewal of the resentment precipitated and provoked by the discrepancy first present in the Torah's own system. The Torah of Moses therefore did more than recapitulate resentment. In age succeeding age the Torah generated the resentment which powered the system—then resolved it.

The proposition of this book—that religion imparts its pattern upon the social world and polity of Jews—stunningly emerges in the simple fact before us: what the record of 586 says happened and what that same record shows happened do not correspond. What really happened was that the Babylonians destroyed Jerusalem and exiled its political classes as well as skilled workers. Large numbers of Jews remained in the land and continued to live out their lives there. The system of the Torah not only presented the pattern of Israel as the covenanted people, whose heightened social reality derived from the experience of exile and return, but also created the pattern, using the experience of those who had gone into exile and who had come back to the land, even though sizable numbers of Jews did not go into exile, or did not return to the land, so the pattern did not describe what had happened to them. The system selected happenings and treated them as events, then ranked events in order of priority, then interpreted important events as part of a larger system: a world view, a way of life, addressed to a particular Israel. The order of the process is first the creation of the system, and then the selection of things that have happened as events, and finally the formation out of events of a pattern that is called history or theology.[17]

17. At this point in the argument the terms are equivalent and the choice of which of the two synonyms we use no longer matters.

FOUR

THE FIRST STAGE IN THE FORMATION OF JUDAISM: THE MISHNAH

FROM 70 TO 200

Pharisaism before, and Judaism after, 70

When, exactly, did the Judaism of the two Torahs originate? While drawing on much older materials, beginning with the Scriptures themselves, the Judaism of the dual Torah began to take shape as we now know it only in the first century. What groups contributed to this Judaism? The Scribes, a profession, and the Pharisees, a sect, contributed the contents and the method of Judaism, respectively. Under what circumstances was this union of established elements in a striking new way accomplished? In the aftermath of the destruction of the Second Temple in Jerusalem in 70, the two groups coalesced and began the process that in the next six centuries yielded Judaism in the form in which we now know it.

In A.D. 66 a Jewish rebellion broke out in Jerusalem against Rome's rule of the country. Initially successful, the rebels in the end were pushed back into the holy city, which fell in August, A.D. 70. The Temple, destroyed in 586 B.C. and rebuilt three generations later, by the time of its second destruction had stood for five hundred years, as long a time as separates us from Columbus. And because of the message of the Judaism of the Torah of Moses, people regarded the fate of the Temple as the barometer of their nation's relationship to God. With the Temple's destruction by the Romans, the foundations of national and social life in the land of Israel were shaken. People related the movement of the seasons and the sun in heaven to the cult in the Temple. They associated the first full moon after the vernal equinox with the rite of the Passover, and the first full moon after the autumnal equinox with that of Tabernacles. They attained personal atonement for their sins of inadvertence by minor offerings, and they believed that in the rite of the Day of Atonement, they reconciled themselves with God. The Temple had served as the basis for the many elements of autonomous self-government and political life left in the Jews' hands by the Romans. The government of the country appealed for legitimacy to the Temple and the priesthood, with which it associated itself. The structure not only of political life and of society, but also of the imaginative life of the country, depended upon the Temple and its worship and cult. It was there that people believed they served God. At the Temple the lines of structure—both cosmic and social—converged. The altar was the point at which the transfer of life from heaven to earth took place: the transaction that sustained the world. Consequently the destruction of the Temple meant not merely a significant alteration in the cultic or ritual life of the Jewish people, but also a profound and far-reaching crisis in their inner and spiritual existence.

When the Temple was destroyed, two distinct groups survived: the scribes with their learning, and the priests with their memories, their sense of what God required for service, and their notion that every Jew stood in relationship to all others within the grid of holiness. Over the next half century or so these two groups began to forge the system that—through and beyond the Mishnah—would become the Judaism of the dual Torah. The period from 70 to the Bar Kokhba war, about 132–135, yielded the foundations of the Mishnaic system, a system derived from the combination of three distinct political forces: Roman rule; a local Jewish authority, called the patriarch, recognized by Rome as the legitimate Jewish administrator of Israel's affairs; and the administration of the patriarch, staffed by knowledgeable clerks, called sages. The system that took shape from 70 onward, originally appeared in Yavneh, a coastal town.

We recall that the Persians, ruling a diverse empire, under Cyrus adopted the policy of identifying local groups and ruling through them, a standard imperial procedure followed when the ruling empire did not choose to settle its own population in a conquered area. Fortunately for Israel the several successor empires—from the Persians, through the Macedonians under Alexander and then the inheritor states of Ptolemies and Seleucids, and, finally the Romans—decided to leave the Land of Israel in the hands of loyal regents. The Romans first supported the Maccabees, and then Herod and his family. That policy remained in effect even after the Jewish wars against Rome in 66 and 132. Roman policy involved finding in native populations trustworthy leaders who would keep the peace and execute Roman policy.

After 70 the Romans gave up on the policy of depending on the family of Herod, which had manifestly failed. They accorded some sort of limited recognition to a Jewish ruler of a different family, a Pharisaic one. Our knowledge of the new ruling figure scarcely extends beyond his name, Gamaliel, though we know that his heirs later sustained the institution of Jewish rule that he began.[1] How and why the Romans turned to Gamaliel we can only guess. He was the son of Simeon b. Gamaliel, a leading figure among the Pharisees before 70 and grandson of yet another such figure. That means that Gamaliel got Roman recognition as a promising local authority of a distinguished family prepared to cooperate with the government. Called the patriarch—in Hebrew the *nasi*, —Gamaliel associated with himself two sorts of survivors of the war. One represented the pre-70 Pharisees, of which he was probably an adherent. The other derived from the important state officials of the period before 70, who in the aggregate, are known as scribes: people who knew and administered the laws. The sages that associated themselves with the patriarchal regime contributed the know-how of government, and such administration, on a local basis, as the Jews of the land of Israel knew, derived from that group. The patriarchal government with its scribal staff from the Roman perspective enjoyed only modest success, because they could not prevent the war of Bar Kokhba from breaking out. But once more the Romans after Bar Kokhba's defeat turned back to the system of ethnarchies and restored the ruling regime, this time with complete success. It endured into the fifth century, at which time the Christian government of Rome determined not to accord it further recognition. An equivalent system employed by the Parthian and then the Sassanian rulers of Iran, across the eastern frontier from Rome, led to the development there of a Jewish ethnarchy, called the exilarchate. Both regimes adopted as their constitution and law the Mishnah produced by Judah the Patriarch, on account of which the document enjoyed immediate acceptance as the Jews' law code after Scripture. Thus the first and most important reason for the development of Judaism was the political choices made by

1. Still later, in the person of Judah the Patriarch, they advanced the claim of descent from David, hence of a messianic character. That claim surfaces, to be sure, in documents redacted no earlier than 400, and may represent merely another sign of the messianization of the Judaism of sages.

outsiders. Later we shall observe that Judaism in the same form endured in part for the same reason: Christendom and Islam tolerated it.
But the other reason matters far more: the Jews wanted to form their
world within the structure of that Judaism—in that form. That was the
Judaism that asked the questions they found urgent and provided the
answers they deemed valid.

In the world beyond Yavneh—the site of the sages' meeting place
where Pharisaism and scribism were joined into a new Jewish regime
under Roman rule—people looked for a coming cataclysm. The Judaism of the Torah had after all accounted for such a calamity as had just
taken place. The pattern of sin, suffering, atonement, reconciliation,
and restoration certainly predominated in peoples' minds. After three
generations had passed, a second war against Rome broke out, that is,
the Bar Kokhba rebellion of 132–135. But the old pattern failed to be
realized. Bar Kokhba's armies, successful for a brief time, confronted
Rome at the height of its power, and lost, despite the bravery of the
Jewish soldiers. For a time the Romans engaged in a policy of repression
of Judaism—which they saw as the source of sedition—but they soon
reverted to their established politics. After the Romans had once more
succeeded in pacifying the country, they again turned to the native
regime and reestablished its authority. The sages—disciples of the
masters of Yavneh and now heirs of a tradition half a century in the
making—thus regained recognition and took over such political power
as Rome allowed the Jews. This time they derived considerably greater
satisfaction from the result, since the patriarchal government administered the Jewish affairs of the land of Israel down to its dissolution in
429 in the aftermath of the Christianization of the Roman Empire.

From the political foundations of the system we turn to its method
and doctrine—its world view and way of life. The character of Pharisaic Judaism before 70 helped ensure the success of the Judaism that
the Pharisees helped to shape. When the Temple was destroyed, it
turned out that the Pharisees had prepared for that tremendous change
in the sacred economy. Even after the destruction of the Temple to
which their laws had applied, lay people pretending to be priests could
continue in the paths of holiness that the Temple had shown for centuries by keeping the laws of purity at home. Israel the people was holy,
not only the place of the Temple and Jerusalem, and not only the rite of
the cult in the Temple. The Pharisees (like the Essenes) had a doctrine
of Israel as the holy people living the holy life which proved remarkably
congruent to the urgent issue posed by the destruction of the Temple.
The answer to the questions of the destruction—who is Israel now? is

Israel yet holy now?—was that Israel is the bearer of the holy, Israel as a whole and not solely the priesthood, Israel in its every day life and not only the priests in the Temple. The destruction of the Temple as a real place found compensation in the pretense that the Pharisees had maintained before 70. True, the buildings were gone, but the critical issue was holiness, and holiness endured; this was a powerful and acutely pertinent answer to the question of the day. The remarkable congruity between the Pharisaic view of Israelite life and the circumstances prevailing after the destruction of the Temple in 70 accounts for the success of the Judaism to which the Pharisees made a major contribution. The political advantages accorded to the Pharisees through Gamaliel after 70 should not obscure the doctrinal ones they enjoyed.

The Mishnah's system inherited important components from the Pharisaism of the period before 70 and therefore could maintain the holiness of the life of Israel after the physical destruction of the building and the cessation of sacrifices. Israel the people was holy, the medium and instrument of God's sanctification. The system instructed Israel to act as if there were a new Temple formed of Israel, the Jewish people. Joined to the Pharisaic mode of looking at life, now centered in the doctrine of the holiness of Israel the people, was the substance of the scribal ideal—the stress on learning the Torah and carrying out its teachings. The emerging system claimed, as did the scribes of old, that it was possible to serve God not only through sacrifice but also through the study of Torah.

The union of the scribe and the priest yielded the sage who bore the honorific title, Rabbi. A priest is in charge of the life of the community, just as the priests had said. But the new priest was qualified not by birth in the priestly caste. Rather, his validation derived from his learning in the Torah: the new priest was a sage. The old sin offerings could still be carried out. But now it was the sacrifice of deeds of loving-kindness in the tradition of wisdom that the sage, the rabbi, taught. Like the prophets and historians in the time of the first destruction, in 586 B.C., the sages or rabbis claimed that it was because the people had sinned and had not kept the Torah that the Temple had been destroyed. The disaster was made to vindicate the rabbinic teaching and to verify its truth. When the people lived up to the teachings of the Torah as the rabbis expressed them, the Temple would be restored in response to the people's repentence and renewal.

The professional ideal of the scribes stressed the study of the Torah and the centrality of the learned person in the religious system. But there was something more. It was the doctrine of Israel that made all the difference. If the world view came from the scribes and the way of life from the Pharisees, the doctrine of who was Israel—and the social reality beyond the doctrine—was fresh and unpredictable. It was Israel surviving, the Jewish people beyond the break marked by the destruction of the Temple. What made the Judaic system after 70 more than the sum of its parts, Pharisaism and Scribism, was the very doctrine which neither Pharisaism nor scribism contributed. The crisis of the destruction centered attention on what had endured, persisting beyond the end—the people itself. The most typical fundamental characteristic of the original paradigm was recapitulated. Israel because of its amazing experience of loss and restoration, death and resurrection, had become remarkably self-conscious. For a nation that had ceased to be a nation on its own land and then had once more regained that condition, the new calamity represented for it once more the paradigm of death and resurrection. Consequently the truly fresh and definitive component of the new system, after 70, in fact restated in contemporary terms the fixed and established doctrine with which the first Judaism, the Judaism of the Torah of Moses after 450, had begun.

The genius of the Judaic system of sanctification that took shape after 70 and reached its full expression in the Mishnah was to recognize that the holy people might reconstitute the Temple in the sanctity of its own community life. Therefore the people had to be made holy, as the Temple had been holy. The people's social life had to be sanctified as the surrogate for what had been lost. That is why the rabbinic ideal for Judaism maintained that the rabbi served as the new priest, the study of the Torah substituted for Temple sacrifices, and deeds of loving-kindness were the social surrogate for the sin offering—personal sacrifice instead of animal sacrifice. All things fitted together to construct out of the old Judaisms the world view and the way of life of the new and enduring system that ultimately became the Judaism of the dual Torah. But not just yet. Before proceeding to the second stage in the formation of Judaism, we have to describe the first stage in its full literary statement. And that brings us to the Mishnah—its contents, character, and system.

The Mishnah: History of Its System

What was new in the Mishnah was the Mishnah, not most of the facts upon which the document drew. What defined the Mishnah's system was the questions the framers addressed to those facts. To appreciate the work of the authors of the Mishnah, we must recognize the antiquity of many of the facts upon which they drew—beginning with Scripture itself.

Three points of ordinary life formed the focus for social differentiation in the Mishnah's system: food, sex, and marriage. What people ate, how they conducted their sexual lives, and whom they married or to whom they gave their children in marriage defined the social parameters of their group. These factors indicated who was kept within the bounds and who was excluded and systematically kept at a distance. The people behind the laws could not tell people other than their associates what to eat or whom to marry, but they could make their own decisions on these important, but humble, matters. Moreover by making those decisions, they could keep outsiders at a distance and could keep those who adhered to the group within bounds. Without political control they could not govern the transfer of property or other matters of public interest, but they could govern the transfer of their women. It was in that intimate aspect of life that the Israelites firmly established the outer boundary of their collective existence. It therefore seems no accident at all that the strata of Mishnaic law which appear to go back to the period before the wars, well before 70, deal specifically with the special laws of marriage (in Yebamot), distinctive rules on when sexual relations may and may not take place (in Niddah), and the laws covering the definition of sources of uncleanness and the attainment of cleanness, with specific reference to domestic meals (in certain parts of Ohalot, Zabim, Kelim, and Miqvaot). Nor is it surprising that for the conduct of the cult and the sacrificial system—about which the group may have had its own doctrines but over which it neither exercised control nor even aspired to—there appears to be no systemic content or development whatsoever.

Much of the law of the Mishnah derived from the age before the document was completed. In the Mishnah we see how a group of jurisprudents drew together a rich heritage of legal and moral traditions and facts and made of them a single system. From Scripture onward, no other composition compared in size, comprehensive treatment of a vast variety of topics, balance, proportion, and cogency.[2] But the authors of

2. Let us review the evidence for the antiquity of numerous facts used by the Mishnah's framers in the construction of their system. Some legal facts in the Mishnah, as in other law codes of its place and age, derive from remote antiquity—the ancient Near Eastern world of Sumeria and its successor empires even prior to the beginnings of ancient Israel. Categories of law and investment, for instance, prove continuous with Akkadian and even Sumerian ones. To cite a single instance, there are the sorts of investments classified as *nikhse melug* or *nikhse son barzel* (M. Yebamot 7:1–2), invest-

the Mishnah reshaped whatever came into their hands. The document upon close reading proves systematic and orderly, purposive and well composed. It is no mere scrapbook of legal facts, arranged for purposes of reference. The critical problem at the center always dictated how the facts were chosen, arranged, and used. The law as it emerged whole and complete in the Mishnah, derived from the imagination and wit of the final two generations, in the second century c.e., of its authors. The system as a whole is described in the section "The Mishnah's Law after the Wars" in this chapter. Let us first trace its growth by its individual parts.

THE LAW BEFORE 70

The Mishnah as we know it originated in its Division of Purities. The Sixth Division is the only one that yields a complete statement of a topic dating from before the war of 66–73. It describes what imparts uncleanness, what kinds of objects and substances may be unclean, and how these objects or substances may regain the status of cleanness. Joined to episodic rulings elsewhere, the principal parts of the Sixth Division speak, in particular, of cleanness of meals: food and drink, pots and pans. Apparently the ideas expressed in the Mishnah began among people who had a special interest in observing cultic cleanness, as dictated by the priestly code. The context for such cleanness was the

---

ments in which the investor shares in the loss or the profit, on the one side, or in which the investor is guaranteed the return of the capital without regard to the actual course of the investment transaction, on the other. (The former would correspond to common stock, the latter to preferred stock or even to a government bond). Another mode of demonstrating that facts in the Mishnah's system derived from a period substantially prior to that of the Mishnah carries us to the data provided by documents redacted long before the Mishnah. For example, details of rules in the law codes found in the library of the Essene community of Qumran (the Temple scroll, the Manual of Discipline) intersect with details of rules in the Mishnah. Accounts of aspects of Israelite life take for granted that issues lively in the Mishnah came under debate long before the completion of the Mishnah. The Gospels' accounts of Jesus' encounter with the Pharisees, among others, encompass topics treated in the Mishnah. The matter of grounds for divorce proves important to sages whose names occur in the Mishnah, and one position of one of these sages accords with the position on the same matter imputed to Jesus. It follows that not only isolated facts but critical matters of jurisprudential philosophy came to the surface long before the completion of the Mishnah. As to the contribution of Scripture, that forms the centerpiece of the matter. We take for granted that whenever the authors of the Mishnah chose a subject for intensive study, they automatically drew into their system the facts concerning that subject supplied by Scripture. Points of difference between scriptural and Mishnaic opinion on a given subject prove trivial and inconsequential.

home, not solely the Temple, about which Leviticus speaks. The issues of the law leave no doubt on that score. Since priests ate heave offering at home, and did so in a state of cultic cleanness, it was a small step to apply the same taboos to food which was not a consecrated gift to the priests.

The keeping of these laws meant that the food eaten at home was as holy as the offering at the Temple. If food not consecrated for the altar was deemed subject to the same purity restrictions as food consecrated for the altar, the character of that food, those who were to eat it, and the conditions in which it was grown and eaten all took on new meaning. First, all food was to be protected in a state of levitical cleanness, thus holiness, or separateness. Second, the place in the land where the food was grown and kept was to be kept cultically clean. Third, the people who were to eat that food were holy, just like the priesthood. Fourth, the act of eating food anywhere in the Holy Land was analogous to the act of eating food in the Temple, by the altar.

All of these inferences point to a profound conviction about the land, the people, the produce, and the condition and context of nourishment. The setting was holy and the actors were holy. And what they did that had to be protected in holiness was eat. For when they ate their food at home, they ate it the way priests did in the Temple. And the way priests ate their food in the Temple was the way God ate his food in the Temple. By eating like God, Israel became like God: a pure and perfect incarnation on earth in the land which was holy in the model of heaven. Eating food was the critical act and occasion, as the priestly authors of Leviticus and Numbers had maintained when they made laws about how people should slaughter beasts and burn their flesh, bake pancakes and cookies with and without olive oil and burn them on the altar, and press grapes and make wine and pour it out onto the altar. The nourishment of the Land—meat, grain, oil, and wine—was set before God and burned ("offered up") in conditions of perfect cultic antisepsis.

This antisepsis provided protection against things deemed the opposite of nourishment and the quintessence of death: corpse matter, people who looked like corpses (Lev. 13); dead creeping things; blood when not flowing in the veins of the living (menstrual blood [Lev. 15]); and other sorts of flux (semen in men, nonmenstrual blood in women) which yield not life but death. What these excrescences have in common, of course, is that they are ambiguous, since they may be one thing or the other. Blood in the living is the soul; blood not in the living is the soul of contamination. The corpse was once a living person, like God; the person with skin like a corpse's and who looks dead was once a person who looked alive; the flux of the zab (Lev. 15) comes from the flaccid penis which under the right circumstances, that is, properly erect, produces semen and makes life. What is at the margin between life and death and can go either way is what is the source of uncleanness. But that is insufficient. For the opposite of unclean in the priestly code is not only clean but also holy. The antonym is not to be missed: death or life, unclean or holy.

So the cult was the point of struggle of the forces of life and nourishment against the forces of death and extinction. When meat was eaten—mainly at the time of festivals or other moments at which sin offerings and peace offerings were made—people who wished to live ate their meat (and at all times ate the staples of wine, oil, and bread) in a state of life and so generated life. They kept their food and themselves away from the state of death as much as possible. And this heightened reality pertained at home as much as in the Temple, where most rarely went on ordinary days. The Temple was the font of life and the bulwark against death, just as we noted earlier (p. 43).

Once the meal became a focus of attention, the other two categories of the law which retained principles or laws deriving from the period before the wars presented precisely the same sorts of rules. Laws on growing and preparing food attract attention as soon as people think about how meals are to be eaten. That accounts for the obviously lively interest in the biblical taboos of agriculture. Since meals are acts of society, they call together a group. Outside of the family—the natural unit—such a group is special and cultic. If a group gets together, it is on a Sabbath or festival, not on a workday. So laws are made to govern the making of meals at those times. Rules controlled aspects of the cult which could also apply outside of the cult such as how a beast must be slaughtered, or the disposition of animals of a special status, such as the firstborn. That the rules for meals pertained not to isolated families but to a larger group is strongly suggested by the other area which evidently was subjected to sustained attention before the war of 66–73, laws governing who could marry whom. The context was the life of a small group of people, defining its life apart from the larger Israelite society while maintaining itself wholly within that society.

THE MISHNAH'S LAW BETWEEN THE WARS OF 66–70 AND 132–135

The period between the wars—called the period of Yavneh—marked a transition in the unfolding of the Mishnaic law and system. The law moved out of its narrow, sectarian framework, but it did not yet attain that full definition, serviceable for the governance of a whole society and the formation of a government for the nation as a whole, that would be realized in the aftermath of the wars. The marks of the former state remained, while the marks of the later Mishnaic system began to appear. In its ultimate shape the system as a whole totally reframed the inherited vision. The Mishnah's final framers made provision for the ordinary condition of Israelite men and women, living everyday lives under their own government. The laws suitable for a sect remained, to be joined by others which wholly revised the character of the whole. The shift after the Bar Kokhba war was from a cultic to a communal conception, and from a center at the altar to a system resting upon the utopian character of the nation as a whole.

In the transitional period of Yavneh there was continuity with the immediate past. What took place after 70 was encapsulated in the expansion of the laws of uncleanness. The destruction of the Temple in no way interrupted the unfolding of those laws; development was continuous. The authorities between the wars developed new areas and motifs of legislation, but these were wholly consonant with the familiar ones. If the destruction of the Temple raised in some minds the question of whether the system of cleanness at home would collapse along with the cult, the rules and system before us in no way suggest this. The destruction of the Temple did mark a new phase in the growth of the law. The range of legislation was rapidly extended and specific rules were provided for matters of purity not defined before 70. So the crisis of 70 in the system of uncleanness gave new impetus to movement along lines laid forth long before.

The points of continuity were many and impressive. The development of the rules on the uncleanness of menstrual blood, the *zab,* and corpse uncleanness was wholly consonant with what had gone before. For example, the thought on the zab (Lev. 15) depended entirely on the materials assigned to the Houses of Shammai and Hillel, which were prior to and independent of what is attributed to the authorities after 70. The transfer of the zab's uncleanness through pressure, forming so large and important a part of the tractate of Zabim, begins not with a reference to the zab at all, but to the menstruating women. The fresh point was a step beyond Scripture's own rule, a shift based on analogical thinking. Rulings on corpse contamination dwelled upon secondary and derivative issues. Once the tent was treated as in some way functional, it was natural to focus upon the process or function of overshadowing in general. What was done was to treat the overshadowing as a function, rather than the tent as a thing. The mode of thought was both contrastive and analogical.

The comparison of the table in the home to the cult in the Temple was an old theme in the Mishnaic system. What was new appears to have been the recognition of two complementary sequences, the removes of uncleanness and the degrees of holiness. The former involved several steps of contamination from the original source of uncleanness. The latter covered several degrees of sanctification—ordinary food, heave offering, food deriving from the altar (holy things), and things involved in the preparation of purification water. Each of the latter was subject to the effects of contamination produced by each of the former, in an ascending ladder of sensitivity to uncleanness.

A new topic for intense analysis was Holy Things. The principal statement of this new system was as follows: The Temple is holy. Its priests are therefore indispensable. But the governance of the Temple now is to be in accord with Torah, and it is the sage who knows Torah and therefore applies it. Since a literal reading of Scripture prevented anyone's maintaining that someone apart from the priest could be like a priest and do the things priests do, it was the next best thing to impose the pretense that priests must obey laymen in the conduct even of the priestly liturgies and services. This was a natural step in the development of the law. A second paramount trait of the version of the system between the wars was its rationalization of the uncontrolled powers inherent in the sacred cult as laid forth by Leviticus. The lessons of Nadab and Abihu and numerous other accounts of the cult's or altar's intrinsic mana (inclusive of the *herem*) were quietly set aside. The altar sanctifies only what is appropriate to it, not whatever comes into contact with its power. In that principle, the sacred was forced to conform to simple conceptions of logic and sense, and its power to strike out uncontrollably was dramatically reduced. This same rationality extended to the definition of the effective range of intention. If one intends to do improperly what is in any event not done at all, one's intention is null. Third, attention was paid to defining the sorts of offerings required in various situations of sin or guilt. Here too the message was not to be missed. When circumstances permit sin is still to be expiated through the sacrificial system. Nothing has changed. There was no surrogate for sacrifice, an exceedingly important affirmation of the cult's continuing validity among people burdened with sin and aching for a mode of atonement. Finally, we observe that the established habit of thinking about gifts to be paid to the priest accounts for the choices of topics on fees paid to maintain the cult. All pertain to priestly gifts analogous to tithes and heave offerings. Tithe of cattle was an important subject, and the rules of firstlings and other gifts to the priests were subject to considerable development. The outcome was that the principal concerns of the Division of Holy Things were defined by the end of the age between the wars.

Systematic work on the formation of a Division of Appointed Times did not begin in the aftermath of the destruction of the Temple. There was some small tendency to develop laws pertinent to the observance of the Sabbath; a few of these laws were important and generated later developments. But the age between the wars may be characterized as a period between important developments. Work on legislation for meals on Sabbaths and festivals had begun earlier. The effort systematically and thoroughly to legislate for the generality of festivals, with special attention to conduct in the Temple cult, would begin later on. In the intervening generations only a little work was done: The established interest in rules governing meals, for example, was carried forward in laws reliably assigned to the time between the wars. But this was episodic and random.

When fully worked out, the Mishnah's Division of Women paid close attention to exchanges of property and documents attendant upon the transfer of a woman from her father's house to her husband's. Authorities between the wars provided only a little guidance for such matters. For a very long time before 70 the national, prevailing law must have defined and governed them. What is significant is that broader and nonsectarian matters, surely subject to a long history of accepted procedure, should have been raised at all. It means that, after the destruction, attention turned to matters which sectarians had not regarded as part of their realm of concern. This may have meant that others who had carried responsibility for the administration of public affairs, such as scribes, now made an appearance. And it also may have meant that the vision of the sectarians themselves had begun to broaden to encompass the administration of the lives of ordinary folk not within the sect. Both meanings are to be imputed to the interest in issues of public administration of property transfers along with the transfer of women to and from the father's home. Concern for definition of personal status devolved upon genealogical questions urgent to the priesthood, and it follows that in the present stratum were contained matters of deep concern to yet a third constituency. But these matters of interest to scribes and priests do not predominate. It is their appearance, rather than their complete expression and articulation, which is of special interest. Various disputes about real estate, working conditions, debts and loans, torts and damages, and other sorts of conflicts which naturally came up in a vital and stable society, were not settled in the Mishnah before 70.

That is why the Division of Damages, dealing with civil law and government, contains virtually nothing assigned to authorities before the wars. Scribes in Temple times served as judges and courts within the Temple government, holding positions in such administrations of the Israelite part of Palestine as the Romans left within Jewish control. The Division of Damages is remarkably reticent on what they might have contributed, after the destruction, out of the heritage of their earlier traditions and established practices. Materials of this period yield little evidence of access to any tradition prior to 70, except (predictably) for Scripture. When people at this time did take up topics relevant to the larger system of Damages, they directed their attention to the exegesis of Scriptures and produced results which clarified what Moses had laid down, or which carried forward problems or topics suggested by the Torah. That is not evidence that thinkers of this period had access (or wished to gain access) to any source of information other than the one provided by Moses. It follows that, in so far as any materials relevant to the later Mishnaic system of Damages did come forth between the wars, the work appears to have begun from scratch. There is no evidence of sustained and systematic thought about the topics assembled in the Division of Damages. We find some effort devoted to the exegesis of Scriptures relevant to the Division. But we cannot say whether those particular passages were selected because of a large-scale inquiry into the requirements of civil law and government, or because of an overriding interest in a given set of Scriptures provoked by some other set of questions entirely.

The net result of the stage in the law's unfolding demarcated by the two wars is that history—the world-shattering events of the day—was kept at a distance from the center of life. The system of sustaining life shaped essentially within an ahistorical view of reality went forward in its own path, above history. Yet the facts of history are otherwise. The people as a whole can hardly be said to have accepted the ahistorical ontology framed by the sages and in part expressed by the systems of Purities, Agriculture, and Holy Things. The people followed the path of Bar Kokhba and took the road to war once more. When the three generations had passed after the destruction and the historical occasion for restoration through historical—political and military—action came to fulfillment, the great war of 132–135 broke forth. A view of being in which people were seen to be moving toward some point within time—the fulfillment and the end of history as it was known—

clearly shaped the consciousness of Israel after 70, just as it had in the decades before 70. So if to the sages of our legal system, history and the end of history were essentially beside the point, the construction of a world of cyclical eternities was the purpose and center, and the conduct of humble things like eating and drinking was the paramount and decisive focus of the sacred—others saw things differently. For those who hoped and therefore fought, Israel's life had other meanings entirely.

The second war proved even more calamitous than the first. In 70 the Temple was lost, in 135 even access to the city. In 70 the people, though they suffered grievous losses, endured more or less intact. In 135 the land of Judah—surely the holiest part of the Holy Land—evidently lost the bulk of its Jewish population. Temple, land, people—all were gone in the forms in which they had been known. In the generation following the calamity of Bar Kokhba, what would be the effect upon the formation of the system of law of the Mishnah? It is to that question that we now turn.

THE MISHNAH'S LAW AFTER THE WARS: THE SYSTEM AS A WHOLE FROM 140 TO 200

The law reached its full and complete statement, as the Mishnah presented it, after the Bar Kokhba war. Over the next sixty years, from about 140 to 200, the system as a whole took shape. The final statement of the Mishnah was divided into six principal topics, called in Hebrew *seder* (plural *sedarim*) and in English divisions. To understand the complete system, we review these divisions as they were finally spelled out.

The Division of Agriculture treats two topics, first, producing crops in accord with the Scriptural rules on the subject, and second, paying the required offerings and tithes to the priests, Levites, and poor. The principal point of the Division is that the land is holy, because God has a claim both on it and upon what it produces. God's claim must be honored by setting aside a portion of the produce for those for whom God has designated it. God's ownership must be acknowledged by observing the rules God has laid down for use of the land. In sum, the Division is divided along these lines: Rules for producing crops in a state of holiness—tractates *Kilayim, Shebiit, Orlah;* Rules for disposing of crops in accord with the rules of holiness—tractates *Peah, Demai, Terumot, Maaserot, Maaser Sheni, Hallah, Bikkurim, Berakhot.*

The Division of Appointed Times forms a system in which the advent of a holy day, like the Sabbath of creation, sanctifies the life of the Israelite village through imposing on the village rules that model those of the Temple. The purpose of the system, therefore, is to bring into alignment the moment of sanctification of the village and the life of the home with the moment of sanctification of the Temple on those same appointed times. The underlying theory of the system is that the village is the mirror image of the Temple. The village is made like the Temple in that on appointed times one may not freely cross the lines distinguishing the village from the rest of the world, just as one may not freely cross the lines distinguishing the Temple from the world. The boundary lines prevent entry into the Temple, so they restrict free egress from the village. On the holy day what one may do in the Temple is precisely what one may not do in the village. Because of the underlying conception of perfection attained through the union of opposites, the village is not represented as conforming to the model of the cult, but of constituting its antithesis. The world thus regains perfection when on the holy day heaven and earth are united, the whole completed and done: the heaven, the earth, and all their hosts. This moment of perfection renders the events of ordinary time, of "history," essentially irrelevant. For what really matters is that moment in time in which sacred time intervenes and effects the perfection formed of the union of heaven and earth, of Temple—in the model of the former—and Israel, its complement. It is not a return to a perfect time but a recovery of perfect being, a fulfillment of creation, which explains the essentially ahistorical character of the Mishnah's Division of Appointed Times. Sanctification is effected by the creator.

The Division in its rich detail is composed of two quite distinct sets of materials. First, it addresses what one does in the sacred space of the Temple on the occasion of sacred time, as distinct from what one does in that same sacred space on ordinary days—a subject worked out in Holy Things. Second, the Division defines how one creates a corresponding space in one's own circumstance for the occasion of the holy day, and what one does within that space during sacred time. The issue of the Temple and cult on the special occasion of festivals is treated in tractates *Pesahim, Sheqalim, Yoma, Sukkah,* and *Hagigah.* Three further tractates, *Rosh Hashshanah, Taanit,* and *Megillah,* are necessary to complete the discussion. The matter of the rigid definition of the outlines in the village, of a sacred space, delineated by the limits within which one may move on the Sabbath and festival, and of the specification of those things which one may not do within that space in sacred time, is in

Shabbat, Erubin, Besah, and *Moed Qatan.* While the twelve tractates of
the Division appear to fall into two distinct groups, joined merely by a
common theme, in fact they relate through a shared metaphor. It is the
comparison—in the context of sacred time—of the spatial life of the
Temple to the spatial life of the village, with activities and restrictions to
be specified for each upon the common occasion of the Sabbath or
festival. The Mishnah's purpose therefore is to correlate the sanctity of
the Temple, as defined by the holy day, with the restrictions of space and
of action which make the life of the village different and holy, also as
defined by the holy day.

The Division of Women defines the women in the social economy of
Israel's supernatural and natural reality. Women acquire definition only
in relationship to men, who impart form to the Israelite social economy.
The status of women is affected by both supernatural and natural, this-
worldly action. What man and woman do on earth provokes a response
in heaven, and the correspondences are perfect. The principal interest
for the Mishnah is the point at which a woman becomes or ceases to be
holy to a particular man, that is, when she enters and leaves the marital
union. These transfers of women are the dangerous and disorderly
points in the relationship of woman to man, and therefore, the Mishnah
states, to society as well.

The formation of marriage comes under discussion in *Qiddushin* and
Ketubot, as well as in *Yebamot.* The rules for the duration of the
marriage are scattered throughout but derive especially from parts of
Ketubot, Nedarim, Nazir, and *Sotah.* The dissolution of the marriage is
dealt with in *Gittin* and *Yebamot.* The essential issues include the
transfer of property, along with women, covered in *Ketubot* and to some
measure in *Qiddushin,* and the proper documentation of the transfer of
women and property, treated in *Ketubot* and *Gittin.* The critical issues
therefore turn upon legal documents—writs of divorce, for example—
and legal recognition of changes in the ownership of property, for
example through the collection of the settlement of a marriage contract
by a widow, through the provision of a dowry, or through the disposition of the property of a woman during the period in which she is
married. Within this orderly world of documentary and procedural
concerns a place is made for the disorderly conception of the marriage
not formed by human volition but decreed in heaven, the levirate
connection. *Yebamot* states that supernature sanctifies a woman to a
man (under the conditions of the levirate connection). What it implies is
that man sanctifies too: man, like God, can sanctify the relationship

between a man and a woman, and can also effect the cessation of the sanctity of that same relationship. Five of the seven tractates of the Division of Women are devoted to the formation and dissolution of the marital bond. Of them, three treat what is done by man here on earth, that is, formation of a marital bond through betrothal and marriage contract and dissolution through divorce and its consequences: *Qiddushin, Ketubot,* and *Gittin.* One of them is devoted to what is done by woman here on earth: *Sotah.* And *Yebamot*—greatest of the seven in size and in formal and substantive brilliance—deals with the corresponding heavenly intervention in the formation and end of a marriage: the effect of death upon both forming the marital bond and dissolving it. The other two tractates, *Nedarim* and *Nazir,* draw into one the two realms of reality, heaven and earth, as they work out the effects of vows, perhaps because vows taken by women and subject to the confirmation or abrogation of the father or husband make a deep impact upon the marital life of the woman who has taken them.

The Division and its system delineate the natural and supernatural character of the woman's role in the social economy framed by man: the beginning, end, and middle of the relationship. The whole constitutes a significant part of the Mishnah's encompassing system of sanctification, for the reason that heaven confirms what men do on earth. A correctly prepared writ of divorce on earth changes the status of the woman to whom it is given, so that in heaven she is available for sanctification to some other man. Without that same writ, in heaven's view, should she go to some other man, she would be liable to be put to death. The earthly deed correlates with the heavenly perspective. That is indeed very much part of larger system, which says the same thing over and over again.

The system of Women thus focuses upon the two crucial stages in the transfer of women and of property from one domain to another: the leaving of the father's house in the formation of a marriage, and the return to the father's house at dissolution of the marriage through divorce or the husband's death. There is yet a third point of interest, though it is much less important than these first two: the duration of the marriage. Finally, included within the Division and at a few points relevant to women in particular are rules of vows and of the special vow to be a nazir. The former is included because, in the scriptural treatment of the theme, the rights of the father or husband to annul the vows of a daughter or wife form the central problem. The latter is included for no very clear reason except that it is a species of which the vow is the genus.

The Division of Damages comprises two subsystems which fit together in a logical way. One part presents rules for the normal conduct of civil society. The rules cover commerce, trade, real estate, and other matters of everyday intercourse, as well as mishaps, such as damages by chattels and persons, fraud, overcharge, interest, and the like, in the conduct of everyday social life. The other part describes the institutions governing civil society, that is, courts of administration, and the penalties at the disposal of the government for the enforcement of the law. The two subjects form a systematic dissertation on the nature of Israelite society and its economic, social, and political relationships, as the Mishnah envisaged them.

The main point of the first part of the Division is expressed in the three *Babas, Baba Qamma, Baba Mesia,* and *Baba Batra.* The point is that the task of society is to maintain perfect stasis, to preserve the prevailing situation, and to secure the stability of all relationships. To this end it is important that there be an essential equality in the interchanges of buying and selling, giving and taking, and borrowing and lending. No party in the end should have more than what he had at the outset, and none should be the victim of a sizable shift in fortune and circumstance. All parties' rights in this stable and unchanging economy of society are to be preserved. When the condition of a person is violated, the law will so far as possible secure the restoration of the antecedent status.

Abodah Zarah, which serves as an appendix to the *Babas,* deals with the orderly governance of transactions and relationships between Israelite society and the outside world, the realm of idolatry, and relationships which are subject to special considerations. These occur because Israelites may not derive benefit (for example, through commercial transactions) from anything which has served in the worship of an idol. Consequently commercial transactions suffer limitations on account of extrinsic considerations of cultic taboos. These cover special occasions, for example fairs and festivals that included idolatrous worship, and general matters, that is, what Israelites may buy and sell. But the main practical illustrations of the principles of the matter pertain to wine. The Mishnah supposes that Gentiles routinely use for a libation a drop of any sort of wine to which they have access. It therefore is taken for granted that wine over which Gentiles have had control is forbidden for Israelite use, and also that such wine is prohibited for Israelites to buy and sell. This other matter—ordinary everyday relationships with the Gentile world, with special reference to trade and commerce—

concludes what the Mishnah has to say about all those matters of civil and criminal law which together define everyday relationships within the Israelite nation and between that nation and others.

The second part of the Division describes the Israelite government institutions and their jurisdiction, with reference to courts, conceived as both judicial and administrative agencies, and it discusses criminal penalties, death, banishment, and flogging. The Mishnah organizes a vast amount of information on what sorts of capital crimes are punishable by each of four modes of execution. Although that information is alleged to derive from Scripture, there are few relevant verses. What the Mishnah clearly contributes to this exercise is a first-rate piece of organization and elucidation of the available facts, but we do not know where the facts come from. The Mishnah tractate *Sanhedrin* further describes the way in which trials are conducted in both monetary and capital cases and pays attention to the possibilities of perjury. The matter of banishment brings the Mishnah to a rather routine restatement about flogging and the application of that mode of punishment, which concludes the discussion.

These matters, worked out in *Sanhedrin* and *Makkot,* are supplemented in two tractates, *Shebuot* and *Horayot,* both emerging from Scripture. Lev. 5 and 6 refer to various oaths which apply mainly, though not exclusively, in courts. Lev. 4 deals with errors of judgment inadvertently made and carried out by the high priest, the ruler, and the people; the Mishnah knows that these considerations apply to Israelite courts too. What for Leviticus draws the chapters together is their common interest in the guilt offering, which is owing for violation of the rather diverse matters under discussion. Tractate *Shebuot* deals with Lev. 5–6, and *Horayot* with Lev. 4, respectively. But here is it from the viewpoint of the oath or erroneous instruction rather than the cultic penalty. In *Shebuot* the discussion is intellectually imaginative and thorough, in *Horayot,* routine. The relevance of both to the issues of *Sanhedrin* and *Makkot* is obvious. For the matter of oaths in the main enriches the discussion of the conduct of the courts. The possibility of error is principally in the courts and other political institutions. So the four tractates on institutions and their functioning form a remarkably unified and cogent set.

The goal of the system of civil law is the recovery of the prevailing order and balance, the preservation of the established wholeness of the social economy. This idea is powerfully expressed in the organization of the three Babas, which treat first abnormal and then normal transactions. The framers deal with damages done by chattels and by human beings, thefts and other sorts of malfeasance against the property of others. The Babas in both aspects pay closest attention to how the property and person of the injured party are so far as possible restored to their prior condition, that is, a state of normality. So attention to torts focuses upon penalties paid by the malefactor to the victim, rather than upon penalties inflicted by the court on the malefactor for what he has done. When speaking of damages, the Mishnah thus takes as its principal concern the restoration of the fortune of victims of assault or robbery. Then the framers take up the complementary and corresponding set of topics, the regulation of normal transactions. When we survey the kinds of transactions of special interest, we see from the topics selected for discussion what we have already uncovered in the deepest structure of organization and articulation of the basic theme.

The other half of this same unit of three tractates presents laws governing normal and routine transactions, many of them of the same sort as those dealt with in the first half. Bailments, for example, occur in both wings of the triple tractate: first, bailments subjected to misappropriation, or accusation thereof, by the bailiff; then, bailments transacted under normal circumstances. Under the rubric of routine transactions are those of workers and householders: the purchase and sale of labor; rentals and bailments; real estate transactions; and inheritances and estates. Of the lot, the one involving real estate transactions is the most fully articulated and covers the widest range of problems and topics. The Babas all together thus provide a complete account of the orderly governance of balanced transactions and unchanging civil relationships within Israelite society under ordinary conditions.

The character and interests of the Division of Damages present probative evidence of the larger program of the philosophers of the Mishnah. Their intention was to create nothing less than a full-scale Israelite government, subject to the administration of sages. This government was fully supplied with a constitution and bylaws (*Sanhedrin, Makkot*). It made provision for a court system and procedures (*Shebuot, Sanhedrin, Makkot*), as well as a full set of laws governing civil society (*Baba Qamma, Baba Mesia, Baba Batra*) and criminal justice (*Sanhedrin, Makkot*). This government, moreover, mediated between its own community and the outside ("pagan") world. Through its system of laws it expressed its judgment of the others and at the same time defined, protected, and defended its own society and social frontiers (*Abodah Zarah*). It even made provision for procedures of remission, to expiate its own errors (*Horayot*).

The (then nonexistent) Israelite government imagined by the second-century philosophers centered upon the (then nonexistent) Temple, and the (then forbidden) city, Jerusalem. For the Temple was one principal focus. There the highest court was in session; there the high priest reigned. The penalties for law infringement were of three kinds, one of which involves sacrifice in the Temple. (The others were compensation, physical punishment, and death.) The basic conception of punishment was that unintentional infringement of the rules of society, whether religious or otherwise, was not penalized but rather expiated through an offering in the Temple. If a member of the people of Israel intentionally infringed against the law that one had to be removed from society and put to death. And if there was a claim of one member of the people against another, that had to be righted, so that the prior, prevailing status could be restored. So offerings in the Temple were given up to appease heaven and restore a whole bond between heaven and Israel, specifically on those occasions on which without malice or ill will an Israelite disturbed the relationship. Israelite civil society without a Temple was not stable or normal, and not to be imagined. The Mishnah was above all an act of imagination in defiance of reality.

The plan for the government involved a clear-cut philosophy of society, a philosophy which defined the purpose of the government and ensured that its task was not merely to perpetuate its own power. What the Israelite government, within the Mishnaic fantasy, was supposed to do was to preserve the state of perfection which, within the same fantasy, the society everywhere attained and expressed. This had at least five aspects. First of all, one of the ongoing principles of the law, expressed in one tractate after another, was that people were to follow and maintain the prevailing practice of their locale. Second, the purpose of civil penalties was to restore the injured party to his prior condition, so far as this was possible, rather than merely to penalize the aggressor. Third, there was a conception of true value, meaning that a given object had an intrinsic worth which had to be paid in the course of a transaction. In this way the seller did not leave the transaction any richer than when he entered it, or the buyer any poorer (parallel to penalties for damages). Fourth, there could be no usury, a biblical prohibition adopted and vastly enriched in the Mishnaic thought, for it was money ("coins"). Any pretense that it had become more than what it was violated the conception of true value. Fifth, when real estate was divided, it had to be done with full attention to the rights of all concerned, so that one party did not gain at the expense of the other. In these and many other aspects the law expressed its obsession with the perfect stasis of Israelite society. Its paramount purpose was to preserve and ensure that that perfection of the division of this world was kept inviolate or restored to its true status when violated.

The Division of Holy Things presents a system of sacrifice and sanctuary: matters concerning the praxis of the altar and the maintenance of the sanctuary. The praxis of the altar involved sacrifice and things set aside for sacrifice and so deemed consecrated. The topic covers these among the eleven tractates of this Division: *Zebahim* and part of *Hullin, Menahot, Temurah, Keritot,* part of *Meilah, Tamid, and Qinnim.* The maintenance of the sanctuary (inclusive of the personnel) was dealt with in *Bekhorot, Arakhin,* part of *Meilah, Middot,* and part of *Hullin.* Viewed from a distance, therefore, the Mishnah's tractates divided themselves up into the following groups (in parentheses are tractates containing relevant materials): rules for the altar and the animals set aside for the cult—*Arakhin, Temurah, Meilah (Bekhorot);* and rules for the altar and support of the Temple staff and buildings—*Bekhorot, Middot (Hullin, Arakhin, Meilah, Tamid).* In a word, this Division spoke of the sacrificial cult and the sanctuary in which the cult was conducted. The law paid special attention to the matter of the status of the property of the altar and of the sanctuary, both materials to be utilized in the actual sacrificial rites, and property the value of which supported the cult and sanctuary in general. Both were deemed to be sanctified, that is, "holy things."

The Division of Holy Things centered upon the everyday and on rules always applicable to the cult: the daily whole offering, the sin offering and the guilt offering which one could bring any time under ordinary circumstances; the right sequence of diverse offerings; the way in which the rites of the whole, sin, and guilt offerings were carried out; what sorts of animals were acceptable; the accompanying cereal offerings; the support and provision of animals for the cult and of meat for the priesthood; and the support and material maintenance of the cult and its building. We have before us the system of the cult of the Jerusalem Temple, seen as an ordinary and everyday affair, a continuing and routine operation. That is why special rules for the cult, both in respect to the altar and in regard to the maintenance of the buildings, personnel, and even the whole city, were elsewhere—in Appointed Times and Agriculture. But from the perspective of Holy Things, those Divisions intersected by supplying special rules and raising extraordinary (Agriculture: land-bound; Appointed Times: time-bound) considerations for that theme which Holy Things claimed to set forth in its most general and unexceptional way: the cult as something permanent and everyday.

The Division of Holy Things thus in a concrete way mapped out the cosmology of the sanctuary and its sacrificial system, that is, the world of the Temple, which had been the cosmic center of Israelite life. A later saying stated matters as follows: "Just as the naval is found at the center of a human being, so the land of Israel is found at the center of the world . . . and it is the foundation of the world. Jerusalem is at the center of the land of Israel, the Temple is at the center of Jerusalem, the Holy of Holies is at the center of the Temple, the Ark is at the center of the Holy of Holies, and the Foundation Stone is in front of the Ark, which spot is the foundation of the world" (*Tanhuma Qedoshim* 10).

The Division of Purities presented a very simple system with three principal parts: sources of uncleanness, objects and substances susceptible to uncleanness, and modes of purification from uncleanness. So it told the story of what made a given sort of object unclean and what made it clean. The tractates on these several topics are as follows: sources of uncleanness—*Ohalot, Negaim, Niddah, Makhshirin, Zabim, Tebul Yom;* objects and substances susceptible to uncleanness—*Kelim, Tohorot, Uqsin;* and modes of purification—*Parah, Miqvaot, Yadayim.* Viewed as a whole, the Division of Purities treated the interplay of persons, food, and liquids. Dry inanimate objects or food were not susceptible to uncleanness. What was wet was susceptible. So liquids activated the system. What was unclean emerged from uncleanness through the operation of liquids, specifically, through immersion in fit water of requisite volume and in natural condition. Liquids thus deactivated the system. Thus water in its natural condition was what concluded the process by removing uncleanness. Water in its unnatural condition, that is, deliberately affected by human agency, is what imparted susceptibility to uncleanness to begin with. The uncleanness of persons was signified by body liquids or flux in the case of the menstruating woman (*Niddah*) and the *zab* (*Zabim*). Corpse uncleanness was conceived to be a kind of effluent, a viscous gas, which flowed like liquid. Utensils received uncleanness when they formed receptacles able to contain liquid. In sum, we have a system in which the invisible flow of fluidlike substances or powers served to put food, drink, and receptacles into the status of uncleanness and to remove those things from that status. Whether or not we call the system "metaphysical," it certainly has no material base but is conditioned upon highly abstract notions. Thus in material terms, the effect of liquid is upon food, drink,

utensils, and man. The consequence has to do with who may eat and
drink what food and liquid, and what food and drink may be con-
sumed from which pots and pans. These loci are specified by tractates
on utensils (*Kelim*) and on food and drink (*Tohorot* and *Uqsin*).

The human being is ambiguous. Persons fall in the middle, between
sources and loci of uncleanness, because they are both. They serve as
sources of uncleanness. They also become unclean. The zab, suffering
the uncleanness described in Leviticus chapter 15, the menstruating
woman, the woman after childbirth, and the person afflicted with the
skin ailment described in Leviticus chapters 13 and 14—all are sources
of uncleanness. But being unclean, they fall within the system's loci, its
program of consequences. So they make other things unclean and are
subject to penalties because they are unclean. Unambiguous sources of
uncleanness never also constitute loci affected by uncleanness. They
always are unclean and never can become clean: the corpse, the dead
creeping thing, and things like them. Inanimate sources of uncleanness
and inanimate objects are affected by uncleanness. Systemically unique,
man and liquids have the capacity to inaugurate the processes of
uncleanness (as sources) and also are subject to those same processes (as
objects of uncleanness). The Division of Purities, which presents the
basically simple system just now described, is not only the oldest in the
Mishnah. It also is the largest and contains by far the most complex laws
and ideas.

The Mishnah's System as a Whole

Let us now stand back and characterize the system as a whole. Overall,
its stress lies on sanctification, understood as the correct arrangement of
all things, each in its proper category, each called by its rightful name,
just as at the creation. Everything having been given its proper name,
God called the natural world very good and God sanctified it. The
Mishnah makes a statement of philosophy, concerning the order of the
natural world in its correspondence with the supernatural world. Later
on, the Midrash compilations and the Talmud of the Land of Israel
would make a statement of theology, concerning the historical order of
society in its progression from creation through salvation at the end of
time. Judaism in the dual Torah constituted a complete statement about
philosophy and nature, theology and history, the one in the oral, the
other in the written Torah. Together the two components constituted
that one whole Torah of Moses, our rabbi. But we have gotten ahead

of our story. Let us return to the Mishnah and its focus upon its modes of sanctification and the orderly rules descriptive of the natural life of Israel in its holy land.

The system of philosophy expressed through concrete and detailed law presented by the Mishnah, consisted of a coherent logic and topic, a cogent world view and a comprehensive way of living. It was a world view which spoke of transcendent things, a way of life responding to the supernatural meaning of what was done, a heightened and deepened perception of the sanctification of Israel in deed and in deliberation. Sanctification thus meant two things: first, distinguishing Israel in all its dimensions from the world in all its ways; second, establishing the stability, order, regularity, predictability, and reliability of Israel in the world of nature and supernature especially in moments and in contexts of danger. Danger meant instability, disorder, irregularity, uncertainty, and betrayal. Each topic of the system as a whole took up a critical and indispensable moment or context of social being. Through what was said in regard to each of the Mishnah's principal topics, what the halakhic system as a whole wished to declare was fully expressed. Yet if the parts severally and jointly gave the message of the whole, the whole could not exist without all of the parts, so well joined and carefully crafted are they all.

It is one thing to state the system as a whole. It is quite another to address the issue of the circumstance addressed by the authorship of the Mishnah. For the Mishnah's authorship did not think it urgent to speak to a particular time or place. They provided no account of the history or authority of their code. They rarely referred to specific circumstances subject to legislation. They spoke in the language of general, descriptive rules, implicitly applicable everywhere and any time. From the first line to the last, the discourse took up questions internal to a system which was never introduced. The Mishnah provided information without establishing a context. It presented disputes about facts hardly urgent outside of a circle of faceless disputants. Consequently, we start with the impression that we join a conversation already long under way about topics we can never grasp anyhow. The Mishnah does not identify its authors. It permits only slight variations, if any, in its authorities' patterns of language and speech, so there is no place for individual characteristics of expression. It nowhere tells us when it speaks. It does not address a particular place or time and rarely speaks of events in its own day. It never identifies its prospective audience. There is scarcely a "you" in the entire mass of sayings and rules. The Mishnah begins nowhere. It

88   CHAPTER FOUR

ends abruptly. There is no predicting where it will commence or explaining why it is done. Where, when, why the document is laid out and
set forth are questions not deemed urgent and not answered.

If then we turn to the contents of the document, we are helped not at
all in determining the place of the Mishnah's origin, the purpose of its
formation, or the reasons for its anonymous and collective plane of
discourse and monotonous tone of voice. For the Mishnah covers a
carefully defined program of topics. But the Mishnah never tells us why
one topic is introduced and another is omitted, or what the combining
of these particular topics is meant to accomplish in the formation of a
system or imaginative construction. Nor is there any way to predict how
a given topic will be treated, or why a given set of issues will be explored
in close detail and another set of possible issues ignored. Discourse on a
theme begins and ends as if all things are self-evident—including the
reason for beginning at one point and ending at another. This strange
and curious book looks like a rulebook. It appears on the surface to be a
book lacking all traces of eloquence and style, revealing no evidence of
system and reflection, and serving no important purpose. Who would
want to have made such a thing? Who would now want to refer to it?

The answer to that question is deceptively straightforward: the
Mishnah is important because it is a principal component of the canon
of Judaism. But that answer begs the question: Why should some of the
ancient Jews of the Holy Land have brought together these particular
facts and rules into a book and set them forth for the Israelite people?
Why should the Mishnah have been received, as much later on it
certainly was received, as a half of the "whole Torah of Moses at Sinai"?
After it was compiled the Mishnah was represented as the part of the
whole Torah of Moses, our rabbi which had been formulated and
transmitted orally, so it bore the status of divine revelation right alongside the Pentateuch. But little in the actual contents of the document
evoked the character or the moral authority of the written Torah of
Moses. None pretended otherwise.

Indeed, most of the authorities named in the Mishnah lived in the
century and a half prior to the promulgation of the document so the
claim that things said by men known to the very framers of the document in fact derived from Moses at Sinai through a long chain of oral
tradition contradicted the well-known facts of the matter. So this claim
presents a paradox even on the surface: How can the Mishnah be
deemed a book of religion, a program for consecration, and a mode of
sanctification? Why should Jews from the end of the second century to
our own day have deemed the study of the Mishnah to be a holy act—a

deed of service to God through the study of an important constituent of God's Torah, God's will for Israel, the Jewish people?

We can derive no answers from the world in which the document emerged. The world addressed by the Mishnah was hardly congruent to the world view presented within the Mishnah. In the aftermath of the war against Rome in 132–135, the Temple was declared permanently prohibited to Jews, and Jerusalem was closed off to them as well. So there was no cult, no Temple, no holy city, to which at this time the description of the Mishnaic laws applied. Therefore a sizable proportion of the Mishnah deals with matters to which the sages had no material access or practical knowledge at the time of their work. The Mishnah contains a division on the conduct of the cult—the fifth—as well as one on the conduct of matters so as to preserve the cultic purity of the sacrificial system along the lines laid out in the book of Leviticus—the sixth division. The fourth division—on civil law—presents an elaborate account of a political structure and system of Israelite self-government, in tractates Sanhedrin and Makkot, not to mention Shebuot and Horayot. This system speaks of king, priest, Temple, and court. But it was not the Jews—their kings, priests, and judges—but the Romans who conducted the government of Israel in the Land of Israel in the time in which the second-century authorities did their work. Well over half of the document speaks of cult, Temple, government, and priesthood. And the Mishnah takes a profoundly priestly and Levitical conception of sanctification. When we consider that, in the very time in which the authorities before us did their work, the Temple lay in ruins, the city of Jerusalem was prohibited to all Israelites, and the Jewish government and administration which had centered on the Temple and based its authority on the holy life lived there were in ruins, the fantastic character of the Mishnah's address to its own catastrophic day becomes clear. Much of the Mishnah speaks of matters not in existence in the time in which the Mishnah was created, because the Mishnah wishes to make its statement on what really matters.

The Mishnah and Judaism

The Mishnah did not encompass everything that its authorship held important, but it does present a Judaic system, for it describes a whole world and tells us the framers' principal concerns. This generative concern involved the ongoing sanctification of Israel. An authorship that had seen the holiness of the life of Israel, the people, as centered on the Temple, and had endured and transcended the destruction of the building and the cessation of sacrifices, found urgent the question of sanctification after the destruction. The Mishnah's system had one fundamental premise: Israel the people was the medium and instrument of God's sanctification. What required sanctification were the modalities of life lived in community (and none conceived of a holy life in any other mode). The system then instructed Israel to act as if it formed a utensil of the sacred. That is why I maintain that, for the Mishnah's authorship, the critical issue was the definition and status of Israel.

Now if we ask ourselves about the sponsorship and source of special interest in the topics just now reviewed, we shall come up with obvious answers. So far as the Mishnah is a document about the holiness of Israel in its land, it expresses the conception of sanctification and the theory of its modes which were shaped among those to whom the Temple and its technology of joining Heaven and Holy Land through the sacred place defined the core of being: the caste of the priests. So far as the Mishnah takes up the way in which transactions are conducted among ordinary folk and takes the position that it is through documents that transactions are embodied and expressed (surely the position of the relevant tractates on both Women and Damages), the Mishnah expresses what was self-evident to scribes. Just as to the priest there was a correspondence between the table of the Lord in the Temple and the locus of the divinity in the heavens, so to the scribe there was a correspondence between the documentary expression of the human will on earth—in writs of all sorts and in the orderly provision of courts for the predictable and just disposition of exchanges of persons and property— and Heaven's judgment of these same matters. So there are scribal divisions—the third and fourth—and priestly divisions—the first, fifth, and sixth; the second is shared between the two groups. These two social groups—the priestly caste and the scribal profession—were not categorically symmetrical with one another. But for both groups the Mishnah made self-evident statements. The scribal profession later became a focus of sanctification. The scribe was transformed into the rabbi, honored man par excellence and locus of the holy through what he knew, just as the priest had been and would remain locus of the holy through what he could claim by genealogy. The divisions of special interest to scribes-become-rabbis and to their governance of Israelite society—those of Women and Damages, together with certain others particularly relevant to utopian Israel beyond the system of the Land— those tractates grew and grew. Many, though not all, of the others remained essentially as they were at the completion of the Mishnah. So we must notice that the Mishnah spoke for the program of topics important to the priests. It took up the persona of the scribes, speaking through their voice and in their manner.

The crisis precipitated by the destruction of the Second Temple affected both the nation and the individual, since, in the nature of things, what happened in the metropolis of the country inevitably touched affairs of home and family. What connected the individual fate to the national destiny was the long-established Israelite conviction that the fate of the individual and the destiny of the Jewish nation depended upon the moral character of both. Disaster came about because of the people's sin, so went the message of biblical history and prophecy. The sins of individuals and of nation alike ran against the revealed will of God, the Torah. So reflection upon the meaning of the recent catastrophe inexorably followed paths laid out long ago, trod from one generation to the next. But there were two factors which at just this time made reflection on the question of sin and history, atonement and salvation, particularly urgent.

First, although there was a deep conviction of having sinned and a profound sense of guilt affecting community and individual alike, the established mode of expiation and atonement for sin proved to be unavailable. The sacrificial system—which the priestly Torah describes as the means by which the sinner attains forgiveness for sin—lay in ruins. So when sacrifice was acutely needed for the restoration of psychological stability in the community at large, sacrifice was no longer possible.

Second, in August, A.D. 70, minds naturally turned to August, 586 B.C. From the biblical histories and prophecies emerged the vivid expectation that sin would be atoned and expiation attained through the suffering of the day. So, people supposed that just as before, whatever guilt had weighed down the current generation and led to the catastrophe would be worked out in three generations through the sacrifice consisting of the anguish of a troubled time. It must follow that somewhere down the road lay renewal. The ruined Temple would yet be rebuilt, the lapsed cult restored, and the Levites' silent song sung once more.

Now these several interrelated themes—suffering, sin, atonement, and salvation—had long been paramount in the frame of the Israelite consciousness. A famous, widely known ancient literature of apocalyptic prophecy had for a long time explored them. The convictions that events carry preponderant meaning, that Israelites could control what happened by keeping or not keeping the Torah, and that in the course of time matters would come to a resolution—these commonplaces were given mythic reality in the apocalyptic literature. Over many centuries in that vast sweep of apocalyptic-prophetic writings all of the changes had been rung for every possible variation on the theme of redemption in history. So it is hardly surprising that, in the aftermath of the burning of the Temple and the cessation of the cult, people reflected upon familiar themes in established modes of thought. They had no choice, given the history of the country's consciousness and its Scriptural frame of reference, but to think of the beginning, middle, and coming end of time.

The second stage in the formation of the earlier phases of rabbinic Judaism coincided with the flowering, in the second century, of that general movement both within Christianity and outside it called Gnosticism. It is as important as was the apocalyptic movement in establishing a base for comparison and interpretation of earlier rabbinic Judaism. One principal theme of the Mishnah and of Judaism involved the affirmation of God's beneficence in creating the world and revealing the Torah. Principal motifs of diverse Gnostic systems were God's malevolence in creating the world, or the malicious character of the creator-god, and the rejection of the Torah. In the Judaism of the sages represented in the Mishnah and later writings we see a direct confrontation on paramount issues of the day between rabbinic Judaism and the family of systems we call Gnosticism.

The second-century Church Fathers referred to Christian heretics called Gnostics, people who believed, among other things, that salvation came from insightful knowledge of a god beyond the creator-god, and of a fundamental flaw in creation revealed in the Scriptures of Moses. Insight into the true condition of the believer derived not from revelation but from self-knowledge, which is knowledge of God. We know no writings of Gnostics who were Jews. We cannot claim that the viewpoint of Gnostic thinkers on two questions of fundamental importance to the Mishnah—creation and revelation—derived from Israelites of the land of Israel. The only certainly is that the Mishnah took a position both specifically and totally at variance with the position framed on identical issues by people writing in exactly the same period. No one can claim that Gnostic and Mishnaic thinkers addressed, or even knew about, one another. But they did confront precisely the same issues, and when placed into juxtaposition with one another, they present a striking and suggestive contrast.

If the apocalyptic prophets focused upon historical events and their meaning, the Gnostic writers of the second century sought to escape from the framework of history altogether. For Israel, Jerusalem had become a forbidden city. The Temple had long stood as the pinnacle of creation but now it was destroyed. The Gnostic thinkers deemed creation, celebrated in the cult, to be a cosmic error. The destruction of the Temple had evoked the prophetic explanations of the earlier destruction and turned attention in the search for meaning to the Torah of God revealed to Moses at Mount Sinai. The Gnostic thinkers declared the Torah to be a deceit handed down by an evil creator. It is as if the cosmic issues vital to the first-century apocalyptic prophets were taken up one by one by the second-century Gnostics and declared closed in a negative decision.

The thinkers of the Mishnah addressed two principal issues also important to Gnostic thought—the worth of the creation and the value of the Torah. They took the opposite position on both matters. The Mishnah's profoundly priestly celebration of creation and its slavishly literal repetition of what is clearly said in Scripture gain significance specifically in that very context in which, to others, these were subjected to a different and deeply negative valuation. We have no evidence that Gnostics were in the land of Israel and formed part of the people of Israel in the period in which the Mishnah reached full expression and final closure. So we speak of a synchronic debate at best. What we know in Gnostic writings is a frame of mind and a style of thought that were characteristic of others than Israelites, living in lands other than the land of Israel. What justifies our invoking two ubiquitous and fundamental facts about Gnostic doctrine in the description of the context in which the Mishnah took shape is the simple fact that, at critical points in its structure, the Mishnaic system counters what are in fact two fundamental assertions of all Gnostic systems. We do not know whether there were Gnostics known to Mishnah's philosophers who in response to the destruction and permanent prohibition of the Temple declared the creation celebrated in the Temple and the Torah to be lies and deceit. But these would be appropriate conclusions to draw. The Temple designed by the Torah for celebrating the center and heart of creation was no more. Would this not have meant that the creator of the known creation and the revealer of the Torah—the allegedly one God behind both—is either weak or evil? And should the elect not aspire to escape from the realm of creation and the power of the demiurge? And who should pay heed to what was written in the revelation of creation, Temple, and Torah? These seem to me conclusions suitable to be drawn from the ultimate end of the thousand-year-old-cult: the final and total discrediting of the long-pursued, eternally fraudulent hope for messianic deliverance in this time, in this world, and in this life. So it would have seemed wise to seek and celebrate a different salvation, coming from a god unknown in this world, unrevealed in this world's revelation, and not responsible for the infelicitous condition of creation.

At the time of the formation of the Mishnah, Christian communities from France to Egypt were taking a position sharply at variance with that of the Hebrew Scriptures on the questions of creation, revelation, and redemption that confronted the Israelite world of the second century. Among the many positions taken up in the systems reported by Christian writers or documented through Christian-Gnostic writings found at Nag Hammadi there are three which are remarkably pertinent. First, the creator-god is evil, because, second, creation is deeply flawed, and third, revelation as Torah is a lie. For one Gnostic-Christian thinker after another these conclusions yielded the simple proposition that redemption is gained in escape; the world is to be abandoned, not constructed, affirmed, and faithfully tended in painstaking detail. It is in the context of this widespread negative judgment on the very matters on which Mishnah's sages registered a highly affirmative opinion, that the choices made by the framers of the Mishnah become fully accessible.

Characterizing the Mishnah's ultimate system as a whole, we may call it both locative and utopian, in that it focuses upon Temple but is serviceable anywhere. In comparison to the Gnostic systems, it was profoundly Scriptural; but it was also deeply indifferent to Scripture. It drew heavily upon the information supplied by Scripture for the construction and expression of its own systemic construction, which in form and language was wholly independent of any earlier Israelite document. It was finally a statement of affirmation of this world, of the realm of society, state, and commerce, and at the same time a vigorous denial that how things were was how things had to be. For the Mishnaic system speaks of the building of a state, government, and civil and criminal system; of the conduct of transactions of property, commerce, and trade; of forming the economic unit of a family through transfer of women and property and the ending of such a family-economic unit; and similar matters, touching all manner of dull details of everyday life.

So the Mishnah's framers deemed the conduct of ordinary life in this world to be the critical focus and central point of tension of all being. At the same time, their account of these matters drew more heavily upon Scripture than upon any more contemporary and practical source. The philosophers designed a government and a state utterly out of phase with the political realities of the day, speaking of king and high priest, but never of sage, patriarch, and Roman official. They addressed a lost world of Temple cult as described by the Torah—of cleanness, support of the priesthood, and offerings on ordinary days and on appointed times in accord with Torah law—and so mapped out vast tracts of a territory whose only reality lay in people's imagination, shaped by Scripture.

Accordingly, for all its intense practicality and methodical application of the power of practical reason and logic to concrete and material things, the Mishnah presents a made-up system which is no more practical or applicable to ordinary life than were the diverse systems of philosophy and myth which fall under the name Gnostic. What the framers of Mishnah have in common with the framers of the diverse world constructions of the Gnostic sort thus is, first, a system building, and second, confrontation with two issues addressed in the diverse Gnostic systems of antiquity—the nature of creation and the creator and the character of the revelation of the creator-god. The position of the Mishnah on these two burning issues of the day was that creation is good and worthy of man's best consideration, and that the creator of the world is good and worthy of man's deepest devotion. So out of creation and revelation will come redemption. The Torah is not only true but the principal source of truth. A system which intersects with the rules of the Torah therefore must patiently restate and reaffirm precisely what Scripture has to say about those same points. A structure coming in the aftermath of the Temple's destruction which doggedly restated rules governing the Temple reaffirmed in the most obvious possible way the cult and the created world celebrated therein.

The real crisis of the age was therefore located in that middle range of life between the personal tragedies of individuals and the national catastrophe of the history of Israel. The pivot had wobbled; everything organized around the Temple had shifted and shaken. Left out were the two things at the extremes of this middle world: private suffering, and national catastrophe in the context of history. That is why, when we contemplate how others of the same time framed the issues of the day, we are struck by the contrast. The obvious and accessible dilemmas of Israel's suffering at the hand of Gentiles, the deeper meaning of the age in which the Temple had been ruined and Israel defeated, the resort to evocative symbols of private suffering and its mystery for expressing public sorrow, the discourse on the meaning of human history in the light of this awful outcome for Israel—none of these accessible and sympathetic themes comes to the surface in those topics which the precursors of the Mishnaic system considered the appropriate focus of discourse. The miserable world of the participants—the people who had fought, lost, and suffered—seems remote. The issue of 70 was framed by the priests and by people who had pretended to be priests and had imitated their cultic routines. To such people the paramount issues of 70 were issues of cult. Israel had originally become Israel and sustained its perpetual vocation by living on the holy Land and organizing all aspects of its holy life in relationship to the conduct of the holy Temple, eating like priests and farming in accord with the cultic taboos and obsessions with order and form, and dividing up time between profane and holy in relationship to the cult's calendar and the temporal division of its own rites. Now Israel remained Israel, loyal to its calling, through continuing to live in the mirror of that cult.

The truly stunning change effected after the wars was the formation of the Mishnah itself which brought together the ideas and laws in circulation before its time, and put them all together into something far more than the sum of its parts. The old, reliable, priestly way of life and world view from the Temple mountain came to be transformed into a social vision framed on the plane of Israel. What is stunning is the shift in perspective, not the change in what was to be seen. From interests limited to the hearth and home the opening lens of social thought took in a larger frame indeed: from home to court, from eating and drinking and beds and pots and pans to exchanges of property and encounters of transactions in material power. What moved the world on its axis, the ball of earth in its majesty? The answer is self-evident: seventy years of wars and the tumult of wars. These shattered a hope which had never had much to do with the Temple at all. There was then a moment of utter despair about things which, from the perspective of the philosophers of the Mishnah, might as well have taken place on another planet. The previous culture of somewhat less than a millennium spun into another orbit, but not because of the gravity of a new civilization of impressive density.

The Mishnah's principal message, which makes the Judaism of this document and of its social components distinctive and cogent, is that man is at the center of creation, the head of all creatures upon earth, corresponding to God in heaven in whose image man is made. The way in which the Mishnah makes this simple and fundamental statement is to impute power to man to inaugurate and initiate those corresponding processes, sanctification and uncleanness, which play so critical a role in the Mishnah's account of reality. The will of man, expressed through the deed of man, is the active power in the world. Will and deed constitute those actors of creation which work upon neutral realms, subject to either sanctification or uncleanness: the Temple and the table, the field and the family, the altar and the hearth, woman, time, space, and transactions in the material world and in the world above. Just as the entire system of uncleanness and holiness awaits the intervention of man, which imparts the capacity to become unclean upon what was formerly inert, or which removes the capacity to impart cleanness from what was formerly in its natural and puissant condition, so in the other ranges of reality man is at the center on earth just as God is in heaven. Man is counterpart and partner and creation, in that, like God he has power over the status and condition of creation, by putting everything in its proper place and calling everything by its rightful name.

So the question taken up by the Mishnah and answered by Judaism is, What can a man do? And the answer laid down by the Mishnah is, man, through will and deed, is master of this world, the measure of all things. Since when the Mishnah thinks of man, it means the Israelite, who is the subject and actor of its system, the statement is clear. This man is Israel, who can do what he wills. In the aftermath of the two wars, the message of the Mishnah cannot have proved more pertinent— or poignant and tragic.

Judaism without Christianity

Before moving toward the fourth century, let us stand back and reflect on the character of the Judaism without a temple that emerged in a world without Christianity. Here we see the Judaism that flowed from the destruction of the Temple. What it did not find necessary—for example, a doctrine of the authority of Scripture and a systematic effort to link the principal document, the Mishnah, to Scripture—is as interesting as what it did define as its principal focus. The system of the Mishnah—a Judaism for a world in which Christianity played a small role—took slight interest in the Messiah and presented a teleology lacking all messianic focus. It laid little stress on the symbol of the Torah, though of course the Torah enjoyed prominence as a scroll, as a matter of status, and as revelation of God's will at Sinai. And it produced a document, the Mishnah, so independent of Scripture that, when the authors wished to say what Scripture said, they chose to do so in their own words and in their own way. They clearly did not intend to explain to the heirs of the Scriptures of Sinai what authority validated the document and how the document related to Scripture.

When we listen to the silences of the Mishnah as much as to its points of stress we hear a single message. It is the message of a Judaism that answered a single encompassing question: What, in the aftermath of the destruction of the holy place and holy cult, remained of the sanctity of the holy caste—the priesthood—the holy land, and above all the holy people and its holy way of life? The answer was that sanctity would endure in Israel the people, in its way of life, in its land, in its priesthood, in its food, in its mode of sustaining life, and in its manner of procreating and so sustaining the nation. But that answer later found itself absorbed within a successor system, with its own points of stress and emphasis. So let us now turn to the Judaism that took shape after 70 but before Constantine's rise to power in 312 (though I think the decisive year much later, namely, 362, when Julian's Christian heir mounted the throne and established for all time the Christian paramountcy in the West). Having seen where Christianity made no difference, we shall now see when Christianity made all the difference in the world.

THE SECOND STAGE IN THE FORMATION OF JUDAISM: THE TALMUD OF THE LAND OF ISRAEL AND MIDRASH-COMPILATIONS

FROM 200 TO 600

The Unfolding of the Mishnah's Tradition

The Judaism of the dual Torah, which emerged at the end of late antiquity and reached its final statement in the Talmud of Babylonia, took shape in response to both internal and external stimuli. The internal questions derived from the character of the Mishnah itself and the external questions from the catastrophic political change brought on by the conversion of the Roman emperor to Christianity and the establishment of the Christian religion as the religion of the state. We begin with the reception of the Mishnah, the issue that dominated in the third and early fourth centuries. Then we move on to the decisive political events of the later fourth and fifth centuries, the challenge of Christianity as the religon of the Roman state.

As soon as the Mishnah made its appearance, the vast labor of explaining its meaning and justifying its authority got under way. The Mishnah presented one striking problem in particular. It rarely cited scriptural authority for its rules. By omitting scriptural proof, texts bore the implicit claim to an authority independent of Scripture, and in that striking fact the document set a new course for itself and raised problems for those who wanted to apply its law to Israel's life. For from the formation of ancient Israelite Scripture into a holy book in Judaism in the aftermath of the return to Zion, and the creation of the Torah book in Ezra's time (about 450 B.C.) as the established canon of revelation, coming generations routinely set their ideas into relationship with

Scripture. They did this by citing proof texts alongside their own rules. Otherwise the new writings could find no ready hearing in the setting of Israelite culture.

Over the six hundred years beginning with the formation of the Torah of Moses in the time of Ezra, from about 450 B.C. to about A.D. 200, four conventional ways to accommodate new writings—new "tradition"—to the established canon of received Scripture had come to the fore. First and simplest, a writer would sign a famous name to his book, attributing his ideas to Enoch, Adam, Jacob's sons, Jeremiah, Baruch, or any number of others, down to Ezra. But the Mishnah bore no such attribution. Implicitly, to be sure, the statement of M. Avot 1 : 1, "Moses received Torah from Sinai," carried the further notion that sayings of people on the list of authorities from Moses to nearly their own day derived from God's revelation at Sinai. But no one made that premise explicit before the time of the Talmud of the Land of Israel. Second, an author might also imitate the style of biblical Hebrew and so try to creep into the canon by adopting the cloak of Scripture. But the Mishnah's authorship does not use biblical syntax or style.[1] Third, an author would surely claim that his work was inspired by God, a new revelation for an open canon. But that claim had no explicit impact on the Mishnah, which contains nothing attributed to God through prophecy, for instance. Fourth, at the very least, someone would link his opinions to biblical verses so Scripture would validate his views. The authorship of the Mishnah did so occasionally, but far more commonly stated on its own authority whatever rules it proposed to lay down.

The solution to the problem of the authority of the Mishnah, that is to say its relationship to Scripture, was worked out in the period after the completion of the Mishnah. Since no one could now credibly claim to sign the name of Ezra or Adam to a book of this kind, the only options lay elsewhere. These were first, to provide a myth of the origin of the contents of the Mishnah, and second, to link each allegation of the

1. The Hebrew of the Mishnah complicated the problem, because it is totally different from the Hebrew of the Hebrew Scriptures. Its verb, for instance, makes provision not only for completed or continuing action, which the biblical Hebrew verb allows, but also for past and future tenses, subjunctive and indicative voices, and much else. The syntax is like that of Indo-European, in that we can translate the word order of the Mishnah into any Indo-European language and come up with perfect sense. None of that crabbed imitation of biblical Hebrew, that makes the Dead Sea scrolls an embarassment to read, characterizes the Hebrew of the Mishnah. Mishnaic style is elegant, subtle, and exquisite in its sensitivity to word order and repetition, balance, and pattern.

Mishnah, through processes of biblical (not Mishnaic) exegesis, to verses of the Scriptures. These two procedures together established for the Mishnah the standing that the uses to which the document was to be put demanded for it: a place in the canon of Israel, and a legitimate relationship to the Torah of Moses. There were several ways in which the work went forward. These are represented by diverse documents that succeeded and dealt with the Mishnah. Let me now state the three principal possibilities: (1) the Mishnah required no systematic support through exegesis of Scripture in light of Mishnaic laws; (2) the Mishnah by itself provided no reliable information and all of its propositions demanded linkage to Scripture, to which the Mishnah must be shown to be subordinate and secondary; (3) the Mishnah is an autonomous document, but closely correlated with Scripture.

The first extreme is represented by the Abot, about A.D. 250, which represents the authority of the sages cited in Abot as autonomous of Scripture. The authorities in Abot do not cite verses of Scripture, but what they say constitutes a statement of the Torah. There can be no clearer way of saying that what these authorities present in and of itself falls into the classification of the Torah. The authorship of the Tosefta, about A.D. 400, takes the middle position. It very commonly cites a passage of the Mishnah and then adds to that passage an appropriate proof text. That is a quite common mode of supplementing the Mishnah. The mediating view is also taken by the Talmud of the Land of Israel, about A.D. 400, among the various documents produced by the Jewish sages of the land of Israel between the end of the second century and the sixth. The Talmud of the Land of Israel ("Palestinian Talmud of the Land of Israel," "Yerushalmi"), like the one made up at the same period—in the third and fourth centuries—in Babylonia, was organized around the Mishnah. It provided a line-by-line or paragraph-by-paragraph exegesis and amplification of the Mishnah. Produced by schools in Tiberias, Sepphoris, Lud (Lydda), and Caesarea, the Talmud of the Land of Israel developed a well-crafted theory of the Mishnah and its relationship to Scripture. The far extreme—that everything in the Mishnah makes sense only as a (re)statement of Scripture or upon Scripture's authority—is taken by the Sifra, a post-Mishnaic compilation of exegeses on Leviticus, redacted at an indeterminate point, perhaps about A.D. 300. The Sifra systematically challenges reason (the Mishnah) unaided by revelation (that is, exegesis of Scripture) to sustain positions taken by the Mishnah, which is cited verbatim, and everywhere proves that it cannot be done.

The final and normative solution to the problem of the authority of the Mishnah, worked out in the third and fourth centuries, produced the myth of the dual Torah, oral and written, which formed the indicative and definitive trait of the Judaism that emerged from late antiquity. Tracing the unfolding of that myth leads us deep into the processes by which that Judaism took shape. The Yerushalmi knows the theory that there is a tradition separate from, and in addition to, the written Torah. This tradition it knows as "the teachings of scribes." The Mishnah is not identified as the collection of those teachings. An ample instantiation of the Yerushalmi's recognition of this other, separate tradition is contained in the following discourse. What is interesting is that, if these discussions take for granted the availability to Israel of authoritative teachings in addition to those of Scripture, they do not also claim that those teachings are contained, uniquely or even partially, in the Mishnah in particular. Indeed, the discussion is remarkable in its supposition that extrascriptural teachings are associated with the views of scribes, perhaps legitimately called sages, but are not in a book to be venerated or memorized as a deed of ritual learning.

Y. Abodah Zarah 2:7:

III. A. Associates in the name of R. Yohanan: "The words of scribes are more beloved than the words of Torah and more cherished than words of Torah: 'Your palate is like the best wine' (Song 7:9)."

    B. Simeon bar Ba in the name of R. Yohanan: "The words of scribes are more beloved than the words of Torah and more cherished than words of Torah: 'For your love is better than wine' (Song 1:2). . . ."

    D. R. Ishmael repeated the following: "The words of Torah are subject to prohibition, and they are subject to remission; they are subject to lenient rulings, and they are subject to strict rulings. But words of scribes all are subject only to strict interpretation, for we have learned there: He who rules, 'There is no requirement to wear phylacteries,' in order to transgress the teachings of the Torah, is exempt. But if he said, 'There are five partitions in the phylactery, instead of four,' in order to add to what the scribes have taught, he is liable [M. San. 11:3]."

    E. R. Haninah is the name of R. Idi in the name of R. Tanhum b. R. Hiyya: "More stringent are the words of the elders than the words of the prophets. For it is written, 'Do not preach'—thus they preach—'one should not preach of such things' (Micah 2:6). And it is written, '[If a man should go about and utter wind and lies, saying,] "I will preach to you of wine and strong drink," he would be the preacher for this people!' (Micah 2:11).

F. "A prophet and an elder—to what are they comparable? To a king who sent two senators of his to a certain province. Concerning one of them he wrote, 'If he does not show you my seal and signet, do not believe him.' But concerning the other one he wrote, 'Even though he does not show you my seal and signet, believe him.' So in the case of the prophet, he has had to write, 'If a prophet arises among you . . . and gives you a sign or a wonder . . .' (Deut. 13:1). But here [with regard to an elder:] '. . . according to the instructions which they give you . . .' (Deut. 17:11) [without a sign or a wonder]."

What is important in the foregoing anthology is the distinction between teachings contained in the Torah and teachings in the name or authority of scribes. These latter teachings are associated with quite specific details of the law and are indicated in the Mishnah's rule itself. Further, at E we have "elders" (that is, sages) as against prophets.

What conclusion is to be drawn from this mixture of word choices that all together clearly refer to a law or tradition in addition to that of Scripture? The commonplace view, maintained in diverse forms of ancient Judaism, that Israel had access to a tradition beyond Scripture, clearly was well known to the framers of the Yerushalmi. The question of how, in that context, these framers viewed the Mishnah is not to be settled by that fact. I cannot point to a single passage in which explicit judgment upon the character and status of the Mishnah as a complete document is laid down. Nor is the Mishnah treated as a symbol or called "the oral Torah." But there is ample evidence, once again implicit in what happens to the Mishnah in the Talmud of the Land of Israel, to allow a reliable description of how the founders of the Talmud of the Land of Israel viewed the Mishnah. The Mishnah rarely cites verses of Scripture in support of its propositions. The Talmud of the Land of Israel routinely adduces scriptural bases for the Mishnah's laws. The Mishnah seldom undertakes the exegesis of verses of Scripture for any purpose. The Talmud of the Land of Israel consistently investigates the meaning of verses of Scripture, and does so for a variety of purposes. Accordingly, the Talmud of the Land of Israel, subordinate as it is to the Mishnah, regards the Mishnah as subordinate to, and contingent upon,

Scripture. That is why, in the view of the Talmud of the Land of Israel, the Mishnah requires the support of proof texts of Scripture. Let me state the upshot: that fact can mean only that, by itself, the Mishnah exercises no autonomous authority and enjoys no independent standing.

What is important in the following abstract is that the search for proof texts in Scripture sustains not only propositions of the Mishnah, but also those of the Tosefta as well as those of the Talmud of the Land of Israel's own sages. This is a stunning fact. It indicates that the search of Scriptures is primary, and the source of propositions or texts to be supported by those Scriptures, secondary. There is no limit, indeed, to the purposes for which Scriptural texts will be found relevant.

Y. SANHEDRIN 10:4:

II.   A. The party of Korach has no portion in the world to come and will not live in the world to come [M. San. 10:4].
           B. What is the Scriptural basis for this view?
           C. "[So they and all that belonged to them went down alive into Sheol;] and the earth closed over them, and they perished from the midst of the assembly" (Num. 16:33).
           D. "The earth closed over them"—in this world.
           E. "And they perished from the midst of the assembly"—in the world to come [M. San. 10:4D-F].
           F. It was taught: R. Judah b. Batera says, "[The contrary view] is to be derived from the implication of the following verse:
           G. "I have gone astray like a lost sheep: seek thy servant [and do not forget thy commandments]" (Ps. 119:176).
           H. "Just as the lost object which is mentioned later on in the end is going to be searched for, so the lost object which is stated herein is destined to be searched for" [T. San. 13:9].
           I. Who will pray for them?
           J. R. Samuel bar Nahman said, "Moses will pray for them:
           K. 'Let Reuben live, and not die, [nor let his men be few]' (Deut. 33:6)."
           L. R. Joshua b. Levi said, "Hannah will pray for them."
           M. This is the view of R. Joshua b. Levi, for R. Joshua b. Levi said, "Thus did the party of Korach sink ever downward, until Hannah went and prayed for them and said, "The Lord kills and brings to life; he brings down to Sheol and raises up' (I Sam. 2:6)."

We have a striking sequence of proof texts, serving, one by one, the cited statement of the Mishnah, A–C, then an opinion of a rabbi in the Tosefta, F–H, and then the position of a Talmudic rabbi, J–K, L–M. The process of providing the proof texts is therefore central, and the differentiation among the passages requiring the proof texts, a matter of indifference. The search for appropriate verses of Scripture vastly transcended the purpose of the study of the Mishnah, the exegesis of its rules, and the provision of adequate authority for the document and its laws. In fact, any proposition to be taken seriously elicited interest in Scriptural support, whether in the Mishnah, in the Tosefta, or in the mouth of a Talmudic sage. So the main thing is that the Scripture was at the center and focus. A verse of Scripture settled all pertinent questions, wherever they were located, whatever their source. That was the Talmud of the Land of Israel's position. We know full well that it was not the Mishnah's position.

This fact shows us in a detail a part of a broad shift that took place in the generations that received the Mishnah, that is, over the third and fourth centuries. If the sages of the second century, who made the Mishnah as we know it, spoke in their own name and in the name of the logic of their own minds, those who followed, certainly the ones who flourished in the later fourth century, took a quite different view. Reverting to ancient authority like others of the age, they turned back to Scripture, deeming it the source of certainty about truth. Unlike their masters in the Mishnah, theirs was a quest for a higher authority than the logic of their own minds. The shift from age to age is clear. The second-century masters took commonplaces of Scripture, well-known facts, and stated them wholly in their own language and context. Fourth-century masters phrased commonplaces of the Mishnah or banalities of worldly wisdom so far as they could in the language of Scripture and its context.

The real issue was not the Mishnah at all, not even its diverse sayings vindicated one by one. Once what a sage said was made to refer to Scripture for proof, it followed that a rule of the Mishnah and of the Tosefta likewise were asked to refer to Scripture. The fact that the living sage validated what he said through Scripture explains why the sage also validated through verses of Scripture what the ancient sages of the Mishnah and Tosefta said. It was one undivided phenomenon. The reception of the Mishnah constituted testimony to a prevalent attitude of mind, important for the age of the Talmud of the Land of Israel and not solely for the Mishnah. The stated issue was the standing of the

Mishnah. But the heart of the matter was the authority of the sage himself, who identified with the authors of the Mishnah and claimed authoritatively to interpret the Mishnah and much else, including Scripture. So the appeal to Scripture in behalf of the Mishnah represented simply one more expression of what proved critical in the formative age of Judaism: the person of the holy man himself. When revelation—Torah—became flesh, Judaism was born.

Systemic Changes in the Fourth Century: Canon, Symbol, Teleology

The documents that carried forward and continued the Mishnah exhibited striking changes, in particular those writings completed at the end of the fourth century. Fundamental in character, those changes marked dramatic shifts in the modes of symbolization of the canon, of the system as a whole, and of the purpose and goal of the system. We shall see that each of the important changes in the documents first redacted at the end of the fourth century responded to a powerful challenge presented by the triumph of Christianity in the age of Constantine. On that basis I maintain that the Judaism of the dual Torah took as its set of urgent questions the issue defined by Christianity as it assumed control of the Roman empire, and that it provided as valid answers a system deriving its power from the Torah, read by sages, embodied by sages, and exemplified by sages.

CANON

The first change revealed in the unfolding of the sages' canon pertained to the use of Scripture. The change at hand was specifically to make books out the collection of exegeses of Scripture. That represented an innovation because the Mishnah, and the exegetical literature that served the Mishnah, did not take shape around the explanation of verses of Scripture. The authorship of the Mishnah and its principal heirs followed their own program, which was a topical one. They arranged ideas by subject matter. But in the third and later fourth centuries, other writings entering the canon took shape around the explanation of verses of Scripture rather than a set of topics. What this meant was that a second mode of organizing ideas now developed.

Let me make the question crystal clear by framing it in negative terms. The problem is not why Jews in general began to undertake exegesis of the Hebrew Scriptures. Judaism in all forms had always done that. Nor was there anything new even in collecting exegeses and framing them for a particular polemical purpose, that is, creating a book out of comments on the Scripture and in the form of a commentary. The Essene library at Qumran presents us with compositions of biblical commentary and exegesis. The school of Matthew provides an ample picture of another sort of exercise in systematic composition based on the amplification and application of Israel's ancient Scriptures.

But within the formation of the holy literature of rabbinic Judaism in particular, so far as we know, no one before the fourth century had produced a composition of biblical exegeses formed into holy books. Why then? Why do it at all? My answer is in two parts. First, making such collections defined the natural next step in the process precipitated by the appearance of the Mishnah and the task of exegesis of the Mishnah. Second, equally pressing in the confrontion with Christianity was the task of showing in a systematic and orderly way how Scripture was to be read in Israel.

With Christianity addressing the world with a systematic exegetical apologetic, beginning of course with the Gospels' demonstration of how events in the life of Jesus fulfilled the prophecies of the shared Scripture, a Judaic response took the form of a counterpart exegesis. When in the Mishnah sages found a systematic exegesis of Scripture unnecessary, it was because they saw no need, since there was no reading contrary to theirs that presented a challenge to them. But the Christians composed a powerful apologetic out of the systematic exegesis of the shared Scripture, and when Christianity made further indifference impolitic and impossible, sages replied with their compositions.

By the fourth century the Church had reached a consensus on the bulk of the New Testament canon, having earlier acccepted as its own the Old Testament. Accordingly, the issue of Scripture had come to the fore, and in framing the question of Scripture, the Church focused sages' attention on the larger matter of systematic exegesis. When, for example, Jerome referred to the Jews' having a "second" Torah, one that was not authoritative, and when a sequence of important fathers of the Church produced exegeses of Scripture in profoundly Christological terms, the issue was raised. It would be joined when sages speaking on their own and to their chosen audience went through pretty much the same processes. This they did by explaining the standing of that "second Torah," and by producing not merely counterpart exegeses to those of the Christians but counterpart compilations of such exegeses.

SYMBOL

The generative symbol of the literary culture of the sages, the Torah, stands for the system as a whole. From the Yerushalmi onward, the symbol of the Torah took on the meaning that would prove indicative when Judaism had reached its final form at the end of this period. It was the doctrine that, when Moses received the Torah at Mount Sinai, it had come down with him in two media, written and oral. The written Torah was transmitted, as its name says, through writing and is now contained in the canon of Scripture. The oral Torah was transmitted through the process of formulation for ease in memorization and then through the memories of sages and their disciples, from Moses and Joshua to the most current generation. That doctrine of the dual Torah—the Torah in two media—came about in response to the problem of explaining the standing and authority of the Mishnah. But the broadening of the symbol of the Torah first took shape around the figure of the sage. That symbolism accounted for the sages' authority. Only later on, in the fourth century, in the pages of the Yerushalmi, did the doctrine of the dual Torah reach expression. So in the unfolding of the documents of the canon of Judaism the symbol of Torah revealed a striking change. Beginning as a rather generalized account of how sages' teachings relate to God's will, the symbol of Torah gained concrete form in its application to the dual Torah, written and oral, Scripture and Mishnah. Within the unfolding of the canonical writings, such a shift represented a symbolic change of fundamental character.

When we speak of Torah in the rabbinical literature of late antiquity, we no longer denote a particular book, or the contents of such a book. Instead we connote a broad range of clearly distinct categories of noun and verb, concrete fact and abstract relationship. Torah stood for a kind of human being, a social status, social group, social relationship, or legal status. The main points of the whole of Israel's life and history came to full symbolic expression in that single word. The Torah symbolized the whole.

After the appearance of the Mishnah, the movement of the Torah from standing for a concrete, material object—a scroll—to symbolizing a broad range of relationships, proceeded in two significant stages. The first was marked off by tractate Abot, the second by the Yerushalmi. Abot regards study of Torah as what a sage does. The substance of Torah is what a sage says. That is so whether or not the saying relates to scriptural revelation. The content of the sayings attributed to sages endows those sayings with self-validating status. The sages usually do not quote verses of Scripture and explain them, nor do they speak in God's name. Yet, it is clear, sages talk Torah. What follows? It is this: if a sage says something, what he says is Torah. More accurately, what he says falls into the classification of Torah. Accordingly, Abot treats Torah learning as symptomatic, an indicator of the status of the sage, hence as merely instrumental. At issue in Abot is not Torah, but the authority of the sage. It is that standing that transforms a saying into a Torah saying, or that places a saying into the classification of Torah. Abot then stands as the first document of incipient rabbinism—the doctrine that the sage embodies the Torah and is a holy man, like Moses "our rabbi," in the likeness and image of God. First came the claim that a saying falls into the category of Torah if a sage says it as Torah. Then came the view that the sage himself was Torah incarnate.

To the rabbis the principal salvific deed was to study Torah, by which they meant memorizing Torah sayings by constant repetition. For some sages it meant profound analytic inquiry into the meanings of those sayings. The innovation now was that the study of Torah imparted supernatural power. For example, by repeating words of Torah, the sage could ward off the angel of death and accomplish other kinds of miracles as well. So Torah formulas served as incantations. Mastery of Torah transformed the man engaged in Torah learning into a supernatural figure who could do things ordinary folk could not do. The category of Torah had already vastly expanded so that through transformation of the Torah from a concrete thing to a symbol, a Torah scroll could be compared to a man of Torah, namely, a rabbi. Now, the principle had been established that salvation would come from keeping God's will in general, as Israelite holy men had insisted for so many centuries. So it was a small step for rabbis to identify their particular corpus of learning—the Mishnah and associated sayings—with God's will expressed in Scripture, the universally acknowledged medium of revelation.

The history of the symbolization of the Torah proceeded to its transformation into something quite different and abstract, quite distinct from the document and its teachings. In the history of the word Torah as abstract symbol, a metaphor serving to sort out one abstract status from another gained concrete and material reality of a new order. The message of Abot was that the Torah served the sage. How so? The Torah indicated who was a sage and who was not. Accordingly, the apology of Abot for the Mishnah was that the Mishnah contained things sages had said. What the sages said formed a chain of tradition extending back to Sinai. Hence it was equivalent to the Torah. The outcome was that words of sages enjoyed the status of the Torah. The small additional step was to claim that what sages said was Torah, as much as what Scripture said was Torah.

A further small step moved matters to the position that there were two media in which the Torah reached Israel: one in writing, the other handed on orally, that is, in memory. This final step, fully revealed in the Yerushalmi, brought the conception of Torah to its logical conclusion. Torah came in several media, written, oral, incarnate. So what the sage said was in the status of the Torah, was Torah, because the sage was Torah incarnate. The abstract symbol now had become concrete and material once again.

The Yerushalmi's theory of the Torah thus carries us through several stages in the symbolization of the word Torah. First transformed from something material and concrete into something abstract and beyond all metaphor, the word Torah finally emerged once more in a concrete aspect—now as the encompassing and universal mode of stating the whole doctrine, all at once, of Judaism in its formative age.

TELEOLOGY

The teleology of a system answers the question of purpose and goal. It explains why someone should do what the system requires. It may also spell out what will happen if someone does not do what the system demands. The Mishnah and its successor documents, Abot, and the Tosefta in particular, present one picture of the purpose of the system as a whole, a teleology without eschatological focus. The two Talmuds— along with some intermediate documents—later laid forth an eschatological teleology. The documents do cohere. The Talmuds, beginning with the former of the two, carried forward not only the exegesis of the Mishnah but also the basic values of the Mishnah's system. But they presented substantial changes too. While what people said about the affective life remained constant, what they said about teleology shifted in substantial ways. The philosophers of the Mishnah did not make use of the Messiah myth in the construction of a teleology for their system. The appearance in the Talmuds of a messianic eschatology fully consonant with the larger characteristic of the rabbinic system— indicated that the encompassing rabbinic system stood essentially autonomous of the prior, Mishnaic system. True, what had gone before was absorbed and fully assimilated. But the talmudic system—expressed in part in each of the non-Mishnaic segments of the canon and fully spelled out in all of them—was different in the aggregate from the Mishnaic system.

The Mishnah and its closely related documents, Abot and the Tosefta, did not appeal to eschatology in their framing of their theory of teleology. They spoke more commonly about preparing in this world for life in the world to come, and the focus was on the individual and his or her personal salvation, rather than on the nation and its destiny at the end of time. So the Mishnah presented an ahistorical teleology, and did not make use of the messiah theme to express its teleology. By contrast, the Talmuds provide an eschatological and therefore a messiah-centered teleology for their system. Theirs is the more familiar teleology of Judaism, which, from the Talmud of the Land of Israel onward, commonly explains the end and meaning of the system by referring to the end of time and the coming of the Messiah. The Judaism that emerged from late antiquity therefore took shape as a profoundly eschatological and messianic statement.

The Mishnah's authorship constructed a system of Judaism in which the entire teleological dimension reached full exposure while hardly invoking the person or functions of a messianic figure of any kind. The Mishnah's noneschatological teleology presented a striking contrast to that of the Yerushalmi, which framed the teleological doctrine around the person of the Messiah. If, as in the Mishnah, what was important in Israel's existence was sanctification, an ongoing process, and not salvation, understood as a one-time event at the end, then no one would find reason to narrate history. Few then would form the obsession about the Messiah so characteristic of Judaism in its later, rabbinic mode.

Since the Mishnah does speak of a goal and end, we ask, where, if not in the end of time, do things end? The answer once more is provided by Abot.[2] Death is the destination. In life we prepare for the voyage. Israel must keep the law in order to make the move required of us all. Abot constructed a teleology beyond time, providing a purposeful goal for every individual. Life is the antechamber, death the destination; what we do is weighed and measured. When we die, we stand on one side of the balance, while our life and deeds stand on the other.

In the Yerushalmi (and afterward the Bavli), the situation changed radically. The figure of the Messiah loomed large in both documents. The teleology of the system portrayed in them rested upon the premise of the coming of the Messiah. If one does so and so, the Messiah will come, and if not, the Messiah will tarry. So the compilers and authors of the two Talmuds laid enormous emphasis upon the sin of Israel and the capacity of Israel through repentance both to overcome sin and to bring the Messiah. "The attribute of justice" delays the Messiah's coming. The Messiah will come this very day, if Israel deserves. The Messiah will come when there are no more arrogant ("conceited") Israelites, when

2. In many ways we must regard Abot as the counterpart and opposite of the Yerushalmi.

judges and officers disappear, when the haughty and judges cease to exist, "Today, if you will obey" (Ps. 95 : 7).

In the hands of the framers of the late canonical literature of Judaism, the Messiah served to keep things pretty much as they were, while at the same time promising dramatic change. The condition of that dramatic change was not richly instantiated. It was given in the most general terms. But it is not difficult to define. Israel had to keep God's will, expressed in the Torah and the observance of the rites described therein. So Israel would demonstrate its acceptance of God's rule. The net effect was to reinforce the larger system of the Judaism of Torah study and the doing of religious duties expressed partially in the Talmuds of the Land of Israel and of Babylonia, with their exegesis of the Mishnah, and partially in the various exegetical compositions organized around the order and program of some of the books of Scripture. It was first in the Yerushalmi that Judaism drew into its sphere the weighty conception embodied in the Messiah myth. The matter of the Messiah remained subordinated: "If you do this or that, the Messiah will come." So the Messiah myth supplied the fixed teleology for the variety of ineluctable demands of the system as a whole. But the symbolic expression of the system's teleology underwent remarkable revision, first surfacing in a late fourth-century composition.

What happened was that the rabbinic system of the Talmuds transformed the Messiah myth in its totality into an essentially ahistorical force. If people wanted to reach the end of time, they had to rise above time and stand off at the side of great ephemeral political and military movements. That was the message of the Messiah myth as it reached full exposure in the rabbinic system of the two Talmuds. At its foundation it was precisely the message of the teleology without eschatology expressed by the Mishnah and its associated documents. We cannot claim that the talmudic system constituted a reaction against the Mishnaic one. To the contrary, we must conclude that in the Talmuds and their associated documents was the restatement, in classical-mythic form, of the ontological convictions that had informed the minds of the second-century philosophers of the Mishnah. The new medium contained the old, enduring message: Israel must turn away from time and change, submit to whatever happens, so as to win for itself the only government worth having—God's rule, accomplished through God's anointed agent, the Messiah.

Judaism in the Encounter with Christianity

The fourth century began with Constantine's conversion to Christianity and ended with the ultimate dissolution of the institutions and social foundations of paganism. There were five events of fundamental importance for the history of Judaism in the fourth and fifth centuries. All of them except for the last were well known in their day. They were as follows: the conversion of Constantine; the fiasco of Julian's plan to rebuild the Temple of Jerusalem; the depaganization of the Roman empire, a program of attacks on pagan temples and, along the way, synagogues; the Christianization of most of the population of Palestine; and the creation of the Talmud of the Land of Israel and of compositions of Scriptural exegeses, Genesis Rabbah and Leviticus Rabbah in particular.

For nearly everyone in the Roman world the most important events of the fourth and fifth centuries were the legalization of Christianity, followed very rapidly by the adoption of Christianity as the state's most favored religion, and then by the delegitimization of paganism and systematic degradation of Judaism. The astonishing arrival of legitimacy and even power provoked Christian intellectuals to rewrite Christian and world history, and to work out theology as a reflection on this new polity and its meaning in the unfolding of human history. A new commonwealth was coming into being, taking over the old and reshaping it for the new age. In 312 Constantine achieved power in the West. In 323 he took the government of the entire Roman empire into his own hands. In 313 he promulgated the edict of Milan, whereby Christianity attained the status of toleration. Christians and all others were given "the free power to follow the religion of their choice." In the next decade Christianity became the most favored religion. Converts from Judaism were protected and could not be punished by Jews. Christians were freed of the obligation to perform pagan sacrifices. Priests were exempted from certain taxes. Sunday became an obligatory day of rest. Celibacy was permitted. From 324 onward Constantine ceased to maintain a formal impartiality, and now intervened in the affairs of the Church. He settled quarrels among believers and called the Church Council at Nicaea (325) to settle issues of the faith. He was baptized only on the eve of his death in 337. Over the next century the pagan cults were destroyed, their priests deprived of support, and their intellectuals bereft of standing.

So far as the Jews of the Land of Israel were concerned, not much changed at the Milvian Bridge in 312, when Constantine conquered in the sign of Christ. The sages' writings nowhere refer explicitly to that event. They scarcely gave testimony to its consequences for the Jews, and continued to harp upon prohibited relationships with pagans in general, as though nothing had changed from the third century to the fourth and fifth. Legal changes affecting the Jews under Constantine's rule were indeed not substantial. Jews could not proselytize; they could not circumcise slaves when they bought them; Jews could not punish other Jews who became Christians. Finally Jews were required to serve on municipal councils wherever they lived, an onerous task involving responsibility for collecting taxes. But those who served synagogues, patriarchs, and priests were still exempted from civil and personal obligations. In the reign of Constantius III (337–361), further laws aimed at separating Jews from Christians were enacted, in 339 in the Canons of Elvira. These laws forbade intermarriage between Jews and Christians, further protected converts, and forbade Jews to hold slaves of Christian or other Gentile origin.

The reversion to paganism on the part of the emperor Julian, about 360, involved a measure of favor to Jews and Judaism. To embarrass Christianity, he permitted the rebuilding of the Temple at Jerusalem, but he died before much progress could be made. If people were looking for a dawn, the emperor Julian's plan to rebuild the ruined Temple in Jerusalem must have dazzled their eyes. For while Constantine had surely raised the messianic question, for a brief hour Emperor Julian appeared to answer it decisively. In 361 the now-pagan Julian gave permission to rebuild the Temple. Work briefly got underway, but stopped because of an earthquake. Julian's intention was quite explicit: to falsify the prophecy of Jesus that "not one stone of the temple would be left upon another." We may assume that since Christ's prophecy had not been proven false, many surely concluded that it had now been shown to be true. We do not know that many Jews then drew the conclusion that Jesus really was the Christ after all. Many Christians said so. In the aftermath of the fiasco of Julian's reversion to paganism, when the Christians returned to power, they determined to make certain that such a calamity would never recur. Over the next century they undertook a sustained attack on institutions and personnel of paganism in all its expressions. The long-term and systematic effort in time overspread Judaism as well. From the accession of Theodosius II in 383 to the death of his son Arcadius in 408, Judaism came under attack. The last pagan emperor's threat to Christianity made urgent the delegitimization of paganism. In the formation of a new and aggressive policy toward outsiders, Judaism too was caught in the net. Jews were to be protected but degraded. But the sword unsheathed against the pagan cult places was untutored, if sharp. It was not capable of discriminating among non-Christian centers of divine service. Nor could those who wielded it—zealots of the faith in church and street—have been expected to. The now-Christian Roman government protected synagogues and punished those who damaged them. Its policy was to extirpate paganism but to protect a degraded Judaism. But the faithful of the church had their own ideas. The assault against pagan temples spilled over into an ongoing program of attacking synagogue property.

In the earlier part of the fifth century, Jews' rights and the standing of their corporate communities were substantially affected. The patriarchate of the Jews of the land of Israel—the ethnarch and his administration—was abolished. From the turn of the fifth century the government policy was meant to isolate Jews, lower their status, and suppress their agencies of self-rule. The later fourth and fifth centuries for Israel in its land marked a time of significant change. Once a mere competing faith, Christianity now became paramount. The Talmud of the Land of Israel and the exegetical compilations came into being in an age first of high hope and then disaster. Vast numbers of Jews now found chimerical the messianic expectation, that they had framed around Julian's plan to rebuild the Temple. So it was a time of boundless expectations followed by bottomless despair. The period from Julian's fall onward presented to Israel problems of a profoundly religious character. In the next half century Palestine gained a Christian majority. Christians were not slow to claim their faith had been proved right. We need not speculate on the depth of disappointment felt by those Jews who had hoped that the project would come to fruition and herald the Messiah they awaited instead of the Christian one.

Still worse from the Jews' viewpoint, a phenomenon lacking much precedent in the preceding thousand years now came into view: random attacks on Jews by reason of their faith, as distinct from organized struggles among contending and equal forces, Jewish and other mobs. The long-established Roman tradition of toleration of Judaism and of Jews, extending back to the time of Julius Caesar and applying both in law and in custom, now drew to a close. A new fact, at this time lacking all basis in custom or in the policy of state and Church, faced Jews: physical insecurity in their own villages and towns. A mark of exceptional piety came to consist in violence against Jews' holy places, their property and their persons. In the last third of the fourth century and the beginning of the fifth, this war against the Jews raised once again those questions about the meaning and end of history that Constantine had forced upon Israel's consciousness at the beginning of the age at hand.

At this time there seems also to have been a sharp rise in the numbers of Christians in the Holy Land. Christian refugees from the West accounted for part of the growth. But we also have some stories about how Jews converted. The number of Christian towns and villages dramatically increased. If Jews did convert in sizeable numbers, then we should have to point to the events of the preceding decades as ample validation in their eyes for the Christian interpretation of history. Instead of being falsified, Jesus' prophecy had been validated. No stone had been left on stone in the Temple, not after 70 and not after 361, just as Jesus had said. Now their synagogues came under threat and, along with them, their own homes and persons. What could be more ample proof of the truth of the Christians' claim than the worldly triumph of their Church? Resisted for so long, that claim now called into question whether it was worth waiting any longer for a messiah that had not come when he was most needed. With followers now proclaiming that the Messiah who had come possessed the world, the question could hardly be avoided.

What happened was a world-historical change, one that could not be absorbed into Israel's available system of theories about the outsiders in general, and about the meaning of the history of the great empires in particular. The Christian empire was fundamentally different from its predecessor in two ways. First, it shared with Israel reverence for exactly the same Holy Scriptures on which Jewry based its existence. Second, established policies of more than a half a millenium—from the time of the Maccabees' alliance with Rome to the start of the fourth century— now gave way. Tolerance of Judaism and an accommodation with the Jews in their Land—disrupted only by the Jews' own violation of the terms of the agreement in 70 and 132—now no longer governed. Instead there was intolerance of Judaism and persecution of Jews through attacks on their persons and property. Whatever the world may have said, Jews themselves surely had to wonder whether history was headed in the right direction, and whether the Christians, emerging from within Israel itself, may not have been right. For the Empire now was Christian. The requirement to construct an apologetics therefore emerged from the condition of Israel, whether or not, in addition, Christian polemicists had a hearing among Jews.

Now to resume my story of the unfolding of the Judaism of the dual Torah, as it took shape in late antiquity. The Talmud of the Land of Israel is a document that was completed approximately a century after the political triumph of Christianity. In the aftermath of the conversion of the Roman Empire to Christianity and the confirmation of the triumph of Christianity in the generation beyond Julian "the apostate," sages worked out in the pages of the Talmud of the Land of Israel and in the exegetical compilations of the age a Judaism intersecting with the Mishnah's but essentially asymmetrical with it. It was a system for salvation, focused on the salvific power of the sanctification of the holy people. The political changes of the age had implications for the meaning and end of history as Israel would experience it. There were new questions and answers: the fresh emphasis on salvation, the introduction of the figure of the Messiah as a principal teleological force, and the statement of an eschatological teleology for the system as a whole. The questions were raised by Christian theologians, and the answers were provided by the Judaic sages. The former held that the Christian triumph confirmed the Christhood of Jesus, the rejection of Israel, and the end of Israel's hope for salvation at the end of time. The latter offered the Torah in its dual media, the affirmation of Israel as children of Abraham, Isaac, and Jacob, and the coming of the Messiah at the end of time. The questions and answers fitted the challenge of the age.

The Judaism without Christianity portrayed in the Mishnah did not present a richly developed doctrine of the Messiah. It worked out issues of sanctification, rather than those of salvation that predominated in important statements of Christianity. The reason is that the Mishnah laid its emphasis upon issues of the destruction of the Temple and the subsequent defeat in the failed war for the restoration. The framers of the Mishnah maintained these issues raised the question of Israel's sanctity: was Israel still a holy people, even without the holy temple, and if so, what were the enduring instrumentalities of sanctification? When sages worked out a Judaism without a Temple and a cult, they produced in the Mishnah a system of sanctification focused on the holiness of the priesthood, the cultic festivals, the Temple and its sacrifices, and the rules for protecting that holiness from levitical uncleanness—four of the six divisions of the Mishnah on a single theme. In the aftermath of the conversion of the Roman Empire to Christianity and the political triumph of Christianity in the generation beyond Julian the apostate, when the Church came to enjoy state sponsorship and backing, sages worked out in the pages of the Talmud of the Land of Israel and in the exegetical compilations of the age a Judaism intersecting with the Mishnah's but essentially asymmetrical with it. That Talmud presented a system of salvation, but one focused on the salvific power of the sanctification of the holy people. The first of the two Talmuds—the one closed at the end of the fourth century—set the compass and locked it into place. The Judaism that was portrayed by the final document of late antiquity—the Talmud of Babylonia—at the end laid equal emphasis on sanctification in the here and now and salvation at the end of time. That shift represents only one chapter in sages' restatement of the Judaism of the dual Torah in the confrontation with triumphant Christianity.

Let us turn back to the beginning of the fourth century and review the Christian challenge. With the triumph of Christianity through the conversion of Constantine in 312 and the favor of his successors in the West, Christianity's explicit claims, now validated in world-shaking events of the age, demanded a reply. The sages of the Talmud of the Land of Israel provided it. At the specific points at which the Christian challenge met head-on old Israel's world view, the sages responded. What did Israel's sages have to present as the Torah's answer to the Cross? It was the Torah. This took three forms. The Torah was first defined in the doctrine of the status of the Mishnah as oral and memorized revelation and by implication of other rabbinical writings. Moreover the Torah was presented as the encompassing symbol of Israel's salvation. Finally the Torah was embodied in the person of the Messiah who would, of course, be a rabbi. The Torah in all three modes confronted the Cross, with its doctrine of the triumphant Christ, Messiah and king, ruler now of earth as of heaven. The outcome was stunning success for that society for which, sages in the view of God cared so deeply: eternal Israel after the flesh. For Judaism in the rabbis' statement did endure in the Christian West, which imparted to Israel the secure conviction that it constituted that Israel after the flesh to which the Torah continued to speak. We know that the Judaism of the sages won because when Islam gained its victory, throughout the Middle East and North Africa Christianity gave way, leaving only pockets of the faithful to live out the long history of Islamic dominance. But sages' Judaism in those same vast territories retained the loyalty and conviction of the people of the Torah. The Cross ruled only where the Crescent and its sword did not. But the Torah of Sinai everywhere and always sanctified Israel in time and promised secure salvation for eternity. The entire history of Judaism is contained within these simple propositions.

The symbolic system of Christianity—with Christ triumphant, with the Cross as the now-regnant symbol, with the canon of Christianity now defined and recognized as authoritative—called forth from the sages of the Land of Israel a symbolic system strikingly responsive to the crisis. This took the form of the symbolic power of the dual Torah, with its explicit claim that sages' authority here and now represented the will of God in heaven. The first change was doctrinal, involving the inclusion into the mishnaic system of the belief in the coming of the Messiah. The second change was the symbol of the Torah expanded to encompass the entirety of the sages' teachings—as much of the written Torah as everyone acknowledged to be authoritative.

The Crisis of the Fourth Century

The fourth century marked the first century of Judaism and of Christianity: the Judaism of the dual Torah would flourish in the West (as well as in the Islamic world), and Christianity in its political formulation would define and govern the civilization of the West. When, in the aftermath of Constantine's legalization of Christianity in 312, Christianity became first the most favored religion, then the established one, and finally, by the end of the fourth century, triumphant, the condition of Israel changed in some ways but not in others. What remained the same was the politics and social circumstance of a defeated nation. What changed was the context of the religious system of Judaism. The worldly situation of Israel did not change, but the setting of Judaism did. For while Israelites in the Land of Israel persisted as a subject people, Judaism confronted a world in which its principal components—interpretation, teleology, symbol—met an effective challenge in the corresponding components of the now-triumphant faith in Christ. Specifically, the Hebrew Scriptures—the written Torah—now demanded a reading as the Old Testament predicting the New. In the Christian view, the reason was that history proved that Scripture's prophetic promises of a king-Messiah pointed toward Jesus, now Christ enthroned. Concomitantly, in the Christians' mind the teleology of the Israelite system of old, focused as it was on the coming of the Messiah, found confirmation and realization in the rule of Jesus, Christ enthroned. And the symbol of the whole—interpretation and teleology alike—rose in heaven's heights: the Cross that had triumphed at the Milvian Bridge.

Why did the conversion of the empire to Christianity make a difference to Israel's sages, although they had paid slight heed to Christianity in its prior apolitical condition? A move of the empire from reverence for Zeus to adoration of Mithra had meant nothing; paganism was what it was, lacking all differentiation in the Jewish eye. Christianity was something else. It was like Judaism. Christians read the Torah and

claimed to declare its meaning. Accordingly, the trend of sages' specula-
tion could not avoid the issue of the place, within the Torah's messianic
pattern, of the remarkable turn in world history represented by the
triumph of Christianity.

What in fact sages did at that time is clear. They composed the
Talmud of the Land of Israel as we know it. They collected exegeses of
Scripture and made them into systematic and sustained account, ini-
tially of the meaning of the Pentateuch.[3]

In the fourth century the sages compiled exegeses of Scripture, as
part of a Jewish apologetic response to what Christians had to say to
Israel. For one Christian message had been that Israel "after the flesh"
had distorted and continually misunderstood the meaning of what had
been its own Scripture. Failing to read the Old Testament in the light of
the New, failing to read the prophetic promises in the perspective of
Christ's fulfillment of those promises, Israel after the flesh had lost
access to God's revelation to Moses at Sinai. If we were to propose a
suitably powerful yet appropriately proud response, it would have two
qualities. First, it would supply a complete account of what Scripture
had meant and must always mean, as Israel read it. Second, it would
do so in such a way as not to dignify the position of the other side with
the grace of an explicit reply at all. The compilations of exegeses and the
Yerushalmi that were accomplished at this time assuredly took up the
challenge of restating the meaning of the Torah revealed by God to
Moses at Mount Sinai. This the sages did in a systematic and thorough
way. At the same time, if the charges of the other side had precipitated
the work of compilation and composition, the consequent collections in
no way suggest it. The issues of the documents were made always to
emerge from the inner life not even of Israel in general but of the sages'
estate in particular. Scripture was thoroughly rabbinized, as earlier it
had been Christianized. None of this suggests that the other side had
won a response for itself. Only the net effect—a complete picture of the
whole, as Israel must perceive the whole of revelation—suggests the
extraordinary utility for apologetics, outside as much as inside the faith,
that was served by these compilations.

The changes at the surface, in articulated doctrines of teleology,
interpretation, and symbolism, responded to changes in the political
condition of Israel as well as in the religious foundations of the politics
of the day. Paganism had presented a different and simpler problem to

---

3. We may assuming dates of the late third through early fifth centuries for Sifra,
the two Sifres, Genesis Rabbah and Leviticus Rabbah.

the sages. Christianity's explicit claims, validated in world-shaking events of the age, demanded a reply. The sages of the Talmud of the Land of Israel provided it. So it is at the very specific points at which the Christian challenge met head on old Israel's world view that the sages' doctrines changed. What did Israel have to present to the Cross? The Torah, in the doctrine of the status of the Mishnah as oral and memorized revelation and, by implication, of other rabbinical writings. The Torah in the encompassing symbol of Israel's salvation. The Torah, finally, in the person of the Messiah, who would of course be a rabbi. The Torah in all three modes confronted the Cross, with its doctrine of the triumphant Christ, Messiah and king, ruler now of earth as of heaven.

The Talmud of the Land of Israel

The Judaism to which the Talmud of the Land of Israel gives testimony forms one plank in the bridge that leads from antiquity to the beginning of the Middle Ages, from the Middle East to Europe, from the end of the classical age to the nascent moment of our own time and place. The Mishnah, in about A.D. 200, described an orderly world in which Israelite society was neatly divided among its castes, arranged in a hierarchy around the center that was the Temple, and systematically engaged in a life of sanctification remote from the disorderly events of the day. The Talmud of the Land of Israel, in about A.D. 400, portrayed the chaos of Jews living among Gentiles, governed by a diversity of authorities, lacking all order and arrangement, and awaiting a time of salvation for which they made themselves ready through sanctification. The Mishnah's Israel in imagination was governed by an Israelite king, a high priest, and the sanhedrin. The Jews of the Talmud of the Land of Israel lived under both rabbis near at hand, who settled everyday disputes of streets and households, and also distant archons of a nameless state, who were to be manipulated and placated on earth as in heaven. The Mishnah's Judaism breathed the pure air of public piazza and stoa; the Talmud of the Land of Israel's breathed the ripe stench of private alleyway and courtyard. The image of the Mishnah's Judaism is evoked by the majestic Parthenon, perfect in all its proportions, and conceived in a single moment of pure rationality. The Talmud of the Land of Israel's Judaism was a scarcely choate cathedral in process, the labor of many generations, each of its parts the conception of diverse moments of devotion, but all of them the culmination of an on-going and evolving process of revelation.

The Mishnah is Judaism's counterpart to Plato's *Republic* and Aristotle's *Politics*, a noble theory of it all. When we study the Mishnah, we contemplate a fine conception of nowhere in particular, addressed to whom it may concern. When we turn to the Talmud of the Land of Israel, we see a familiar world, as we have known it from the Talmud of the Land of Israel's day to our own. We perceive something of our own day as those of us who study Judaism recognize continuity with those times. So the Mishnah marked the end of the ancient and Near Eastern, while the Talmud of the Land of Israel marked the beginning of the modern and the Western (as well as the Near Eastern) epoch in the history of Judaism.

The Talmud of the Land of Israel testified to the existence of a coherent world view and way of life embodied in a distinct and distinctive society, or estate, of Jews: the rabbis—masters and disciples—of the third and fourth century in the Land of Israel. Before us in the Yerushalmi is not a complete system of Judaism, contained in a single document. The Yerushalmi is not like the Mishnah, which provides a full and exhaustive account of its system and its viewpoint. Whatever we know about the Mishnah's system is in that book itself. The Judaism to which the Yerushalmi testifies defines the matrix in which, among other documents, the Yerushalmi came into being. The Yerushalmi and the Mishnah are really not comparable to one another. The Yerushalmi is continuous with the Mishnah. But the character of the document, and therefore also the world to which its evidence pertains, was a mirror image of the Mishnah. The Mishnah exhaustively answered any and all questions about its Judaism. But the Yerushalmi, while it answered many questions about the Judaism represented in its pages, was by no means the sole source of answers. Numerous questions dealt with by the Judaism to which Yerushalmi attests were answered—in the same or similar ways—in other documents altogether. The evidence of the Yerushalmi about the Judaism attested in its pages must be described in a way quite different from the way in which we lay out evidence of the Mishnah about the Judaism expressed within the Mishnah. The one gives evidence of a world beyond itself, a world of which it was an important component. The other gives evidence only about itself and the world view contemplated within its words.

In our consideration of the formation of Judaism in response to the crisis of the fourth century, we should review the doctrine of the Messiah as it emerged in the Talmud of the Land of Israel. In the Talmud of the Land of Israel, two historical contexts framed discussion of the

Messiah—the destruction of the Temple and the messianic claim of Bar Kokhba.[4] Rome played a role in both, and the authors of the materials gathered in the Talmud made a place for Rome in the history of Israel. In conformity to their larger theory of who was Israel, they did this by assigning to Rome a place in the family. As to the destruction of the Temple, we find a statement that the Messiah was born on the day that the Temple was destroyed. The Talmud's doctrine of the Messiah therefore found its place in its encompassing doctrine of history. What was fresh in the Talmud was the perception of Rome as an autonomous actor, as an entity with a point of origin (just as Israel had a point of origin) and a tradition of wisdom (just as Israel had such a tradition). So as Rome was Esau, so Esau was part of the family and therefore played a role in history. And since Rome played a role in history, Rome also found a position in the eschatological drama. This sense of poised opposites, Israel and Rome, came to expression in two ways. First, Israel's own history called into being its counterpoint, the antihistory of Rome. Without Israel, there would be no Rome—a wonderful consolation to the defeated nation. For if Israel's sin had created Rome's power, then Israel's repentance would bring about Rome's downfall. Here is the way in which the Talmud presented the match:

Y. Avodah Zarah 1:2

[IV E]   Saturnalia means "hidden hatred" [*sina'ah temunah*]: The Lord hates, takes vengeance, and punishes.

[F]   This is in accord with the following verse: "Now Esau hated Jacob" [Gen. 27:41].

[G]   R. Isaac b. R. Eleazar said, "In Rome they call it Esau's Saturnalia."

[H]   Kratesis: It is on the day on which the Romans seized power.

[K]   Said R. Levi, "It is the day on which Solomon intermarried with the family of Pharaoh Neccho, King of Egypt. On that day Michael came down and thrust a reed into the sea, and pulled up muddy alluvium, and this was turned into a huge pot, and this was the great city of Rome. On the day on which Jeroboam set up the two golden calves, Remus and Romulus came and built two huts in the city of Rome.

---

4. The Talmud of the Land of Israel totally ignores whatever messianic hopes and figures took part in the fiasco of Julian's projected rebuilding of the Temple.

On the day on which Elijah disappeared, a king was appointed in Rome: "There was no king in Edom; a deputy was king" [1 Kings 22:47].

The important point is that Solomon's sin provoked heaven's founding of Rome. The entire world and what happens in it enter into the framework of meaning established by Israel's Torah. So what the Romans did, their historical actions, could be explained in terms of Israel's conception of the world.

The concept of two histories, balanced opposite one another, came to particular expression, within the Talmud of the Land of Israel, in the balance of Israelite sage and Roman emperor. Just as Israel and Rome, God and no-god, compete, so do sage and emperor. In this age, it appeared that the emperor had the power. God's Temple, in contrast to the great churches of the age, lay in ruins. But just as sages could overcome the emperor through their inherent supernatural power, so too would Israel and Israel's God control the course of events in the coming age. In this doctrine we see the true balance: sage as against emperor. In the age of the Christian emperors, the polemic acquired power. The sage, in his small-claims court, weighed in the balance against the emperor in Constantinople—a rather considerable claim. So two stunning innovations appeared: first, the notion of emperor and sage in mortal struggle; and second, the idea of an age of idolatry and an age beyond idolatry. The world had to move into a new orbit indeed for Rome to enter into the historical context formerly defined wholly by what happened to Israel. How did all this relate to the Messianic crisis at hand? The doctrine of sages, directly pertinent to the issue of the coming of the Messiah, held that Israel could free itself of control by other nations only by humbly agreeing to accept God's rule. The nations—Rome, in the present instance—rested on one side of the balance, while God rested on the other. Israel had to choose between them. There was no such thing for Israel as freedom from both God and the nations, total autonomy and independence. There was only a choice of masters, a ruler on earth or a ruler in heaven.

Once the figure of the Messiah came on stage, there arose discussion on who, among the living, the Messiah might be. The identification of the Messiah began with the person of David himself: "If the Messiah-King comes from among the living, his name will be David. If he comes from among the dead, it will be King David himself" (Y. Ber. 2:3 V P). A variety of evidence announced the advent of the Messiah as a figure in the larger system of formative Judaism. The rabbinization of David constituted one kind of evidence. Serious discussion within the framework of the accepted document of Mishnaic exegesis and the law, concerning the identification and claim of diverse figures asserted to be messiahs, presented still more telling proof.

Y. BERAKHOT 2:4 (translated by T. Zahavy)

    A. Once a Jew was plowing and his ox snorted once before him. An Arab who was passing and heard the sound said to him, "Jew, loosen your ox and loosen the plow and stop plowing. For today your Temple was destroyed."

    B. The ox snorted again. He [the Arab] said to him, "Jew, bind your ox and bind your plow, for today the Messiah-King was born."

    C. He said to him, "What is his name?"

    D. "Menahem."

    E. He said to him, "And what is his father's name?"

    F. The Arab said to him, "Hezekiah."

    G. He said to him, "Where is he from?"

    H. He said to him, "From the royal capital of Bethlehem in Judea."

    I. The Jew went and sold his ox and sold his plow. And he became a peddler of infants' feltcloths [diapers]. And he went from place to place until he came to that very city. All of the women bought from him. But Menahem's mother did not buy from him.

    J. He heard the women saying, "Menahem's mother, Menahem's mother, come buy for your child."

    K. She said, "I want to bring him up to hate Israel. For on the day he was born, the Temple was destroyed."

    L. They said to her, "We are sure that on this day it was destroyed, and on this day of the year it will be rebuilt."

    M. She said to the peddler, "I have no money."

    N. He said to her, "It is of no matter to me. Come and buy for him and pay me when I return."

    O. A while later he returned to the city. He said to her, "How is the infant doing?"

    P. She said to him, "Since the time you saw him a spirit came and carried him away from me."

    Q. Said R. Bun, "Why do we learn this from [a story about] an Arab? Do we not have explicit scriptural evidence for it? 'Lebanon with its majestic trees will fall' [Isa. 10:34]. And what follows this? 'There shall come forth a shoot from the stump of Jesse' [Isa. 11:1]. [Right after an allusion to the destruction of the Temple the prophet speaks of the messianic age.]"

This is a set-piece story, adduced to prove that the Messiah was born on the day the Temple was destroyed. The Messiah was born when the Temple was destroyed; hence God prepared for Israel a better fate than had appeared.

A more concrete matter—the identification of the Messiah with a known historical personality—was associated with the name of Aqiba. He is said to have claimed that Bar Kokhba, the leader of the second-century revolt, was the Messiah. The important aspect of the story, however, was the rejection of Aqiba's view. The discredited messiah figure (if Bar Kokhba was actually such in his own day) found no apologists in the later rabbinical canon. What is striking in what follows, moreover, is that we really have two stories. At G, Aqiba is said to have believed that Bar Kokhba was a disappointment. At H-I, he is said to have identified Bar Kokhba with the King-Messiah. Both cannot be true, so what we have is simply two separate opinions of Aqiba's judgment of Bar Kokhba/Bar Kozebah.

Y. TAANIT 4:5.X

> G. R. Simeon b. Yohai taught, "Aqiba, my master, would interpret the following verse: 'A star (*kokhab*) shall come forth out of Jacob' [Num. 24:17] 'A disappointment (*Kozeba*) shall come forth out of Jacob.'"
>
> H. R. Aqiba, when he saw Bar Kozeba, said, "This is the King Messiah."
>
> I. R. Yohanan b. Toreta said to him, "Aqiba! Grass will grow on your cheeks before the Messiah will come!"

The important point is not only that Aqiba had been proved wrong. It is that the very verse of Scripture adduced in behalf of his viewpoint could be treated more generally and made to refer to righteous people in general, rather than to the Messiah in particular. And that leads us to the issue of the age, as sages had to face it: what makes a messiah a false messiah? When we know the answer to that question, we also uncover the distinctively rabbinic version of the Messiah theme that the Talmud of the Land of Israel contributed.

What matters is not the familiar doctrine of the Messiah's claim to save Israel, but the doctrine that Israel would be saved through total submission to God's yoke and service under the Messiah's gentle rule. In the model of the sage, the Messiah would teach Israel the power of submission. So God was not to be manipulated through Israel's humoring heaven in rite and cult. The notion of keeping the commandments so as to please heaven and get God to do what Israel wanted was totally incongruent to the text at hand. Keeping the commandments as a mark of submission, loyalty, and humility before God was the rabbinic system of salvation. So Israel could not save itself. Israel could never control its own destiny, either on earth or in heaven. The only choice was whether to cast one's fate into the hands of cruel, deceitful men, or to trust in the living God of mercy and love. We now understand the stress on the centrality of hope. Hope signifies patient acceptance of God's rule, and as an attitude of mind and heart, it is something that Israel could sustain on its own—the ideal action. We shall now see how this critical position—that Israel's task was humble acceptance of God's rule—was spelled out in the setting of discourse about the Messiah in the Talmud of the Land of Israel. Bar Kokhba weighed in the balance against the sage, much as the Roman emperor weighed in the balance against the sage, and for the same reason. The one represented arrogance, and the other, humility. Bar Kokhba exemplified arrogance against God. He lost the war because of his arrogance. In particular, he ignored the authority of sages—a point not to be missed, since it formed the point of critical tension of the tale:

Y. TAANIT 4:5

> XJ. Said R. Yohanan, "Upon orders of Caesar Hadrian, they killed eight hundred thousand in Betar."
>
> K. Said R. Yohanan, "There were eighty thousand pairs of trumpeeters surrounding Betar. Each one was in charge of a number of troops. Ben Kozeba was there and he had two hundred thousand troops who, as a sign of loyalty, had cut off their little fingers.
>
> L. "Sages sent word to him, 'How long are you going to turn Israel into a maimed people?'
>
> M. "He said to them, 'How otherwise is it possible to test them?'
>
> N. "They replied to him, 'Whoever cannot uproot a cedar of Lebanon while riding on his horse will not be inscribed on your military rolls.'
>
> O. "So there were two hundred thousand who qualified in

one way, and another two hundred thousand who quali-
fied·in another way."

P. When he would go forth to battle, he would say, "Lord of
the world! Do not help and do not hinder us! 'Hast thou
not rejected us, O God? Thou dost not go forth, O God,
with our armies'" [Ps. 60:10].

Q. Three and a half years did Hadrian besiege Betar.

R. R. Eleazar of Modiin would sit on sackcloth and ashes and
pray every day, saying "Lord of the ages! Do not judge in
accord with strict judgment this day! Do not judge in
accord with strict judgment this day!"

S. Hadrian wanted to go to him. A Samaritan said to him,
"Do not go to him until I see what he is doing, and so hand
over the city [of Betar] to you. [Make peace . . . for you.]"

T. He got into the city through a drain pipe. He went and
found R. Eleazar of Modiin standing and praying. He
pretended to whisper something into his ear.

U. The townspeople saw [the Samaritan] do this and brought
him to Ben Kozeba. They told him, "We saw this man
having dealings with your friend."

V. [Bar Kokhba] said to him, "What did you say to him, and
what did he say to you?"

W. He said to [the Samaritan], "If I tell you, then the king will
kill me, and if I do not tell you, then you will kill me. It is
better that the king kill me, and not you.

X. [Eleazar] said to me, 'I should hand over my city.' ['I shall
make peace. . . .']"

Y. He turned to R. Eleazar of Modiin. He said to him, "What
did this Samaritan say to you?"

Z. He replied, "Nothing."

AA. He said to him, "What did you say to him?"

BB. He said to him, "Nothing."

CC. [Ben Kozeba] gave [Eleazar] one good kick and killed him.

DD. Forthwith an echo came forth and proclaimed the following verse:

EE. "Woe to my worthless shepherd, who deserts the flock!
May the sword smite his arm and his right eye! Let his arm
be wholly withered, his right eye utterly blinded! [Zech.
11:17].

FF. "You have murdered R. Eleazar of Modiin, the right arm
of all Israel, and their right eye. Therefore may the right

arm of that man wither, may his right eye be utterly
blinded!"

GG. Forthwith Betar was taken, and Ben Kozeba was killed.

We notice two complementary themes. First, Bar Kokhba treats heaven
with arrogance, asking God merely to keep out of the way. Second, he
treats an especially revered sage with a parallel arrogance. The sage had
the power to preserve Israel. Bar Kokhba destroyed Israel's one protection. The result was inevitable.

In the Talmud of the Land of Israel, we witness, among the Mishnah's heirs, a striking reversion to biblical convictions about the centrality of history in the definition of Israel's reality. The heavy weight of
prophecy, apocalypse, and biblical historiography, with their emphasis
upon salvation and on history as the indicator of Israel's salvation, stood
against the Mishnah's quite separate thesis of what truly mattered.
From the sages' viewpoint what demanded description and analysis and
required interpretation? It was the category of sanctification for eternity. The true issue framed by history and apocalypse was how to move
toward the foreordained end of salvation, and how to act in time to
reach salvation at the end of time. The Mishnah's teleology was beyond
time and its eschatology was without a place for a historical Messiah.
Thus it took a position beyond that of the entire antecedent sacred
literature of Israel. Only one strand, the priestly one, had ever taken so
extreme a position on the centrality of sanctification and the peripheral
nature of salvation. Wisdom had stood in between, with its own concerns, drawing attention both to what happened and to what endured.
But to Wisdom what finally mattered was not nature or supernature,
but rather abiding relationships in historical time.

But we should not conclude that the Talmud at hand had simply
moved beyond the Mishnah's orbit. The opposite is the case. What the
framers of the document did was to assemble materials in which the
eschatological, and therefore messianic, teleology was absorbed within
the ahistorical, and therefore sagacious one. The Messiah turned into a
sage was no longer the Messiah embodied in the figure of the arrogant
Bar Kokhba (in the Talmud's representation of the figure). The reversion to the prophetic notion of learning history's lessons carried in its
wake a reengagement with the Messiah myth. But the reengagement
did not represent a change in the unfolding system. Why not? Because
the climax came in an explicit statement that the conduct required by
the Torah would bring the coming Messiah. That explanation of the
holy way of life focused upon the end of time and the advent of the

Messiah—both of which therefore depended upon the sanctification of Israel. So sanctification took priority and salvation depended on it. The framers of the Mishnah had found it possible to construct a complete and encompassing teleology for their system with scarcely a word about the Messiah's coming when the system would be perfectly achieved.

So because of their interest in explaining events and accounting for history, the third- and fourth-century sages represented in these units of discourse invoked what their predecessors had found to be of peripheral consequence to their system. The following contains the most striking expression of this viewpoint.

Y. TAANIT 1:1

XJ. "The oracle concerning Dumah. One is calling to me from Seir, 'Watchman, what of the night? Watchman, what of the night?' [Isa. 21:11]."

K. The Israelites said to Isaiah, "O our Rabbi, Isaiah, what will come for us out of this night?"

L. He said to them, "Wait for me, until I can present the question."

M. Once he had asked the question, he came back to them.

N. They said to him, "Watchman, what of the night? What did the Guardian of the ages tell you?"

O. He said to them, "The watchman says: 'Morning comes; and also the night. If you will inquire, inquire; come back again' [Isa. 21:12]."

P. They said to him, "Also the night?"

Q. He said to them, "It is not what you are thinking. But there will be morning for the righteous, and night for the wicked, morning for Israel, and night for idolaters."

R. They said to him, "When?"

S. He said to them, "Whenever you want, He too wants [it to be]—if you want it, he wants it."

T. They said to him, "What is standing in the way?"

U. He said to them, "Repentance: 'Come back again' [Isa. 21:12]."

V. R. Aha in the name of R. Tanhum b. R. Hiyya, "If Israel repents for one day, forthwith the son of David will come.

W. "What is the scriptural basis? 'O that today you would hearken to his voice!' [Ps. 95:7]."

X. Said R. Levi, If Israel would keep a single sabbath in the proper way, forthwith the son of David will come.

Y. "What is the scriptural basis for this view? 'Moses said, "Eat it today, for today is a sabbath to the Lord; today you will not find it in the field"' [Exod. 16:25].

Z. "And it said, 'For thus said the Lord God, the Holy One of Israel, "In returning and rest you shall be saved; in quietness and in trust shall be your strength." And you would not' [Isa. 30:15]."

A discussion of the power of repentance would hardly have surprised a Mishnah sage. What is new is at V–Z, the explicit linkage of keeping the law with achieving the end of time and the coming of the Messiah. That motif stands separate from the notions of righteousness and repentance, which surely did not require it. We must not lose sight of the importance of this passage, with its emphasis on repentance, on the one side, and the power of Israel to reform itself, on the other. The Messiah will come any day that Israel makes it possible.

Now, two things are happening here. First, the system of religious observance, including study of Torah, is explicitly invoked as having salvific power. Second, the persistent hope of the people for the coming of the Messiah is linked to the system of rabbinic observance and belief. Here a teleology lacking all eschatological dimension gave way to an explicitly messianic statement that the purpose of the law was to attain Israel's salvation: "If you want it, God wants it too." The one thing Israel commanded was its own heart; the power it yet exercised was the power to repent. These would suffice. The entire history of humanity would respond to Israel's will, to what happened in Israel's heart and soul. With the Temple in ruins, repentance could take place only within the heart and mind.

Israel could contribute to its own salvation by the right attitude and the right deed. But Israel bore responsibility for its present condition. So what Israel did would make history. This lesson, sages maintained, derived from the very condition of Israel even then, its suffering and its despair. How so? History taught moral lessons. Historical events entered into the construction of a teleology for the Talmud of the Land of Israel's system of Judaism as a whole. What the law demanded reflected the consequences of wrongful action on the part of Israel. So Israel's own deeds defined the events of history. Rome's role, like Assyria's and Babylonia's, depended upon Israel's provoking divine wrath as it was executed by the great empire. The paradox of the Talmud of the Land of Israel's system of history and Messiah lay in the fact that Israel could free itself of control by other nations only by humbly agreeing to accept

God's rule. The nations—Rome, in the present instance—rested on one side of the balance, while God rested on the other. Israel had to choose between them. There was no such thing for Israel as freedom from both God and the nations, total autonomy and independence. There is only a choice of masters, a ruler on earth or a ruler in heaven. In the Talmud's theory of salvation, therefore, the framers provided Israel with an account of how to overcome the unsatisfactory circumstances of an unredeemed present, so as to accomplish the movement from here to the much-desired future.

Keeping the law in the right way was not represented as merely right or expedient. It was the way to bring the Messiah, the son of David. This was stated by Levi, as follows:

Y. TAANIT 1:1.IX

    X. Said R. Levi, "If Israel would keep a single Sabbath in the proper way, forthwith the son of David would come.

    Y. "What is the Scriptural basis for this view? 'Moses said, Eat it today, for today is a sabbath to the Lord; today you will not find it in the field' (Ex. 16:25)."

    Z. And it says, "For thus said the Lord God, the Holy One of Israel, 'In returning and rest you shall be saved; in quietness and in trust shall be your strength. And you would not' (Is. 30:15)."

Here, in a single saying, we find the entire talmudic doctrine set forth. How like, yet how different from, the Mishnah's view. Keeping the law of the Torah represented the visible form of love of God.

What is most interesting in the Talmud of the Land of Israel's picture is that the hope for the Messiah's coming was joined to the moral condition of each individual Israelite. Hence the messianic fulfillment was made to depend on the repentance of Israel. The entire drama, envisioned by others in earlier types of Judaism as a world-historical event, was reworked in context into a moment in the life of the individual and the people of Israel collectively. The coming of the Messiah depended not on historical action but on oral regeneration. So from a force that moved Israelites to take up weapons on the battlefield, the messianic hope and yearning were transformed into motives for spiritual regeneration and ethical behavior. The energies released in the messianic fervor were linked to rabbinical government, through which Israel would form the godly society. When we reflect that the message, "If you want it, He too wants it to be," came in a generation confronting a dreadful disappointment, its full weight and meaning become clear.

Genesis Rabbah

Genesis Rabbah in the aggregate responds to the question of the meaning of history, in particular, the history of Israel confronted by the triumph of its sibling-enemy. To find that meaning at the end, sages turned to the picture of creation in the beginning. That is why, in the book of Genesis, as the sages who composed Genesis Rabbah saw things, God set forth to Moses the entire scope and meaning of Israel's history among the nations and salvation at the end of days. They read Genesis not as a set of individual verses, one by one, but as a single and coherent statement, whole and complete. In a few words let me restate the conviction of the framers of Genesis Rabbah about the message and meaning of the book of Genesis:

We now know what will be in the future. How do we know it? Just as Jacob had told his sons what would happen in time to come, just as Moses told the tribes their future, so we may understand the laws of history if we study the Torah. And in the Torah, we turn to beginnings: the rules as they were laid out at the very start of human history. These we find in the book of Genesis, the story of the origins of the world and of Israel.

The Torah tells us not only what happened but why. The Torah permits us to discover the laws of history. Once we know those laws, we may also peer into the future and come to an assessment of what is going to happen to us—and, especially, of how we shall be saved from our present existence. Because everything exists under the aspect of a timeless will, God's will, and all things express one thing, God's program and plan, in the Torah we uncover the workings of God's will. Our task as Israel is to accept, endure, submit, and celebrate.

To the rabbis who created Genesis Rabbah, the book of Genesis told the story of Israel, the Jewish people, in the here and now. The principle was that what happened to the patriarchs and matriarchs signaled what would happen to their descendants: the model of the ancestors sent a message for the children. So the importance of Genesis, as the sages of Genesis Rabbah read the book, derived not from its lessons about the past but its message for Israel's present—and, especially, future. Their conviction was that what Abraham, Isaac, and Jacob did shaped the future history of Israel. In line with the Mishnah's view, sages maintained that the world reveals not chaos but order, and God's will works itself out not once but again and again. Bringing to the stories of Genesis the conviction that the book of Genesis told not only the story of yesterday but also the tale of tomorrow, the sages transformed a picture of the past into a prophesy for a near tomorrow.

At the turn of the fifth century, sages entertained deep forebodings about Israel's prospects. In Genesis Rabbah every word of Genesis was read against the background of the world-historical change that had taken place in the time of the formation of the document. The people who compiled the materials made a statement through what they selected and arranged. Let me give one concrete example of how sages responded in Genesis Rabbah. Rome now claimed to be Israel, that is Christian and heir to the testament of the founders. Sages of Genesis Rabbah did not deny it, they affirmed it: Rome is Esau, or Moab, or Ishmael. "We are Israel." To them Genesis talked about the here and now, "about us, Israel, and about our sibling, Rome." That concession—Rome is a sibling, a close relative of Israel—represented an implicit recognition of Christianity's claim to share the patrimony of Judaism, to be descended from Abraham and Isaac. To deal with the glory and the power of our brother, Esau and to assess today the future history of Israel, the salvation of God's first, best love, sages took the simple tack of restating matters already clear in Scripture. That is, it was not by denying Rome's claim but by evaluating it.

In Genesis Rabbah sages represented Rome as Israel's brother, counterpart, and nemesis. Rome was the one thing standing in the way of Israel's ultimate salvation and the world's. It was not a political Rome but a messianic Rome that was at issue: Rome as surrogate for Israel, Rome as obstacle to Israel. The reason of course was that Rome now confronted Israel with a crisis, and Genesis Rabbah constituted a response to that crisis. In the fourth century Rome became Christian. Sages responded by facing that fact quite squarely and saying, "Indeed, it is as you say, a kind of Israel, an heir of Abraham as your texts explicitly claim. But we remain the sole legitimate Israel, the bearer of the birthright—we and not you. So you are our brother: Esau, Ishmael, Edom." By rereading the story of the beginnings, sages discovered the answer and the secret of the end. Rome claimed to be Israel, and indeed, sages conceded, Rome shared the patrimony of Israel. That claim took the form of the Christians' appropriation of the Torah as the Old Testament, so sages acknowledged a simple fact in acceding to the notion that, in some way, Rome too formed part of Israel. But it was the rejected part, the Ishmael, the Esau, not the Isaac, not the Jacob. The advent of Christian Rome precipitated the sustained, polemical, and rigorous, and well-argued rereading of beginnings in light of the end. Rome then marked the conclusion of human history as Israel had known it. Beyond lay the coming of the true Messiah, the redemption of Israel, the salvation of the world, and the end of time.

Let us consider a simple example of how ubiquitous the shadow of

Ishmael/Esau/Edom/Rome was. Wherever sages reflected on future history, their minds turned to their own day. They found the hour difficult, because Rome, now Christian, claimed the very birthright and blessing that they understood to be theirs alone. Christian Rome posed a threat without precedent. Now another dominion besides Israel's claimed the rights and blessings that sustained Israel. Wherever in Scripture they turned, sages found comfort in the message that the birthright, the blessing, the Torah, and the hope all belonged to them and to none other. Here is a striking statement of that constant proposition.

Genesis Rabbah LIII : XIL

1.   A. "[So she said to Abraham, 'Cast out this slave woman with her son, for the son of this slave woman shall not be heir with my son Isaac.'] And the thing was very displeasing to Abraham on account of his son" (Gen. 21:11).
      B. That is in line with this verse: "And shuts his eyes from looking upon evil" (Is. 33:15). [Freedman, p. 471, n. 1: He shut his eyes from Ishmael's evil ways and was reluctant to send him away.]
2.   A. "But God said to Abraham, 'Be not displeased because of the lad and because of your slave woman; whatever Sarah says to you, do as she tells you, for through Isaac shall your descendants be named'" (Gen. 21:12).
      B. Said R. Yudan bar Shillum, "What is written is not 'Isaac' but 'through Isaac.' [The matter is limited, not through all of Isaac's descendants but only through some of them, thus excluding Esau.]"

Among the descendants of Isaac will be found Abraham's heirs, but not all the descendants of Isaac will be heirs of Abraham. Number 2 explicitly excludes Esau, that is Rome. As the several antagonists of Israel stood for Rome in particular, so the traits of Rome, as sages perceived them, characterized the biblical heroes. Easu provided a favorite target. Israel and Rome contended from the womb. Specifically, Esau hated Israel even while he was still in the womb. Jacob, for his part, revealed from the womb those virtues that would characterize him later on. He was as eager to serve God as Esau was eager to worship idols. The ambiguous status of Rome as Christian brought sages to compare Rome to the swine, which in one trait appeared to be acceptable but in reality was unacceptable.

LXV:I.

1.   A. "When Esau was forty years old, he took to wife Judith, the daugher of Beeri, the Hittite, and Basemath the daughter of Elon the Hittite; and they made life bitter for Isaac and Rebecca" (Gen. 26:34–35).

B. "The swine out of the wood ravages it, that which moves in the field feeds on it" (Ps. 80:14).

C. R. Phineas and R. Hilqiah in the name of R. Simon: "Among all of the prophets, only two of them spelled out in public [the true character of Rome, represented by the swine], Asaf and Moses.

D. "Asaf: 'The swine out of the wood ravages it.'

E. "Moses: 'And the swine, because he parts the hoof' (Deut. 14:8).

F. "Why does Moses compare Rome to the swine? Just as the swine, when it crouches, puts forth its hoofs as if to say, 'I am clean,' so the wicked kingdom steals and grabs, while pretending to be setting up courts of justice.

G. "So Esau, for all forty years, hunted married women, ravished them, and when he reached the age of forty, he presented himself to his father, saying, 'Just as father got married at the age of forty, so I shall marry a wife at the age of forty.'

H. "'When Esau was forty years old, he took to wife Judith, the daughter of Beeri, the Hittite, and Basemath the daughter of Elon the Hittite'."

The exegesis of course once more identified Esau with Rome. The roundabout route linked Esau's taking a wife with Roman duplicity. Whatever the government did it claimed to do in the general interest. But it really had no public interest at all. Esau for his part spent all forty years pillaging women and then, at the age of forty, pretended to his father to be upright. That, at any rate, was the parallel clearly intended by this obviously unitary composition. The issue of the selection of the intersecting verse does not present an obvious solution to me; it seems to me that only the identification of Rome with the swine accounts for the choice.

Identifying Rome as Esau was a fresh idea. In the Mishnah, two hundred years earlier, Rome appeared as a place, not as a symbol. But in Genesis Rabbah, Rome was symbolized by Esau. Why Esau in particular? Because Esau was sibling: relation, competitor, enemy, brother. In choosing Rome as the counterpart to Israel, sages simply opened Genesis and found there Israel, that is Jacob, and his brother, his enemy Esau. So why not understand the obvious: Esau stood for Rome, Jacob for Israel, and their relationship represented what Israel and Rome would work out even then, in the fourth century, the first century of Christian rule. So Esau ruled now, but Jacob possessed the birthright. Esau/Rome was the last of the four great empires (Persia, Media, Greece, Rome). On the other side of Rome? Israel's age of glory. And why was Rome now brother? Because, after all, the Christians did claim a common patrimony in the Hebrew Scriptures and did claim to form part of Israel. The claim was not ignored; it was answered: yes, part of Israel, the rejected part. Jacob bore the blessing and transmitted the blessing to humanity, Esau did not. Such a message bore meaning only in its context. So in a concrete way Genesis talked about "us," Israel, and about "our sibling," Rome. That concession—Rome was a sibling, a close relative of Israel—represented an implicit recognition of Christianity's claim to share the patrimony of Judaism, to be descended from Abraham and Isaac. So how to deal with the glory and the power of our brother, Esau? And what were they to say about the claim of Esau to enthrone Christ? And how to assess the future history of Israel, the salvation of God's first, best love? It was not by denying Rome's claim but by evaluating it, not by turning a back to the critical events of the hour but by confronting those events forcefully and authoritatively.

Leviticus Rabbah

Leviticus Rabbah deals with a biblical book, not a Mishnah tractate. But it approaches that book with a fresh plan, one in which exegesis does not dictate rhetoric, and in which amplification of an established text (whether Scripture or Mishnah) does not supply the underlying logic by which sentences are made to compose paragraphs, or completed thoughts. The framers of Leviticus Rabbah treated topics, not particular verses. They made generalizations which were freestanding. They expressed cogent propositions through extended compositions, not episodic ideas. Earlier, things people wished to say were attached to predefined statements based on an existing text, and constructed in accord with an organizing logic independent of the systematic expression of a single, well-framed idea. Now the authors collected and arranged their materials so that an abstract proposition emerged. The proposition was not expressed only or mainly through episodic restatements assigned to

an order established by a basetext. Rather it emerged through a logic of
its own. The framers of the composition undertook to offer propositions in which they said what they had in mind through the exegesis of
verses of Scripture not in the order of Scripture, but through an order
dictated by their own sense of the logic of syllogistic composition. To
begin with, they laid down their own topical program, related to but
essentially autonomous of that of the book of Leviticus. Second, in
expressing their ideas on these topics, they never undertook simply to
cite a verse of Scripture and then to claim that the verse stated precisely
what they had in mind to begin with. The framers said what they
wished to say in their own way—just as had the authors of the Mishnah
itself. In so doing the composers of Leviticus Rabbah treated Scripture
as had their predecessors; to them as to those who had gone before,
Scripture provided a rich treasury of facts.

Statements in the Leviticus Rabbah became intelligible not on the
strength of an established text, but on the basis of a deeper logic of
meaning. Leviticus Rabbah is topical, not exegetical. Each of its thirty-
seven parashiyyot pursues its given topic and develops points relevant to
that topic. In Leviticus Rabbah, rabbis took up the problem of saying
what they wished to say not in an exegetical, but in a syllogistic and
freely discursive logic and rhetoric. Just as the Mishnah marked a
radical break from all prior literature produced by Jews, so Leviticus
Rabbah marked a stunning departure from all prior literature produced by rabbis. Since these rabbis defined Judaism as we have known it
from their time to ours, we rightly turn to the book at hand for evidence
about how the Scripture entered into, was absorbed by, and reached full
status as the foundation document of the Judaism taking shape at this
time.

The dominant exegetical construction in Leviticus Rabbah was the
base-verse/intersecting-verse exegesis. In this construction, a verse of
Leviticus was cited (hence base verse), and then another verse from such
books as Job, Proverbs, Qohelet, or Psalms was cited. The latter, not the
former, was subjected to detailed and systematic exegesis. But the
exegetical exercise ended up by leading the intersecting verse back to
the base verse and reading the latter in terms of the former. In such an
exercise, what in fact do we do? We read one thing in terms of something else. To begin with, it is the base verse in terms of the intersecting
verse. But it also is the intersecting verse in other terms as well—a
multiple-layered construction of analogy and parable. The intersecting
verse's elements always turn out to stand for, to signify, and to speak of,
something other than that to which they openly refer. Nothing says

what it means. Everything important speaks elliptically, allegorically, and symbolically. All statements carry deeper meaning, which belongs to other statements altogether. The profound sense of the base verse emerges only through restatement within and through the intersecting verse—as if the base verse spoke of things that we do not see on the surface.

People who see things this way do not call a thing as it is. They have become accustomed to perceiving more or less than is at hand. Perhaps that was a natural mode of thought for the Jews of this period, so long used to calling themselves God's first love, yet now seeing others claiming that same advantaged relationship with greater worldly reason. The radical disjuncture between the way things were and the way Scripture said things were supposed to be and would some day become surely imposed an unbearable tension. It was one thing for the slave born to slavery to endure. It was another for the free man sold into slavery to accept that same condition. The vanquished people had lost its city and its temple and had produced another nation from its midst to take over its Scripture and much else; it could not bear too much reality. So the defeated people found refuge in a mode of thought that trained vision to see things otherwise than as the eyes perceived them. Among the diverse ways by which the weak and subordinated accommodate to their circumstance, the one of iron-willed pretense in life is most likely to yield the mode of thought at hand: things never are what they seem because they cannot be.

Reading a thing in terms of something else, the builders of the document systematically adapted for themselves the reality of the Scripture, its history and doctrines. They transformed that history from a sequence of one-time events, leading from one thing to another, into an ever-present mythic world. No longer was there one Moses, one David, or one set of happenings of a distinctive and never-to-be-repeated character. Now whatever happened of which the thinkers proposed to take account had to enter and be absorbed into that established and ubiquitous pattern and structure founded in Scripture. It was not that biblical history repeated itself. But biblical history was no longer a story of things that had happened once, long ago, and pointed to one moment in the future. Rather it became an account of things that happen every day in an ever-present mythic world.

We turn from the mode of thought to the message of the document for the age of its formulation, the fourth and early fifth centuries. The recurrent message may be stated in a single paragraph:

God loves Israel, and so gave them the Torah, which defines their life and governs their welfare. Israel is alone in its category, so what is a virtue to Israel is a vice to the nation, life-giving to Israel, but poison to the Gentiles. Israel sins, but God forgives that sin, having punished the nation on account of it. Such a process has yet to come to an end, but it will culminate in Israel's complete regeneration. Meanwhile, Israel's assurance of God's love lies in his many expressions of special concern for even the humblest and most ordinary aspects of the national life: the food the nation eats, and the sexual practices by which it procreates. These life-sustaining, life-transmitting activities draw God's special interest, as a mark of his general love for Israel. Israel must achieve its life in conformity with the marks of God's love. These indications also signify the character of Israel's difficulty, namely, subordination to the nations in general but to the fourth kingdom, Rome in particular. Both food laws and skin diseases stand for the nations. The social category of sin is also collective and brings about collective punishment. Bad treatment of people by one another, gossip, and small-scale thuggery draw down divine penalty. The nation's fate therefore corresponds to its moral condition. The moral condition emerges not only from the current generation. Israel's richest hope lies in the merit of the ancestors, thus in the scriptural record of the merits attained by the founders of the nation, those who originally brought it into being and gave it life. The world to come upon the nation is so portrayed as to restate these same propositions. Merit overcomes sin, and doing religious duties or supererogatory acts of kindness will win merit for the nation that does them. Israel will be saved at the end of time, and the world to follow will be exactly the opposite of this one. Much that we find in the account of Israel's national life recurs in slightly altered form in the picture of the world to come.

The one-time events of the flood, Sodom and Gomorrah, the patriarchs and the sojourn in Egypt, the exodus, the revelation of the Torah at Sinai, the golden calf, the Davidic monarchy and the building of the Temple, Sennacherib, Hezekiah, and the destruction of northern Israel, Nebuchadnezzar and the destruction of the Temple in 586, the life of Israel in Babylonian captivity, Daniel and his associates, Mordecai and Haman—and these events occurred over and over again. They served as patterns of sin and atonement, steadfastness and divine intervention, and equivalent lessons. We find, in fact, a fairly standard repertoire of scriptural heroes or villains, on the one side, and conventional lists of Israel's enemies and their actions and downfall, on the other. The boastful, for instance, included (VII:VI) the generation of the flood, Sodom and Gomorrah, Pharaoh, Sisera, Sennacherib, Nebuchadnezzar, and the wicked empire (Rome)—contrasted to Israel, "despised and humble in this world." The four kingdoms recurred again and again, always ending with Rome, and with the repeated message that after Rome will come Israel. But Israel had to make this happen through its faith and submission to God's will. Lists of enemies rang the changes on Cain, the Sodomites, Pharaoh, Sennacherib, Nebuchadnezzar, and Haman.

The mode of thought brought to bear upon the theme of history remained exactly the same as before: list-making, with similar traits drawn together into lists based on common traits. The lists were repeated to make a single enormous point or prove a social law of history. The catalogues of exemplary heroes and historical events served a further purpose: They provided a model of how contemporary events were to be absorbed into the biblical pattern. Since biblical events exemplified recurrent happenings—sin and redemption, forgiveness and atonement—they lost their one-time character. Current events found a place within the ancient but eternally present pattern. No new historical events demanded narration because what was happening in the times of the framers of Leviticus Rabbah came under consideration through what was said about the past. This mode of dealing with biblical history and contemporary events produced two reciprocal effects. One was the mythicization of biblical stories, their removal from the framework of ongoing, unique patterns of history and sequences of events, and their transformation into accounts of things that happened all the time. The other was that contemporary events lost all of their specificity and entered the framework of established mythic existence. So the Scripture's myth happens every day, and every day produces reenactment of the Scripture's myth.

The message of Leviticus Rabbah attached itself to the book of Leviticus, as if that book had come from prophecy and addressed the issue of salvation. But it really came from the priesthood and spoke of sanctification. Salvation would come through sanctification. The Messiah would come not because of what a pagan emperor did nor because of Jewish action either, but because of Israel's own moral condition. When Israel entered the right relationship with God, then God would respond to Israel's condition by restoring things to their proper balance. Israel could not and did not need to act so as to force the coming of the Messiah. Israel could attain the condition of sanctification by forming a moral and holy community and God's response would follow the established prophecy of Moses and the prophets. So the basic doctrine of Leviticus Rabbah was the metamorphosis of Leviticus. Instead of holy caste we deal with holy people. Instead of holy place, we deal with holy community in its holy land. The deepest exchange between reality and inner vision came at the very surface: the rereading of Leviticus in terms of a different set of realities from those to which the book related on the surface. No other biblical book would have served so well; it had to be Leviticus. Only through what the framers did with that particular book could they deliver their astonishing message and vision.

The complementary points of stress in Leviticus Rabbah—the age to come would come, but Israel had to reform itself beforehand—addressed the context defined by Julian, on the one side, and by the new anti-Judaic Christian policy of the later fourth and fifth centuries, on the other. The repeated reference to Esau and Edom and how they marked the last monarchy before God's through Israel underlined the same point: These truly form the worst of the four kingdoms, but they also come at the end. If we only shape up, so will history. We therefore grasp an astonishing correspondence between how people were thinking, what they wished to say, and the literary context—rereading a particular book of Scripture in terms of a set of values different from those expressed in that book—in which they delivered their message. Given the mode of thought, the crisis that demanded reflection, and the message found congruent to the crisis, we must find entirely logical the choice of Leviticus and the treatment accorded to it. So the logic and the doctrine prove to accord remarkably with the society and politics that produced and received Leviticus Rabbah.

The Success of Judaism

Before the fourth century, Judaism and Christianity (as defined by their intellectuals) had comprised different people talking about different things to different people. In the fourth century the shape of discourse shifted. Because of a political event that Israel could not ignore and the Church deemed probative, discourse between Judaism and Christianity found different people talking to different people about some of the same things. The reason for the shift and for the particular topics was a common politics. There was a second factor: common premises, deriving from common Scriptures, about the importance of politics, that is, history. Both parties to the common argument shared a single canon— the Hebrew Scriptures (Old Testament or written Torah) and both parties confronted the same political facts and had to deal with them. The common argument proved possible, therefore, because the intellectuals of the two parties shared a single intellectual and social world.

The fourth century produced true confrontation between Judaic and

Christian intellectuals—actual debate on issues defined in the same terms, through the same modes of argument, and with appeal to the same facts. This had not happened before and it never happened again until our own time. In the fourth century—the age of Constantine—Judaic sages and Christian theologians met in a head-on argument on a shared agenda and confronted the fundamental issues of the historical existence of politics and society in the West: doctrine, specifically the meaning of history; teleology, specifically the eschatological teleology formed by the messianic doctrine identifying Jesus as Christ; and the symbolism of the godly society, specifically the identity of God's social medium—Israel—in the making of the world. Before that time, the Christian theologians and Judaic sages had not managed to frame a single program for debate. Earlier Judaic sages had talked about their issues to their audience, and Christian theologians had pursued their arguments on their distinctive agenda. The former had pretended the latter did not exist. The latter had framed doctrines concerning the former solely within the logical requirements of the internal arguments of Christianity. There had been no confrontation of an intellectual character, since neither party had addressed the issues important to the other in such a way that the issues could find a mutually agreeable definition and the premises of argument could form a mutually acceptable protocol of discourse. Later on the confrontation would shift again, so that no real debate could unfold on a shared set of issues, defined in the same way by both parties. The politics no longer required it, and the circumstance prevented it.

But in the fourth century, issues urgent for Christian thinkers were of acute concern for Judaic ones as well. Those issues became urgent only when matters of public policy, specifically the ideology of state (empire for the Christians; supernatural nation or family for the Jews) demanded a clear statement on the questions at hand. When the Roman empire and Israelite nation had to assess the meaning of epochal change, when each had to reconsider the teleology of society and system as the identity of the Messiah defined that teleology, and when each had to reconsider the appropriate metaphor for the political unit—people, nation, extended family—only then did chronic disagreement become acute difference. What was decisive was the progressive but remarkable change in the character of the Roman government: at the beginning of the century pagan and hostile to Christianity, at the end of the century Christian and hostile to paganism. In the age of Constantine the terms of the confrontation between Judaism and Christianity reached conclusive formulation.

In the first century Christians and Jews did not argue with one

another. Each—the family of Christianities and the family of Judaisms—went its own way. When Christianity came into being in the first
century, one important strand of the Christian movement laid stress on
salvation, in the Gospels maintaining that Jesus was Christ, come to save
the world and impose a radical change on history. At the same time, an
important group within the diverse Judaic systems of the age, the
Pharisees, emphasized issues of sanctification, maintaining that the task
of Israel was to attain the holiness of which the Temple was a singular
embodiment. When we find in the Gospels the record of the Church
placing Jesus into opposition with the Pharisees, we witness the confrontation of different people talking about different things to different
people. The issues presented to Jews by the triumph of Christianity,
which informed the documents shaped in the Land of Israel in the
period of that triumph, did not play an important role in prior components of the unfolding canon of Judaism, in particular the Mishnah and
closely allied documents which were completed before the fourth century. These presented a Judaism in utter indifference to Christianity.
The contrast between the Mishnah and the Judaic system that emerged
in the fourth century documents tells the tale.

The shift in the condition of Israel marked by Christianity's rise to
political power and the Torah's loss of a place in political institutions
defined the context and setting of Judaism from then to nearly the
present day. And the response of the day—represented by the Judaism
defined in the documents of the late fourth and fifth centuries—proved
remarkably successful. Judaism did endure, and the Jews did persist,
from then to now. So the Judaism that emerged from the fourth century—principally in the pages of the Talmud of the Land of Israel—
and that two hundred years later reached fruition and full statement in
the Talmud of Babylonia, enjoyed stunning success. The fourth century
also marked the first century of Christianity as the West would know it.
When Rome became Christian, Judaism as it would flourish in Western
civilization reached the familiar form and definition that we know
today. Judaism was born in the matrix of Christianity triumphant, or to
use theological language of a sort, Christ enthroned and triumphant
dictated not only the dominant faith but also the successful one.

Judaism endured in the Christian West (as well as in the Muslim
East) for two reasons. First, Christianity (and Islam) permitted it;
second, Israel—the Jewish people—wanted it to. The fate of paganism
in the fourth century (and of Zoroastrianism and "Sabaeism" in the
seventh and eighth under Islam) shows the importance of the first
factor. It was not the intellectual power of sages alone that secured the

long-term triumph of Judaism. It also was the character of the Christian emperors' policy toward Judaism that afforded to Jews and their religion such toleration as they would enjoy then and thereafter. The religion of Judaism was never prohibited. Pagan sacrifice, by contrast, came under interdict in 341. Festivals went on into the fifth century, but the die was cast. When, after 350, Constantius won the throne over a contender who had enjoyed pagan support, he closed all the temples in the empire, prohibited access to them under penalty of death, and tolerated the storming and destruction of the temples. Churches took the place of pagan temples. That is not to suggest that paganism was extirpated overnight, or that all the laws were kept. It is an indication of an on-going policy. The Christian emperors never instituted a parallel policy toward Judaism and the synagogue.

Pagan intellectuals, counterparts to the Judaic sages, responded with profound and systematic answers to Christian doctrine. No one familiar with their writing can suppose paganism lacking the power of ideas afforded to Israel by the Judaic sages. Iamblichus, a principal figure in the first half of the fourth century, accomplished what Geffcken calls "the inner strengthening of paganism." He did this not by a negative statement on Christianity but by a positive reassertion of pagan doctrine, in a profoundly philosophical idiom bearing deep overtones of religious feeling. Geffcken cites the following statement, "It is the fulfillment of ineffable rites the fitting accomplishment of which surpasses an intellectual understanding and the power of unspeakable signs which are intelligible to the gods alone that effect theurgic union." Iamblichus inspired Julian, and for a brief moment it appeared that paganism would enjoy a renaissance. On purely intellectual grounds it might have. But afterward a severe repression set in, and the Christian emperors Gratian, Valentinian II, and Theodosius undertook a systematic counterattack.

The institutions of paganism lost their foundations. That was a fact of state policy and politics to which pagan doctrine hardly pertained. The outcome, as Geffcken says, was the end of pagan cult: "For without the substructure of religious observance within the framework of the state, there could be no pagan cult, no ancestral worship." True enough, Christian people, led by monks, implemented the spirit of the laws through their own actions, destroying temples as well as synagogues. For their part, pagan intellectuals at the end of the century, typified by Libanius, responded with a program of argument and rhetoric. But the issue was not to be resolved through rhetoric nor was the fate of the temples to be settled by mobs. It was a political attack that paganism confronted, and with the throne in Christian hands the policy of the Church settled matters. Antipagan legislation won the day, not everywhere and all at once, but ultimately and completely. The same might have happened to Judaism, but it did not, in part because the Church-state did not choose to extirpate Judaism. The other reason we have located in the intellectual achievements of the Judaic sages.

The formative events in the history of the Judaic encounter with the Christian West require only a rapid reprise. With the triumph of Christianity through Constantine and his successors in the West, Christianity's explicit claims, now validated in the world-shaking events of the age, demanded a reply. The sages of the Talmud of the Land of Israel, Genesis Rabbah, and Leviticus Rabbah provided it. The sages responded at the specific points at which the Christian challenge met Israel's world view head on. What did Israel's sages have to present as the Torah's answer to the Cross? It was the Torah, with its doctrine of history, Messiah, and Israel. History in the beginning, in Genesis, accounted for the events of the day. The Messiah would be a sage of the Torah. Israel today comprised the family, after the flesh, of the founders of Israel. The Torah therefore served as the encompassing symbol of Israel's salvation. The Torah would be embodied in the person of the Messiah who would of course be a rabbi. The Torah confronted the Cross, with its doctrine of the triumphant Christ, Messiah and king, ruler now of earth as of heaven. In the formulation of the sages who wrote the fourth- and early fifth-century documents, the Talmud of the Land of Israel and Genesis Rabbah and Leviticus Rabbah, the Torah thus confronted the challenge of the Cross of Christianity as the Torah, with its ample doctrines of history, Messiah, and Israel, would later meet and overcome the Sword and Crescent of Islam. Within Israel, the Torah everywhere triumphed. That is why, when Christianity came to power and commenced to define the civilization of the West, Judaism met and overcame its greatest crisis before modern times. And it held. As a result, Jews remained within the Judaic system of the dual Torah. That is why they continued for the entire history of the West to see the world through the world view of the dual Torah and to conduct life in accord with the way of life of the Torah as the rabbis explained it.

The consequence was stunning success for that society for which God cared so deeply: eternal Israel after the flesh. For Judaism in the rabbis' statement did endure in the Christian West, imparting to Israel the secure conviction of constituting the Israel after the flesh to which the Torah continued to speak. How do we know sages' Judaism won? Because when, in turn, Islam gained its victory, Christianity gave way throughout the Middle East and North Africa. But sages' Judaism in those same vast territories retained the loyalty and conviction of the people of the Torah. The Cross would rule only where the Crescent and its sword did not. But the Torah of Sinai everywhere and always sanctified Israel in time and promised secure salvation for eternity. So Israel believed and so does faithful Israel, those Jews who also are Judaists, believe today. The entire history of Judaism is contained within these simple propositions.

The Classical System of Theology

Before concluding this account of the formation of Judaism of the dual Torah, we should consider the principal theological positions that characterized that system. The best place in which to discover the religious beliefs of the Judaism of the dual Torah is in the Jewish prayerbook, the Siddur. The accepted prayerbook is a document of public piety. The Siddur contains descriptions and interpretations of Judaism's view of the world. Among the principal theological positions of the classical system are the following.

THE DOCTRINE OF ONE GOD

God Is One: The great teaching, the dogma, of Judaism is that God is one. That is not meant as a philosophical declaration, alleging the unity of the Divinity as against the claim of the plurality of Divinity. It is a religious affirmation, to be discerned from the language of the prayer. The Shema constitutes the credo of the Judaic tradition. Morning and evening, the Judaist responds to the natural order of the world with thanks and praise of God who created the world and who actively guides the daily events of nature. Whatever happens in nature gives testimony to the sovereignty of the creator. And that testimony is not in unnatural disasters, but in the most ordinary events, sunrise and sunset. These, especially, evoke the religious response. God is purposeful. The works of creation serve to justify—to testify to Torah—the revelation of Sinai. Torah is the mark not merely of divine sovereignty, but also of divine grace and love, source of life here and now and in eternity. Revelation takes concrete and specific form in the Judaic tradition: God the creator revealed his will for creation through the Torah, given to Israel his people.

That Torah contains the laws of life. The commandments are the means of divine service, and of reverence and love for God. Israel sees itself as chosen, close to God, because of the Torah, and it finds in its devotion to the Torah the mark of its chosenness. The covenant made at Sinai, a contract on Israel's side to do and hear the Torah, and on God's side to be the God of Israel—that covenant is evoked by natural events, and then confirmed by human deeds and devotion. The Shema presents a view of the world in three parts: creation, revelation, and redemption. The opening blessings, prior to the recitation of the Shema, refer to creation and revelation. The unity that is affirmed is the oneness of nature and history, the conviction that all reality is the creation of God and finds unity in the oneness of the Creator. Above all things, behind all things, is the one God who made heaven and earth and who regulates nature and history. The rising and the setting of the sun testify to the oneness and the orderliness of creation. The Torah contains and expresses the orderliness of human history. Redemption, at the end of days, will complete the unity of being.

THE DOCTRINE OF THE DUAL TORAH

Having seen the doctrine of the dual Torah in its literary formulation, let us return and examine the same matter as a theological position. The doctrine of the dual Torah is the one important idea of Judaism that is absolutely unique to Judaism. No other scriptural religion possesses the doctrine. Central to Judaism is the belief that the Scriptures constituted Torah, divine revelation, but only a part of it. At Sinai, God had handed down revelation in two media: the written part widely known, and the oral, memorized part preserved by the great scriptural heroes, passed on by prophets in the obscure past, and finally and most openly handed down to the rabbis who ultimately created the Palestinian and Babylonian Talmuds. The whole Torah thus consisted of both written and oral parts. The rabbis taught that the whole Torah was studied by David, augmented by Ezekiel, legislated by Ezra, and embodied in the schools and by the sages of every period in Israelite history from Moses to the present. It is a singular, linear conception of a revelation, preserved only by the few, pertaining to the many, and in time capable of bringing salvation to all.

The rabbinic conception of Torah further regards Moses as "our rabbi," the first and prototypical figure of the ideal Jew. It holds that whoever embodies the teachings of Moses our rabbi thereby conforms to the will of God—and not to God's will alone but also to God's way. Rabbinic Judaism teaches that in heaven, God and the angels study Torah just as rabbis do on earth. God dons phylacteries like any Jew. God prays in the rabbinic mode. God carries out the acts of compassion called for by Judaic ethics. God guides the affairs of the world according to the rules of Torah, just as does the rabbi in his court. One exegesis of the creation legend taught that God had looked into the Torah and had created the world guided by the Torah.

The symbol of Torah is multidimensional. It includes the striking detail that whatever the most recent rabbi is destined to discover through proper exegesis of the tradition is as much a part of the Torah revealed to Moses as is a sentence of Scripture itself. It is therefore possible to participate even in the giving of the law by appropriate, logical inquiry into the law. God himself, studying and living by Torah, is believed to subject himself to the same rules of logical inquiry. When an earthly court overruled the testimony, delivered through miracles, of the heavenly one, God rejoiced, crying out, "My sons have conquered me!"—so the sages believed. In a word, before us is a mythicoreligious system in which earth and heaven correspond to one another, with Torah—in place of Temple—the model of both. The heavenly pattern is embodied upon earth in Moses our rabbi. Moses sets the pattern for the ordinary sage. And God himself participates in the system, for it is God's image which forms that cosmic paradigm in the end. The faithful Jew constitutes the projection of the divine on earth. That is why honor is due to the learned rabbi even more than to the holy scroll of the Torah, for through his learning and logic the sage may alter the very content of Mosaic revelation. The sage is Torah, not merely because he lives by it, but because at his best he forms as compelling an embodiment of the heavenly model as does a Torah scroll itself.

TORAH AND SALVATION

The critical idea in the rabbinic conception of Torah concerns salvation. Through learning and living by the Torah, Israel will be saved—from the nations' rule, for God's dominion. This idea takes many forms. One salvific teaching holds that if Israel had not sinned—disobeyed the Torah—the Scriptures would have closed with the story of the conquest of Palestine. From that time onward the sacred community would have lived in eternal peace under the divine law. Keeping the Torah was therefore the veritable guarantee of salvation. The opposite is said in many forms as well. Since Israel had sinned, God had called the Babylonians in 586 B.C., and then Romans in A.D. 70, to destroy the Temple of Jerusalem. But in his mercy he would restore the fortunes of the people when they had expiated the result and the cause of their sin through their suffering and repentance.

So in both negative and positive forms, the rabbinic idea of Torah tells of a necessary connection between the salvation of the people and the state of Torah among them. It is at this point that the Messiah strand of ancient Israelite tradition came into play. The coming of the Messiah, meaning the end of the difficult world that Israel endured, was tied to the system of the Torah. If people wanted the Messiah to come—and they surely did—they should study the Torah and carry out its teachings. For example, if all Israel would properly keep a single Sabbath, the Messiah would come. Of special interest here is the rabbinic saying that the rule of the pagans depends upon the sin of Israel. If Israel constituted a full and complete replication of "Torah," that is, of heaven, then pagan rule would come to an end. It would end because all Israel then, like a few rabbis even now, would attain to the creative powers inherent in Torah. Just as God had created the world through Torah, so saintly rabbis could create a sacred community. When Israel made itself worthy through its embodiment of Torah, that is, through its perfect replication of heaven, then the end would come. But before that great day ever came, the Judaism of the dual Torah would achieve rich and complete expression here on earth. It was in the life of the Jews in both Christendom and Islam from the end of the formative age in the seventh century, to the beginning of modern times in the nineteenth, that the Judaism of the dual Torah defined Judaism.

THE CLASSICAL PERIOD OF JUDAISM

FROM 640 TO 1789

Why Judaism Triumphed in Christendom and Islam

The Judaism of the dual Torah constructed for Israel a world in which the experience of the loss of political sovereignty and the persistence of the condition of tolerated subordination attested to the importance and centrality of Israel in the human situation. So the long-term condition of the conquered people found more than mere explanation in precisely the pattern that had first defined God's will in the Torah for Israel after the first catastrophe and restoration. That condition turned out to afford reassurance and make the truths of the system certain. The success of Judaism derived from this reciprocal process. On the one side, the Judaism of the dual Torah restated for Israel in an acutely contemporary form, in terms relevant to the situation of Christendom and Islam, the experience of loss and restoration, death and resurrection, that the first Scripture had set forth as a pattern. The people had attained a self-consciousness that continuous existence in a single place under a single government had denied others (and had denied Israel before 586, as the Yahwist and the Deuteronomist testify). Israel thus found a renewed sense of its own distinctive standing among the nations of the world.

But at the same time, that Judaism taught the Jews the lesson that its subordinated position itself gave probative evidence of the nation's true standing: the low would be raised up, the humble placed into authority, the proud reduced, and the world made right. So the Judaism of the dual Torah did more than reassure and encourage. It acted upon and determined the shape of matters. That Judaism defined the politics and policy of the community for a long time. It instructed Israel on the rules for the formation of the appropriate world and it laid forth the design for the attitudes and actions that would yield an Israel that was subordinate and tolerated, on the one side, but also proud and hopeful, on the other. The Judaism of the dual Torah began in the encounter with a successful Christianity and persisted in the face of a still more successful Islam. But for Israel that Judaism persevered because, long after the conditions that originally precipitated the positions and policies deemed normative, that same Judaism not only reacted to, but also shaped, Israel's condition in the world. Making a virtue of a policy of subordination that was not always necessary or even wise, the Judaism of the dual Torah defined the Jews' condition and set the limits to its circumstance.

The religion of a small, weak group, Judaism more than held its own against the challenge of triumphant Christendom and Islam. The reason for the success of the Judaism of the dual Torah was that the system answered the question of why God's people, in exile, held a subordinated, but tolerated position within the world framed by the sibling-rivals, Ishmael of Isaac and Esau of Jacob. The appeal to exile accounted for the dissonance between present unimportance and promised future greatness: "today if only you will." So the question was urgent, and the answer self-evidently true. Here was the family of Abraham, Isaac, and Jacob: Israel. Now tolerated, sometimes oppressed, in exile—in time to come the family would come home to its own land. The road back was fully mapped out. People now had to remember who they were, where they were going, and what they had to do in order to get from here to there.

The framing of the world as a system of families—with Israel unique but Israel's siblings related to it—admirably accounted for the state of Israel. The way of life of the Judaism of the dual Torah, with its stress on the ongoing sanctification of the every day, the world view with its doctrine of the ultimate salvation of the holy people—these realized in concrete and acutely relevant form the fundamental system. The consequence was total and enduring success. So long as Christianity defined the civilization of the West and Islam that of North Africa, the Near and Middle East, and Central Asia, Judaism in its fourth-century, classical statement triumphed in Israel, the Jewish people, located in Christendom and Islam. The questions deemed urgent and the answers found self-evidently true defined the world for Israel. In the West from the eighteenth century onward, as part of the secularization of politics and culture, Christendom lost its standing as a set of self-evident truths. Then in the same countries Judaism in its classical statement also found itself facing competition from other Judaisms: different systems, each one asking its distinctive, urgent questions and producing its own self-evidently true answers. For these other Judaisms neither questions nor answers bore any relationship whatever to those of the received system, even when they episodically exploited proof texts drawn from the inherited holy writings. In Christian lands it was only until the eighteenth century that the Judaism of the dual Torah both set the standard for accepted innovation and also defined the shape and structure of heresy. From that time onward, continuator-Judaisms competed with essentially new and unprecedented systems, which in no way stood in a linear and incremental relationship with the Judaism of the dual Torah.

In the Muslim countries, because the palpable self-evidence of Islam never gave way, but has defined reality in pretty much its own way from the beginning to the present day, the equivalently obvious standing of truth accorded by Jews to the received system of the Judaism of the dual Torah for Israel endured. Judaism in the received statement of the fourth century, as given its definitive version in the Talmud of Babylonia in the seventh, persisted from the beginning of Islam to the end of the life of Israel in Islam in 1948. In Muslim countries whatever variations and developments marked the history of Judaism from the fourth century to today worked themselves out within the received system and its norms.

The reasons for the difference between the uninterrupted history of Judaism in Islam and the diverse histories of Judaisms in modern and contemporary Christendom lies in the different modern and contemporary histories of Islam—so long the victim of imperialism—and Christianity—equally long the beneficiary of the same politics. In its fourth century formulation Judaism thrived within imperial systems in accord with the conditions of its circumstance—uninterruptedly in the one world, conditionally in the other. But the reason was the same: Judaism explained for Israel its subordinated but tolerated condition, and indeed made that condition into God's will. The acceptance of that condition in the heart as much as in the mind was part of the definition of virtue. In its version of the dual Torah Judaism brought to its ultimate statement the original, scriptural Judaism of the Torah of Moses, which was completed in the time of Ezra. The message of the Judaism of the dual Torah addressed precisely the situation envisaged by the original system: the people are special, its life is contingent, its relationship to the land is subject to conditions, and its collective life is lived at a level of heightened reality.

The outside world works out its affairs in order to accommodate God's will for Israel, and Israel has complete control of its relationship to the larger world—but in a paradoxical way. For what Israel must do is accept, submit, accommodate, and receive with humility the will and word of God in the Torah. The power to govern the fate of the nation rested with the nation, but only so far as the nation accorded that power to God alone. Were people perplexed about who is Israel? The Torah answered the question: God's people here and now, living out the holy life prescribed by God. Did people wonder how long that people would have to endure the government of Gentiles? The Torah addressed that issue: so long as God willed. The system laid emphasis upon the everyday as a sequence of acts of sanctification. It promised remission and resolution—salvation—in consequence of the correct and faithful performance of those acts of sanctification. The system therefore served to attest to the true status of Israel, small and inconsequential now, but holy even now and destined for great reward at the end of time.

The power of Judaism therefore lay in its remarkable capacity to define and create the world of Israel, the Jewish people. Israel understood that the nation that had ceased to be a nation on its own land and had once more regained that condition could and would once more reenact that paradigm. The original pattern imparted on events the meaning that made ample and good sense for Israel. That is why I have maintained that in the case of the Judaism of the dual Torah the social world recapitulated religion, and that religion did not merely recapitulate the givens of society.

In the mid-seventh century Islam found a powerful adversary in the Judaism of the system of the dual Torah. After the death of Muhammed the Muslim armies swept over the Middle East and North Africa, subduing the great empire of Iran to the east and much of Byzantine Rome to the west, cutting across Egypt, Cyrenaica, and what we know as Tunisia and North Africa, and reaching into Spain. Ancient Christian bishoprics fell, as vast Christian populations accepted the new monotheism though they were not compelled to do so. We have no evidence that similar sizable conversions decimated the Jewish community. That Judaism stood firm. The reason is clear. Having dealt with the political triumph of Christianity, the system of the dual Torah found itself entirely capable of coping with the military (and political) victory of Islam as well. Indeed, given the apparent stability of the Jewish communities in the newly-conquered Islamic countries and the decline of Christianity in those same, long-Christian territories—Syria, Palestine, Egypt, Cyrenaica, and the western provinces of North Africa, not to mention Spain—we observe a simple fact. The Judaism of the dual Torah satisfactorily explained the events of the day for Israel, while the Christianity triumphant through the sword of Constantine withstood the yet-sharper sword of Muhammed only with difficulty. One may surmise that the great Christian establishments of the Middle East and North Africa fell away on that account. Since Judaism and Christianity enjoyed precisely the same political status, the evident success of the one and the failure of the other attests to what the fourth century sages had accomplished for Israel, the Jewish people.

The situation of Jews as tolerated minority in Christendom and Islam, and that of Christianity in Islam, likewise accorded subordinated but tolerated standing, meant that only a free male Muslim enjoyed the rank of a full member of society.[1] Jews and Christians could accept Islam or submit; they could pay a tribute and accept Muslim supremacy, but continue to practice their received religions. Lewis characterizes the policy toward the conquered people in these terms: "This pattern was not one of equality but rather of dominance by one group and, usually, a hierarchic sequence of the others. Though this order did not concede equality, it permitted peaceful coexistence. While one group might dominate, it did not as a rule insist on suppressing or absorbing the others . . . Communities professing recognized religions were allowed the tolerance of the Islamic state. They were allowed to practice their religions . . . and to enjoy a measure of communal autonomy."[2] The Jews fell into the category of *dhimmis,* communities "accorded a certain status, provided that they unequivocally recognized the primacy of Islam and the supremacy of the Muslims. This recognition was expressed in the payment of the poll tax and obedience to a series of restrictions defined in detail by the holy law."[3] The situation of Judaism in Muslim countries therefore corresponded overall with that in the Christian ones. In some ways, to be sure, it proved easier, there being no emotional hostility directed against either Jews or Judaism such as flourished in Christendom.[4] But the Jews were a subject group and had to accommodate themselves to that condition, just as they had learned to make their peace with the remarkable success of Christianity in fourth-century Rome. And that brings us to the question of the basis for the remarkable success of Judaism in its classical form.

From the fourth century in Christendom, and from the seventh in Islam, Judaism enjoyed remarkable success in the very world that it had both created and also selected for itself—the world of Israel, the Jewish

1. Bernard Lewis, *The Jews of Islam* (Princeton: Princeton University Press, 1984), p. 8.
2. Lewis, *Jews of Islam,* pp. 19–20.
3. Lewis, *Jews of Islam,* p. 21.
4. Lewis, *Jews of Islam,* p. 32.

people. Both Islam and Christendom presented a single challenge: the situation of subordination along with toleration. The power of Judaism lay in its capacity to do two things. First, in its classical statement, shaped in the fourth-century Talmud of the Land of Israel and then fully articulated by the sixth-century Talmud of Babylonia, Judaism presented doctrines that both explained and drew renewal from the condition of subordination and toleration. So the facts of everyday life served to reenforce the claims of the system. Second, the same Judaism taught an enduring doctrine of the virtues of the heart that did more than make Israel's situation acceptable. The doctrine so shaped the inner life of Israel as to define virtue in the very terms that were imposed by politics. In age succeeding age Israel recreated within the exact condition of humility and accommodation that the people's political circumstance imposed from without. So the enduring doctrine of virtue not only made it possible for Israel to accept its condition, but also that same condition in the psychological structure of Israel's inner life, so bringing political facts and psychological fantasies into exact correspondence. Judaism triumphed in Christendom and Islam because of its power to bring into union heart and mind, inner life and outer circumstance, psychology and politics. The Judaism of the dual Torah not only matched the situation of Israel the conquered but (ordinarily) tolerated people, but also created that same condition within the psychological heritage of Israel. The condition was the acceptance of a subordinated but tolerated position, while awaiting the superior one.

The Power of the Classical Doctrine of Virtue

In the view of the sages of the dual Torah, attitudes or virtues of the heart—emotions—fitted together with the encompassing patterns of society and culture, theology, and the religious life. The affective rules formed an integral part of the way of life and world view put forward to make sense of the existence of the social group. That simple fact accounts for the long-term world-creating power of Judaism in Israel. What Jews were supposed to feel matched what they were expected to think. In this way the individual linked his deepest personal emotions to the cosmic fate and transcendent faith of the social group of which he or she formed a part. Emotions laid down judgments. They derived from rational cognition. The individual Israelite's innermost feelings, the microcosm, corresponded to the pubic and historic condition of Israel, the macrocosm.

That stunning accomplishment of the Judaism of the dual Torah accounts for its power not only to respond to, but to define and shape, the condition of Israel, the Jewish people. What the dual Torah taught the private person to feel linked the individual's heart to what Judaism stated about the condition of Israel in history and of God in the cosmos. All formed one reality, in supernatural world and nature, in time and in eternity wholly consubstantial. In the innermost chambers of deepest feelings, the Israelite therefore lived out the public history and destiny of the people, Israel. The genius of Judaism, the reason for its resilience and endurance, lay in its power to teach Jews to feel in private what they also had to think in public about the condition of both self and nation. The world within and the world without were so bonded that one was never alone. The individual's life was always lived with the people.

The sages' repertoire of approved and disapproved feelings remained constant through the four-century-long unfolding of the canon of Judaism from the Mishnah through the Talmud of Babylonia, 200–600. After that point, the same doctrine of virtue persisted in molding both the correct attitudes of the individual and the public policy of the community. The reason is clear.

First, the emotions encouraged by Judaism in its formative age, such as humility, forbearance, accommodation, and a spirit of conciliation, exactly corresponded to the political and social requirements of the Jews' condition in that time.

Second, the reason that the same repertoire of emotions persisted with no material change through the unfolding of the writings of the sages of that formative age was the constancy of the Jews' political and social condition.

In successfully joining psychology and politics, inner attitudes and public policy, sages discovered the source of power that would sustain their system. The reason that Judaism enjoyed the standing of self-evident truth for so long in both Islam and Christendom, derives not from the cogency of its doctrines, but principally from the fusion of heart and mind, emotion and intellect, attitude and doctrine—and the joining of the whole in the fundamental and enduring politics of the nation, wherever it located itself.

The sages' notion of the centrality of human feelings in the religious life presented no surprises. Scripture was explicit on both sides of the matter. The human being was commanded to love God. The biblical record of God's feelings and God's will about the feelings of humanity—wanting human love, for example—left no room for doubt. The Judaism of the rabbis of late antiquity made it explicit that God always wants the heart. God commanded that humanity had to love God with full heart, soul, mind and might. That was the principal duty of humanity. But the sages' contribution, from the Mishnah forward, proved

distinctive and definitive. For they imparted the distinctive pattern of
their mind upon the doctrine that emotions matter: they defined which
ones mattered.

Early, middle, and late, a single doctrine and program dictated what
people had to say on how Israel should tame its heart. So far as the
unfolding components of the canon of Judaism portrayed matters,
emotions formed part of an iron tradition. As successive documents
were completed, each one added its improvements, while leaving the
structure basically the same. Like a cathedral that takes a thousand
years to build but always looks uniform and antique, so the view of the
affective life over centuries remained not only cogent but essentially
uniform. Sages' doctrine of affections remained a constant in an age of
change.

While the Mishnah casually referred to emotions—tears of joy or
tears of sorrow—where feelings mattered it was always in a public and
communal context. For one important example, where there was an
occasion of rejoicing, one form of joy was not to be confused with
another, or one context of sorrow with another. Accordingly, marriages
were not to be held on festivals (M. M.Q. 1:7). Likewise mourning was
not to take place then (M. M.Q. 1:5, 3:7–9). Where emotions played a
role, it was because of the affairs of the community at large—rejoicing
on a festival or mourning on a fast day (M. Suk. 5:1–4). The single
underlying principle affecting all forms of emotion for the Mishnah
was that feelings had to be kept under control and must never be fully
expressed without reasoning about the appropriate context. Emotions
always had to lay down judgments. When emotions played a systemic
role and not merely a tangential one the basic principle was the same: to
frame our feelings so as to accord with the appropriate role.

In only one case did emotion play a decisive role in settling an issue,
and that had to do with whether or not a farmer was happy that water
came upon his produce or grain. That case underlined the conclusion
just now drawn. If people felt a given sentiment, it was a matter of
judgment,[5] and therefore invoked the law's penalties. So in this system
emotions were not treated as spontaneous, but as significant aspects of a
person's judgment. The very fact that the law applied came about
because the framers judged the farmer's feelings to constitute, on their
own and without associated actions or even conceptions, final and
decisive judgments on what had happened.

5. It would be difficult to find a more striking example of that view than at M.
Makh. 4:5 and related passages.

Following the Mishnah, tractate Abot presented the single most comprehensive account of religious affections. The reason is that in that document how we feel defines a critical aspect of virtue. The issue proved central, and not peripheral. The doctrine emerged fully exposed. A simple catalogue of permissible feelings comprised humility, generosity, self-abnegation, love, a spirit of conciliation of the other, and eagerness to please. A list of impermissible emotions was made up of envy, ambition, jealousy, arrogance, sticking to one's opinion, self-centeredness, a grudging spirit, and vengefulness. People had to aim at eliciting acceptance and good will from others and had to avoid confrontation, rejection, and humiliation of the other. This they did through conciliation and giving up their own claims and rights. So both catalogues form a harmonious and uniform whole, aiming at the cultivation of the humble and malleable person, one who accepts everything and resents nothing. In this tractate as in the system as a whole, these virtues derived from knowledge of what really counted, which was what God wanted. But God favored those who pleased others. The virtues appreciated by human beings proved identical to the ones to which God responded. And what single virtue of the heart encompassed the rest? Restraint, the source of self-abnegation and humility, served as the antidote for ambition, vengefulness, and, above all, for arrogance. It is restraint of our own interest that enables us to deal generously with others, and humility about ourselves that generates a liberal spirit towards others.

The emotions prescribed in tractate Abot provided variations of a single feeling, the sentiment of the disciplined heart, whatever affective form it may take. And where does the heart learn its lessons, if not in relationship to God? "Make his wishes yours, so that he will make your wishes his" (Abot 2:4). Applied to the relationships between human beings, this inner discipline of the emotional life will yield exactly those virtues of conciliation and self-abnegation, humility and generosity of spirit, that the framers of tractate Abot spell out in one example after another. Imputing to heaven exactly those responses felt on earth, for example, "Anyone from whom people take pleasure, God takes pleasure" (Abot 3:10), makes the point at the most general level.

When the authors or compilers of the Tosefta finished their labor of amplification and complement, they had succeeded in adding only a few fresh and important developments of established themes. What was striking was first the stress upon the communal stake in an individual's emotional life. Still more striking was the Tosefta's authors' explicit effort to invoke an exact correspondence between public and private feelings. In both realms emotions are to be tamed and kept in hand and within accepted proportions. Public sanctions for inappropriate or disproportionate emotions entail emotions, for instance, such as shame. It need hardly be added that feeling shame for improper feelings once again underlined the social judgmental character of those feelings. For shame is public, guilt private. People are responsible for how they feel, as much as for how they express feeling in word or deed. Hence an appropriate penalty derived from the same aspect of social life, that is, the affective life.

I cannot imagine a more stunning tribute to the power of feeling than the allegation, surfacing in the Tosefta, that the Temple was destroyed because of vain hatred. Given the critical importance accorded to the Temple cult, sages could not have made more vivid their view that how a private person feels shapes the public destiny of the entire nation. So the issues came to expression in high stakes. But the basic position of the authors of the Mishnah, inclusive of their first apologists in Abot, seems entirely consistent. What Tosefta's authors accomplished is precisely what they claimed, which was to amplify, supplement, and complement established principles and positions.

In the Yerushalmi emotions not taken up earlier now did not come under discussion. Principles introduced earlier enjoyed restatement and extensive exemplification. Some principles of proper feelings even generated secondary developments of one kind or another. The system proved essentially complete in the earliest statement of its main points. Where the Mishnah introduced into its system issues of the affective life, the Yerushalmi's authors and compilers took up those issues. But they rarely created them on their own and never said much new about those they did treat. What we find is instruction to respect public opinion and cultivate social harmony. What is most interesting in the Yerushalmi is the recognition that there are rules descriptive of feelings, as much as of other facts of life. The effects of emotions, as much as of opinions or deeds, came within the rule of law. People were assumed to frame emotions, as much as opinions, in line with common and shared judgments. In no way did emotions form a special classification, one expressive of what was private, spontaneous, individual, and beyond the law and reason.

The Bavli carried forward with little change the now traditional program of emotions, listing the same ones catalogued earlier and no new ones. The authors said about those feelings what had been said earlier. A fresh emphasis in the Bavli favored mourning and disapproved of rejoicing. We can hardly maintain that that view came to expression only in the latest states in the formation of the canon. The contrary is the case. The point remained consistent throughout. Excessive levity marks arrogance, deep mourning characterizes humility. So many things came down to one thing. The nurturance of an attitude of mourning should mark both the individual and the community, in mourning for the Temple, but also mourning for the condition of nature, including the human condition, signified in the Temple's destruction. Humble acceptance of suffering is a mark of humility. The ruin of the Temple served as a guarantee that just as the prophetic warnings had come to realization, so too would prophetic promises of restoration and redemption. In the realm of feelings, the union of opposites came about through the same mode of thought. Hence God's love comes to fulfillment in human suffering, and the person who joyfully accepts humiliation or suffering will enjoy the appropriate divine response of love.

Another point at which the authors of the Bavli introduced a statement developing a familiar view derived from the interpretation of how to love one's neighbor. It was by imposing upon one's neighbor the norms of the community, by rebuking the other for violating accepted practice. In this way the emotion of love would take on concrete social value in reenforcing the norms of the community. Since the verse at hand invites exactly that interpretation, we can hardly regard the Bavli's paragraph on the subject as innovative.

The strikingly fresh medium for traditional doctrines in the Bavli took the form of prayers composed by sages. Here the values of the system came to eloquent expression. Sages prayed that their soul would be as dust for everyone to tread upon. They asked for humility in spirit, congenial colleagues, good will, and good impulses. They asked God to notice their humiliation, and to spare them from disgrace. The familiar affective virtues and sins—self-abnegation as against arrogance— made their appearance in liturgical form as well. Another noteworthy type of material, also not new, in which the pages of the Bavli are rich, portrayed the deaths of sages. One dominant motif was uncertainty in the face of death, a sign of humility and self-abnegation. The basic motif—theological as much as affective—that encompassed all materials was simple. Israel was estranged from God, and therefore needed to exhibit the traits of humility and uncertainty, acceptance and conciliation. When God recognized the proper feelings in Israel's heart, as much as in the nation's deeds and deliberation, God would respond by ending the estrangement that marked the present age. So the single word alienation encompassed the entire affective doctrine of the canon of Judaism. No one can miss the psychological depth of the system, which joined the human condition to the fate of the nation and the world, and linked the whole to the broken heart of God.

The Judaic doctrine of affections may be stated in a few simple propositions which strikingly correspond with the literary rules of interpretation of Leviticus Rabbah: the system required Israel to see the world "as if"—things were not what they seemed to be. The way to get something, was to want its opposite. To be rich, accept what you have. To be powerful, conciliate your enemy. To be endowed with public recognition express humility. So the doctrine of the emotional life expressed in law, scriptural interpretation, and tales of sages was be uniform and simple. Emotions well up uncontrolled and spontaneous. Anger, vengeance, pride, arrogance—these people feel by nature. So feelings as much as actions had to become what by nature they were not. But how do you seek the opposite of wealth? By accepting what you have. And how do you pursue humility? By doing nothing to aggrandize yourself. So the life of the emotions, in conformity to the life of reflection and of concrete deed, consisted in the transformation of what things seem into what they ought to be. Both the heart and the mind belonged to the human being's power to form reasoned viewpoints. Coming from sages, such an opinion surely cohered with the context and circumstance of those who held it.

This theory meant that it was as if a common object or symbol really represented an uncommon one. Nothing said what it meant. All statements carried deeper meaning, which inhered in other statements altogether. So too each emotion bore a negative and a positive charge, as each matched and balanced the other: humility and arrogance, love and hate. If a negative emotion was natural to the heart, then the individual had the power to sanctify that negative, sinful feeling and turn it into a positive, holy emotion. Ambition had to be tamed and so transformed into humility; hatred and vengeance had to be changed into love and acceptance.

Given the situation of Israel—vanquished on the battlefield, broken in the turning of history's wheel—we need hardly wonder why wise men advised conciliation and acceptance. Exalting humility made sense because there was little choice. Whether or not these virtues found advocates in other contexts for other reasons, the policy of forebearance proved entirely appropriate to the politics and social condition at hand. If Jewry cultivated the strong-minded individual, it would sentence such a person to a useless life of ineffective protest. The nation required not strong-minded leadership but consensus. The social virtues of con-

ciliation reenforced the bonds that joined the nation lacking frontiers—
the people without a politics of its own. For all there was to hold Israel
together and sustain its life as a society would have to come forth out of
sources of inner strength. So consensus, conciliation, self-abnegation
and humility, and the search for acceptance outside the group—these
defined appropriate emotions in the literary culture at hand because
they dictated wise policy and shrewd politics.

Life in "exile," viewed as living in other peoples' countries and not in
their own land, meant for Israel a long span of endurance—a test of
patience to end only with the end of time. That life in exile required
Israel to live in accord with the will of others. Under such circumstances
the virtues of the independent citizen sharing command of affairs of
state, and the gifts of innovation, initiative, and independence of mind,
proved beside the point. From the end of the Second Revolt against
Rome in 135 to the creation of the state of Israel in 1948, Israel faced a
different task. The human condition of Israel therefore defined a special heroism, one filled with patience, humiliation, and self-abnegation.
To turn survival into endurance and pariah status into an exercise in
godly living, the sages' affective program served well. Israel's hero saw
power in submission, wealth in the gift to be grateful, and wisdom in
the confession of ignorance. Like the Cross, ultimate degradation was
made to stand for ultimate power. Like Jesus on the Cross, Israel in exile
served God through suffering. True, the policy represented a scandal to
the nations and foolishness to some Jews. But Israel's own version of the
doctrine endured and defined the nation's singular and astonishing
resilience. For Israel did endure and endures today.

The Jewish people rarely enjoyed instruments of civil coercion that
were capable of preserving social order and coherence. Governments
afforded Jews limited rights over their own affairs. When, at the start of
the fifth century, the Christian-Byzantine Roman government ended
the existence of the patriarchate of the Jews of the Land of Israel, people
may well have recognized the parlous condition of Jewish authorities. A
government in charge of itself and its subjects, a territorial community
routinely able to force individuals to pay taxes and otherwise conform
where necessary—these normal political facts rarely marked the condition of Israel between 429 and 1948. What was left was another kind of
power, civil obedience generated by force from within. The stress on
pleasing others and conforming to the will of the group and the belief
that God likes people whom people like substituted for the civil power
of political coercion and imparted to the community of Israel a different
power of authority.

In the rules of the sages both sources of power—the one in respect to the public world beyond and the other in respect to the social world within—gained force through the primal energy of emotion. A system that made humility a mark of strength and a mode of gaining God's approval, a social policy that imputed ultimate virtue to feelings of conciliation, restraint, and conformity to social norms, such a system had no need of the armies and police it did not have. The heart would serve as the best defense, inner affections as the police who were always there when needed. The remarkable inner discipline of Israel through its difficult condition in history from the beginnings of the sages' system to today began in those feelings that met the misery with grandeur of soul. Israel's victory would come through the triumph of the broken heart, now mended with the remedy of moderated emotion.

Judaisms within Judaism (1): The German Pietists of the Middle Ages

The Judaism of the dual Torah bore the power to encompass diverse Judaisms within the classical system, each with its choice of elements to emphasize and amplify. We see the power of the system when we consider the Judaisms that it both precipitated and accommodated. From the fourth century to the present time, derivative systems took shape, restating in distinctive ways the fundamental convictions of the Judaism of the dual Torah, or adding their particular perspective or doctrine to that system. Heresies attained heretical status specifically by rejecting important components of the received system, for example its doctrine of the dual Torah or of the Messiah as a sage and model of the Torah fully observed. So long as the self-evidence of the established Judaism persisted, each of the derivative systems—orthodox or heretical—placed itself into relationship with that fundamental statement of matters. Only when the received Judaism no longer enjoyed virtually unique standing as the valid answer to obviously urgent questions did Judaic systems take shape that were utterly out of phase with the one that reached its initial version in the fourth century and its final version in the Talmud of Babylonia.

Within the received system, diverse systems found for themselves ample space. Some of these concerned new doctrines which had to be made to accord with the received ones. For example a massive rethinking of the very modes of thought of Judaism, moving from mythic to philosophical thinking, took shape over a long period of time. The philosophical movement presented striking testimony to the power of the received system, for it took as its task the validation and vindication

of the received system inclusive of the law and doctrine of the oral
Torah. Each continuator-Judaism laid its stress on a received component of the original system or else explicitly reaffirmed the whole
system, while adding to it in interesting ways. All of the continuator-
Judaisms claimed to stand in a linear and incremental relationship to
the original. They made constant reference to the established and authoritative canon. They affirmed the importance of meticulous obedience to the law. Each one in its way proposed to strengthen or purify
or otherwise confirm the dual Torah of Sinai.

That is why the Judaic systems of the long age from the fourth
century to the nineteenth in Europe and to the mid-twentieth in the
Muslim world in retrospect served to affirm the normative standing of
the classic system. One system after another took shape and made its
own distinctive statement, but every one of them affirmed the definitive
symbolic system and structure of the original. Among many candidates
for study of how Judaism generated systemically cogent and coherent
Judaisms I have chosen two, one medieval, the other modern. Both fall
into the category of sects within the "church" of the dual torah. The
first shows how a distinctive group worked out a legitimate Judaism,
systemically harmonious with the inherited one. The second shows
how, even in the conditions of modern times, an essentially original
system, with its own quite distinctive world view and doctrine, could
make a place for itself within the received system. The first Judaism was
that of the Jewish Pietists in medieval Germany, and the second Judaism was that of the Hasidim of eighteenth-century Poland.

What marks a Judaism as an autonomous system is not its doctrine
or mode of thought but its address to a distinct social group, an Israel. In
the late twelfth century, Jewries in the Rhineland produced a pietistic
circle "characterized by its own leadership and distinctive religious
outlook."[6] What made this Judaism a system within the larger system?
First, the Pietists produced their own viewpoints and doctrines, defining a distinctive way of life for their group. Second, their principal
authority remained the canon of the dual Torah and its values. The
writers defined a distinctive world view, described by Marcus as
"grounded in their new understanding of the hidden and revealed will
of God." Their ideas became influential later on, but what is interesting
for us is the entirely comfortable position the Pietists found for themselves in the received Judaism; they formed a Judaism within Judaism.

6. Ivan G. Marcus, *Piety and Society: The Jewish Pietists of Medieval Germany*
(Leiden: E. J. Brill, 1981), p. 1. The entire account that follows draws on Marcus.

What first marked the group as a distinctive was their doctrines, not their way of life. But as matters unfolded, practice as much as profession would distinguish the group from others within the larger, harmonious world of Israel. They developed an ascetic way of life to balance their doctrine: "The Pietists continuously weigh this-worldly inward enjoyment and try to reduce it so as not to diminish otherworldly reward. The locus of obedience is not primarily external behavior . . . but the degree of the Pietist's inward zeal or sinful motivation." Their system differed from the established system because, as Marcus states, they held that "God's will consists of more than what was explicitly revealed in Scripture, more than the rabbinically derived expanded meanings which form the basis of rabbinic law." The Pietists identified themselves with Abraham at the binding of Isaac and with Job in his trials. The Pietist accepted anguish and pain as part of the price of serving God: "Infinite in scope, the larger will consists of a third dimension encoded in Scripture but which is obligatory for the Pietist. Complementing the idea of God's larger will is the infinite obligation which the Pietist assumes of searching for and discovering it . . . The Pietist . . . must be engaged continuously in a search for the hidden will by striving to discover new prohibitions and make new proscriptive safeguards around the forbidden. In so doing, the Pietist shows his true fear of God, which is understood as being afraid that one not love Him self-lessly, sacrificially, totally." [7] We see here the power of the sect to carry to an extreme the convictions of the "church"—the community as a whole. The stress on keeping the law more perfectly and on studying the Torah more perspicaciously—that defined not a heresy but a Judaism within the Judaism of the community at large. But although a sect, the Pietists in the German Rhineland made persistent efforts to take over the community at large and run it. In general the Pietists did not succeed and consequently they tended to segregate themselves from the larger world of Judaism: "For it is difficult for someone who wants to be a Pietist to see someone his own age in town pursuing a different way of life. If he does not also follow the others, he will be embarassed, and he would be better off living in a different town." [8]

One characteristic of the Pietists was their stress on sin and atonement, which Marcus describes as "a logical and psychological extension of their pietistic ideal." The familiar category of virtuous attitudes defined the correct attitude as one of repentance, confession of sins, and

7. Marcus, *Piety and Society,* p. 12.
8. Marcus, *Piety and Society,* p. 95.

returning to God: "Atonement requires not only contrite repentance and confession as well as proofs of same, but in addition demands that the sinner must impose penances on himself which are designed to rebalance the divine scales which sinning has tipped towards punishment." Sin encompassed both what one had done and one's attitude or motivation. Keeping the laws covered the former and doing so with "the whole heart," the latter. The life of repentance, penance, and reconciliation with God formed the concrete counterpart to the doctrines. The whole comprised the "way"—the path to personal salvation.[9] The group formed a distinctive fellowship in their rejection of the Jewish society made up of outsiders to their system. They tried to take over the community or they withdrew from it; they remained in uneasy balance with the larger Judaic world. That is what I mean by a Judaism within Judaism. With their heavy emphasis on sin and atonement, the Pietists selected, out of the original system, the theme that in theological terms stated most exactly Israel's condition after 586—and before the final end of time. Study of the Torah now encompassed doctrines not in the received documents: "'One must be resourceful in the fear of God.' Since a person is punished even when he does not know what God requires, it is necessary to know and study Torah, including pietism. Moreover, you will not be able to tell the Ruler that you did a sin unintentionally out of ignorance. Therefore I decided to write a book for those who fear God so that they are not punished for sinning out of ignorance and think that it was for no reason."[10] Once more we observe that Torah defined and dominated, but Torah of a special sort. In the end European Jewry was reshaped by the practices and norms which began in the Pietist group. The Pietists wove a new religious ideology into the fabric of Jewish law.[11] The sect did not become part of the "church," but it remade the church in its own image. So the Torah that had taken shape in the encounter with triumphant Christianity broadened and deepened in its scope and found room for distinctive emphases and even new doctrines.

Judaisms within Judaism (2): Hasidism

What was interesting in Hasidism—a mystical movement that took shape in the eighteenth century and came to fruition in the nineteenth

9. Marcus, *Piety and Society*, p. 15.
10. Marcus, *Piety and Society*, p. 72.
11. Marcus, *Piety and Society*, p. 132.

and twentieth—was the power of the movement to reenforce the observance and study of the Torah. That fact is astonishing, given the fresh
character of the doctrines of the movement, on the one side, and the
powerful opposition precipitated by it, on the other. The power of the
original system to absorb diverse viewpoints and quite novel doctrines
and matters of emphasis and make them its own finds testimony in the
ultimate character of Hasidism. The mystic circles in Poland and
Lithuania among whom Hasidism developed in the eighteenth century
carried on practices that marked them as different from other Jews—
for example, special prayers and distinctive ways of observing certain
religious duties. The first among the leaders of the movement of ec-
statics and antiascetics was Israel b. Eliezer Baal Shem Tov, "the Besht,"
who worked as a popular healer. From the 1730s onward he undertook
travels and attracted to himself circles of followers in Podolia, Poland
and Lithuania, and elsewhere. When he died in 1760 he left behind not
only disciples but also a broad variety of followers and admirers in
southeastern Poland and Lithuania. Leadership of the movement
passed to a succession of holy men, about whom stories were told and
preserved. In the third generation, from the third quarter of the eighteenth century into the first quarter of the nineteenth, the movement
took hold and spread. Diverse leaders called zaddikim, who were holy
men and charismatic figures, developed their own standing and
doctrine.

Given the controversies that swirled about the movement, we might
expect that many of the basic ideas were new. But that was hardly the
case. The movement drew heavily on available mystical books and
doctrines, which from medieval times onward had won a place within
the faith as part of the Torah. Emphasis on a given doctrine on the part
of Hasidic thinkers should not obscure the profound continuities between the modern movement and its medieval sources. To take one
example of how the movement imparted its own imprint on an available idea, Menahem Mendel of Lubavich, noted that God's oneness—
surely a given in all Judaisms—meant more than that God is unique. It
meant that God is all that is. "There is no reality in created things. This
is to say that in truth all creatures are not in the category of something or
a thing as we see them with our eyes. For this is only from our point of
view, since we cannot perceive the divine vitality. But from the point of
view of the divine vitality which sustains us, we have no existence and
we are in the category of complete nothingness like the rays of the sun in
the sun itself . . . From which it follows that there is no other existence
whatsoever apart from his existence, blessed be he. This is true unifica-

tion."[12] Since all things are in God, the suffering and sorrow of the world cannot be said to exist. So to despair is to sin.

Hasidism lay great stress on joy and avoiding melancholy. Like their earlier counterparts in the medieval Rhineland, the Hasidim of modern times maintained that the right attitude must accompany the doing of religious deeds: the deed could be elevated only when carried out in a spirit of devotion. The doctrine of Hasidism further held that "In all things there are 'holy sparks' waiting to be redeemed and rescued for sanctity through man using his appetites to serve God. The very taste of food is a pale reflection of the spiritual force which brings the food into being."[13] Before carrying out a religious deed, the Hasidim would recite the formula, "For the sake of the unification of the Holy One, blessed be he, and his shekhinah [presence in the world]." On that account they were criticized. But the issues were defined by the fundamental pattern of life and the received world view contained in the holy canon of Judaism. Hasidism therefore constituted a Judaism within Judaism— distinctive, yet in its major traits so closely related to the Judaism of the dual Torah as to be indistinguishable except in trivial details.

But one of the details mattered a great deal, and that was the doctrine of *zaddikism*—the doctrine of the holy man as mediator. The *zaddik*, holy man, had the power to raise the prayers of the followers and to work miracles. The zaddik was the means through which grace reached the world, the one who could control the universe through his prayers. The zaddik would bring humanity nearer to God and God closer to humanity. The Hasidim were well aware that this doctrine of the zaddik—the pure and elevated soul that could reach to the realm of heaven in which only mercy reigns—represented an innovation. So Jacobs:

> But if such powers were evidently denied to the great ones of the past how does the zaddik come to have them? The rationale is contained in a parable attributed to the Maggid of Mezhirech . . . When a king is on his travels he will be prepared to enter the most humble dwelling if he can find rest there, but when the king is at home, he will refuse to leave his palace unless he is invited by a great lord who knows how to pay him full regal honors. In earlier generations only the greatest of Jews could attain to the holy spirit. Now that the *Shekhinah* [divine presence] is in exile, God is ready to dwell in every soul free from sin.[14]

12. Cited by Louis Jacobs, "Basic Ideas of Hasidism," *Encyclopaedia Judaica* 7: 1404.
13. Jacobs, "Basic Ideas," col. 1405.
14. Jacobs, "Basic Ideas," col. 1406.

Although it was apparently a complete innovation, the doctrine of the zaddik in fact carried forward a theme of the Zohar, a mystical document of the thirteenth century. The principal figure of that document, Simeon b. Yohai, an important rabbi in talmudic times, was seen by the Hasidim as the model for the veneration offered to the zaddik. In that way they linked themselves to the most ancient past of what to them was the Torah.[15] Nahman of Bratzslav was identified with Simeon b. Yohai and was held by his disciples to have formed the reincarnation of the talmudic authority. The conclusion drawn from that fact, Green points out, is not the one that would distinguish the zaddik and his followers from the rest of Judaism: "Nahman was very cross with those who said that the main reason for the *zaddik*'s ability to attain such a high level of understanding was the nature of his soul. He said that this was not the case, but that everything depended first and foremost upon good deeds, struggle, and worship. He said explicitly that everyone in the world could reach even the highest rung, that everything depended upon human choice."[16] While the zaddik was a superior figure, a doctrine such as that of Nahman brought the Hasidic movement into close touch with the rest of Jewry, with its stress on the equal responsibility of all Israel to carry on the work of good deeds and worship (not to mention study of the Torah). What was special became its most appealing trait. So Green describes the legacy of Nahman of Bratslav, citing the record of the master's last great message: "'Gevalt! Do not despair!' He went on in these words: 'There is no such thing as despair at all!' He drew forth these words slowly and deliberately, saying, 'There is no despair.' He said the words with such strength and wondrous depth that he taught everyone, for all generations, that he should never despair, no matter what it is that he has to endure." Green notes that the master had left "the example of a man who had suffered all the torments of hell in his lifetime, but had refused to give in to ultimate despair."[17] Rightly seeing this as emblematic of the master, we may also note how thoroughly in agreement the authors of the Yerushalmi, Genesis Rabbah, and Leviticus Rabbah found themselves. That is what I mean when I call Hasidism a Judaism within Judaism: it was both a restatement of the familiar in a fresh idiom and a reconsideration of the profane under the aspect of the holy.

By the 1830s the original force of the movement had run its course,

15. Arthur Green, *Tormented Master: A Life of Rabbi Nahman of Bratslav* (University: University of Alabama Press, 1979), p. 12.

16. Green, *Tormented Master*, p. 14.

17. Quoted in Green, *Tormented Master*, p. 265.

and the movement, which had begun as a persecuted sect, now defined the way of life of the Jews in the Ukraine, Galicia, and central Poland, with offshoots in White Russia and Lithuania on the one side, and Hungary on the other. The waves of emigration from the 1880s onward carried the movement to the West, and in the aftermath of World War II, to the United States and the land of Israel as well. Today the movement forms a powerful component of Orthodox Judaism, and that fact is what is central to our interest. For by the end of the eighteenth century, powerful opposition, led by the most influential figures of East European Judaism, characterized Hasidism as heretical. Its stress on ecstasy, visions, and miracles of the leaders and its enthusiastic way of life—these were seen as delusions, and the veneration of the zaddik was interpreted as worship of a human being. The stress on prayer, to the denigration of study of the Torah, likewise called into question the legitimacy of the movement. In the war against Hasidism the movement found itself anathematized, its books burned, and its leaders vilified: "They must leave our communities with their wives and children . . . and they should not be given a night's lodging; . . . it is forbidden to do business with them and to intermarry with them or to assist at their burial."

Under these circumstances, the last thing anyone could have anticipated was that Hasidism would find a place for itself within what was later considered Orthodoxy. But it did. For example, one of the most influential and important organizations within contemporary Orthodoxy, Agudat Israel, finds its principal membership in Hasidim. The acceptance of the movement came about through the development within Hasidism of centers of study of the Torah. The joining of Hasidic doctrine with the received tradition legitimated what had begun outside of that tradition altogether (or at least outside in the view of those who deemed themselves insiders). The first Hasidic center of Torah study came into being in the mid-nineteenth century, and by the end of that time the Lubavich sect of Hasidism had founded still more important centers. What had begun as a heretical movement had within the span of a century gained entry into the centers of the normative faith, and within another century had come to constitute the bulwark of that faith. I can imagine no greater testimony to the remarkable power and resilience of the Judaism of the dual Torah than the capacity of that system to make a place for so vigorous and original a movement as Hasidism.

Heresies Against Judaism (1): Karaism as a Systemic Heresy

The heresies generated by the Judaism of the dual Torah present still more striking evidence of the power of the received system to thrive. Judaism in its ascendancy also defined the limits of heresy, imposing its values upon the contrary-minded statements of the age. One heresy rejected the doctrine of the dual Torah, while another rejected the doctrine of the sage-Messiah. In the age of the dominance of the Judaism of the dual Torah, we look in vain for evidence that the system faced heresies essentially alien to its structure and system. From the fourth to the nineteenth century in Christendom, and to the mid-twentieth century in the Muslim world, Judaic "heresies"[18] commonly took up a position on exactly the program and agenda of the Judaism of the dual Torah. What made a heresy heretical was the rejection of one or another of the definitive doctrines of the norm. In the nineteenth- and twentieth-century West, by contrast, new Judaisms—not merely heresies cleaved out of the old—took shape wholly outside of the system and structure of the old Judaism. That fact attests to the contemporary world's systemic change of monumental proportions.

We consider two systemic heresies, each addressing a fundamental plank in the platform of the Judaism of the dual Torah: Karaism, which denied the myth of the dual Torah, and Sabbateanism, which rejected the doctrine of the Messiah as defined in the classical system and created a new doctrine within the received structure and system—a Messiah outside of the law. I cannot think of two more characteristic components of the Judaism of the dual Torah than its belief in the oral Torah, on the one side, and its expectation of a Messiah who would master and carry out the teachings of the Torah of Sinai, on the other. Both of these heresies took exactly the opposite position to the Judaism of the dual Torah, thereby not only challenging that Judaism but also testifying to its power to define reality for all Israel. As in our consideration of the Judaisms within Judaism, we take up both medieval and early modern phenomena in order to show the uninterrupted and uniform history of Judaisms from the fourth to the nineteenth century. Karaite Judaism flourished in medieval times and the Sabbatean system in the early

18. I treat heresy as an inappropriate but necessary word choice. Within the theory of this book on the diversity of Judaisms, none can be more or less authentic than any other. Descriptively, a heresy becomes a heresy when it takes up a position on an issue defined by a dominant Judaism which is different from the position of that Judaism. It thus confirms the dominance of the paramount system of the time and place.

modern age. So the correspondence between the systemically harmonious Judaisms and the systemically contradictory ones is exact.

The indicative trait of the Judaism of the dual Torah was the doctrine that at Sinai, God had revealed the Torah to be transmitted thorough two media, written and oral. Focusing upon that central belief, Karaism denied that God had revealed to Moses at Sinai more than the written Torah, and explicitly condemned belief in an oral one. Karaism took shape in the eighth century, beginning after the rise of Islam, and advocated the return to Scripture as against tradition, including rabbinic tradition. The sect originated in Babylonia in the period following the formation of the Talmud of Babylonia, on the one side, and the rise of Islam, on the other. In his classic account of the matter, Zvi Ankori explains the origin of the movement as follows:

> The forceful promotion of talmudic legislation by the central Jewish institutions under Muslim domination . . . could not but call forth defiance in the distant peripheries of the Jewish Diaspora. Claiming to be the last link in an uninterrupted chain of oral transmission, the central Jewish administration, residing in Babylonia, considered itself the only legitimate heir and sole competent interpreter of that unique national experience: the lawgiving communication at Sinai . . . The protest against the central Jewish authorities did perforce assume the form of opposition to the Oral Law which was embodied in the Talmud and effectively enforced by the exilarchic office and the continuous activity of . . . lawmakers. Indeed, regional customs, rites and observances persisted in the fringe areas of Jewish Dispersion in spite of their having been ordered out of existence by the levelling action of Babylonian talmudic legislation. In reaffirming adherence to these practices, the forces of protest would register their dissatisfaction with the exilarchic and [sages'] administration and repudiation of its legal and social policies which were identified with the talmudic legislation.[19]

Ankori judges that the dynamics of sectarian life found definition "within or against its normative environment."[20] For our purpose that observation proves critical, for it was the dual Torah that defined, in doctrinal and mythic terms, the normative environment.

The movement itself claimed to originate in biblical times and to derive its doctrine from the true priest, Zadok. The founder of the movement then recovered that original Torah. The founder, Anan b. David, imposed rules concerning food that were stricter than those of

19. Zvi Ankori, *Karaites in Byzantium* (New York: Columbia University Press, 1959), pp. 1–3.
20. Ankori, *Karaites*, p. 9.

the rabbis, and in other ways legislated a stricter version of the law than the talmudic authorites admitted. Ankori says of Anan:

Anan ben David led the forces of anti-Rabbanite rebellion out of the remote frontiers of the Muslim-dominated Jewish Dispersion into the heart of ex-ilarchic and geonic [sages, that is rabbinic-talmudic] dominion. Until that time open defiance was in evidence only in the outlying provinces of the Caliphate in which Muslim heterodoxy was thriving also. Anan's answer to the challenge of disillusionment with militant Palestino-centric messianism was national asceticisim anchored in the diasporic community of the pious . . . Anan's widely heralded fundamentalism and exclusive reliance on the letter of the Written Law are largely a misnomer. Rather, his was an ex post facto attempt to read into the Bible (the full twenty-four volumes of it and not the Pentateuch alone) the customs and observances already practiced by the sectarians . . . Normative leadership in Babylonia, awakened to the danger of sectarian subversion in its own home while campaigning for the extension of Babylonian jurisdiction over all provinces of the Jewish dispersion, must have struck back with all its force.[21]

By the ninth century the movement had established itself firmly. From the seventh to the twelfth century the main centers were located in Baghdad, Nehavend, Basra, and Isfahan and elsewhere in Iran, and there were centers of the faith in the Holy Land and Egypt as well. Later on the movement moved its focus to the Byzantine empire, especially in the twelfth through sixteenth centuries. In the seventeenth and eighteenth centuries it moved to Poland and nearby regions, and in the nineteenth and twentieth centuries it was found in the Crimea. What makes the movement interesting is its principle: "Search thoroughly in the Torah and do not rely on my opinion," so said Anan. The Scriptures formed the sole principle of the law.

Overall, in its formative century, the Karaite Judaism formed "a conglomeration of various anti-rabbanite heresies." Exhibiting differences among themselves, they claimed that the differences proved their authenticity: "[The Rabbanites] believe that their laws and regulations have been transmitted by the prophets; if that was the case, there ought not to exist any differences of opinion among them, and the fact that such differences of opinion do exist refutes their presumptuous belief. We on the other hand arrive at our views by our reason, and reason can lead to various results."[22] The principle that predominated was that Scriptures were to be studied freely, independently, and individually.

21. Ankori, Karaites, pp. 14, 17, 21.
22. Al Kirkisani, quoted by Joseph Elijah Heller and Leon Nemoy in "Karaites," Encyclopaedia Judaica 10:766.

No uniformity of view could then emerge. Given the stress of the Judaism of the dual Torah on the authority of the Talmud and related canonical documents, we could not expect a more precise statement of the opposite view. Each party considered the other to be Jews, until the eighteenth century, but in the nineteenth century in the Russian empire they were treated as distinct from one another. Karaites took the title "Russian Karaites of the Old Testament Faith." On that account the Germans spared their lives during World War II. But after the rise of the state of Israel, the Karaites in Islamic lands moved to the state of Israel, where 7,000 of them live today.[23]

The principal doctrine that the Bible serves as the sole source of faith and law made a place for tradition. But it was to be kept subordinate. The emphasis lay not on the consensus of sages, characteristic of the Judaism of the dual Torah, but on the individual's task of finding things out for himself. Anan, the founder, said exactly that. So the doctrine balanced the principles of "rigidity and immutability of tradition" and "an absence of restrictions on individual understanding of the Scriptures."[24] The anarchy that resulted yielded ground to systemization later on. Heller and Nemoy list the four principles for the determination of the law: the literal meaning of the biblical text; the consensus of the community; the conclusions derived from Scripture by the method of logical analogy; and knowledge based on human reason and intelligence.

Apart from the rejection of the oral Torah, one would look in vain for important differences in creed. God is the sole creator, and God made the world out of nothing; God is uncreated; formless; incomparable in unity; incorporeal; unique; sent Moses and the prophets; and gave the Torah through Moses, to which there will be no further complement or alteration; the dead will be raised on a day of judgment; there is reward and punishment, providence, freedom of will, and immortality of the soul; and God will send a Messiah when Israel in exile has been purified. The followers of the oral Torah would have found themselves entirely at home in these principles of the faith. On the other hand, the calendar did distinguish the Karaites from the other Jews, since the Karaites developed their own calendar and therefore observed holy occasions on different days from those selected by the rabbanites. Some minor details of the law of ritual slaughter differed, and the rules of consanguineous marriage are more strict than those of

23. Heller and Nemoy, "Karaites," col. 777.
24. Heller and Nemoy, "Karaites," col. 777.

the rabbanites. In structure the liturgy does not vastly differ from that of the rabbanites: the Shema is recited, the Torah is read, and so on. So the fundamental point of heresy was simple: the authority of the oral tradition. The Karaites claimed that their Torah conveyed the pure faith of Moses, and the belief in a dual revelation was the point that separated them permanently from the Judaism of the dual Torah. This was made explicit in the beginning, though later on Karaites could admit, "Most of the Mishnah and the Talmud comprises genuine utterances of our fathers, and . . . our people are obligated to study the Mishnah and the Talmud." [25] But that was the issue that had led to the original division.

Heresies Against Judaism (2): Sabbateanism as a Systemic Heresy

From the perspective of our search for a theory for the entire history of Judaism, what is important about the Sabbatean movement, a seventeen-century messianic movement organized around the figure of Shabbetai Zevi, 1626–1676, [26] is a simple fact. The Sabbatean movement defined the Messiah not as a sage who kept and embodied the law, but as the very opposite. The Torah defined the framework of debate. Sabbateans responded with the Messiah as a holy man who violated the law in letter and in spirit. In positing a Messiah in the mirror image of the sage-Messiah of the Judaism of the dual Torah, the Sabbatean movement, like Karaism, paid its respects to the received system. Scholem finds the power of the movement in its link to earlier doctrines of the Jewish Kabbalah, in which the hope for the Messiah was joined to mystical religious experience, thus, in Scholem's language, "introducing a new element of tension into the Kabbalah, which was of a much more contemplative nature." The Kabbalah that took shape in the sixteenth century, associated with the name of Luria and the locale of Safed, linked the doing of the religious duties of the Torah, the recitation of prayer, and the messianic hope. Specifically, the link is drawn as follows: "All being has been in exile since the very beginning of creation and the task of restoring everything to its proper place has been given to the Jewish people, whose historic fate and destiny symbolize the state of the Universe at large. The sparks of Divinity are dispersed everywhere . . . but are held captive by . . . the power of evil and must be redeemed.

25. Heller and Nemoy, "Karaites," col. 781.
26. Gershom G. Scholem, "Shabbetai Zevi," *Encyclopaedia Judaica* 14:1219–1254. All quotations and citations are from this article.

This final redemption . . . cannot be achieved by one single messianic act, but will be effected thorough a long chain of activities that prepare the way."[27] The Jews' redemption through the messiah will serve as "external symbols of a cosmic process which in fact takes place in the secret recesses of the universe." The doctrine of the sixteenth-century Kabbalists, that the final stages of redemption were now near, made the Judaic world ready for the messianic figure who came to the fore in 1665.

Shabbetai Zevi, born in Smyrna/Ismir in 1626, mastered talmudic law and lore and enjoyed respect for his learning even among his opponents. A manic-depressive, during his manic periods he deliberately violated religious law with actions called, in the doctrine of his movement, "strange or paradoxical actions." In depressed times he chose solitude "to wrestle with the demonic powers by which he felt attacked and partly overwhelmed." During a period of wanderings in Greece and Thrace, he placed himself in active opposition to the law, declaring the commandments to be null and saying a benediction "to Him who allows what is forbidden." In this way he distinguished himself even before his meeting with the disciple who organized his movement, Nathan of Gaza. In 1665 the two met and Nathan announced to Shabbetai that the latter was the true Messiah. This independent confirmation of Shabbetai's own messianic dreams served, in Nathan's doctrine, "to explain the peculiar rank and nature of the Messiah's soul in the kabbalistic scheme of creation."[28] In May 1665, Shabbetai announced that he was the Messiah, and various communities, hearing the news, split in their response to that claim. Leading rabbis opposed him, but others took a more sympathetic view. Nathan proclaimed that the time of redemption had come. In 1666 the grand vizier offered Shabbetai Zevi the choice of accepting Islam or imprisonment and death. On 15 September 1666, Shabbetai Zevi converted to Islam.

Nathan of Gaza explained that the apostasy marked a descent of the Messiah to the realm of evil, outwardly to submit to its domination but actually to perform the last and most difficult part of his mission by conquering that realm from within.[29] The Messiah was engaged in a struggle with evil, just as in his prior actions in violating the law he had undertaken part of the labor of redemption. The apostate Messiah then formed the center of the messianic drama, meant to culminate soon in

27. Scholem, "Shabbetai Zevi," col. 1220.
28. Scholem, "Shabbetai Zevi," col. 1224.
29. Scholem, "Shabbetai Zevi," col. 1238.

the triumph. Down to his death in 1672 Shabbetai Zevi carried out his duties as a Muslim and also observed Jewish ritual. He went through alternating periods of illumination and depression, and in the former periods he founded new festivals and taught that accepting Islam involved "the Torah of grace," as against Judaism, "the Torah of truth." Scholem summarizes the doctrine as follows: "In a way, every soul is composed of the two lights, and by its nature bound predominantly to the thoughtless light which aims at destruction, and the struggle between the two lights is repeated over and over again in every soul. But the holy souls are helped by the law of the Torah, whereas the Messiah is left completely to his own devices. These ideas . . . responded precisely to the particular situation of those who believed in the mission of an apostate Messiah, and the considerable dialectical force with which they were presented did not fail to impress susceptible minds."[30] The Sabbatean movement persisted for another century or so. Some believers joined Islam and others reverted to Judaism. The main stream of followers persisted in the antinomianism of the founder and took the view that the "new spiritual or Messianic Torah entailed a complete reversal of values . . . This included all the prohibited sexual unions and incest." The story of Sabbateanism, both in the life of Shabbetai and Nathan and afterward, carries us far afield. The one consequential fact for the history of Judaism lies in the trait of the system that defined it as a heresy. The messianic doctrine that had stood at the head of the Judaism of the dual Torah—the Messiah as sage and master of the law—found as its counterpart and heretical opposite the doctrine of the Messiah as master of the law but at the same time the quintessential sinner in committing those very sins that the law designated as sinful. The Messiah, who was supposed to come to fulfil and complete the law, ended up denying it. From the viewpoint of the Judaism of the dual Torah there can have been no greater heresy than that. Only when we encounter the Judaisms of the twentieth century, wholly out of phase with the received system of the dual Torah, shall we appreciate the full power of the received system to dictate to heretical groups the terms and doctrines of their heresies, for the doctrine of the dual Torah created Karaism and the Messiah-sage defined Sabbateanism.

The Power and Pathos of Judaism

In the nineteenth century the Judaism of the dual Torah found for itself adaptations and continuations. In the twentieth century, for the first

30. Scholem, "Shabbetai Zevi," col. 1243.

time since the fourth, the same Judaism met with competition from Judaisms that defined themselves—their terms and classifications—wholly out of relationship with those of the Judaism fo the dual Torah. The new Judaisms no longer fell into the category of heresies of the received one. They asked different questions and proposed as valid, answers that had no bearing upon the issues of the dual Torah. The Judaism of the dual Torah exercised power for so long as people found its questions urgent and its answers obvious and beyond the need for argument. The same Judaism ceased to define the system for substantial communities of Jews when those questions gave way to others and those answers became irrelevant.

The power of Judaism derived from the world as it was defined by its rivals and heirs, Christianity and Islam. Christianity and Islam formulated the questions that Christianity, Judaism, and Islam would confront. The pathos of the Judaism of the dual Torah derived from its incapacity to address questions that lay totally outside of its powers of imagination. But those were the questions of the twentieth century, and no religious world view and way of life would prove able to cope with them. When humanity lost the vision of itself as having been created in the image of God, "in our image, after our likeness," then Judaism, Islam, and Christianity had to fall silent. For the great religions of Scripture took as their critical question what it meant for humanity to be in God's image, after God's likeness. The power of Judaic religious systems, like that of Christian and Islamic religious systems, were the same as the pathos of the three faiths of Abraham. Their strength—the transcendant vision of humanity—also marked their weakness: the measure of trivial humanity, there to be murdered in its masses. The death of Judaism, where it died, formed a chapter in this century's tale of civil war within humanity, first in the West in World War I, and then in the world in World War II and afterward. But our task is to tell only that small paragraph in the history of Judaism that attests to the larger meaning in the story of humanity.

Since the Judaism of the dual Torah faced significant competition only in the West,[31] let us speak of Christendom in particular as we approach modern and contemporary times. The critical Judaic compo-

31. The impact of imperialism on Judaism in the Islamic world cannot be ignored, for example, in French Algeria and Morocco. But Islam overall retained its self-evident standing as revealed truth, and the Judaism of the colonized world of Islam thrived, as did Islam. The development in the French colonies of a Francophone Israel affected only the urban middle and upper classes while the larger numbers were essentially untouched by Western secularism. Neither Reform nor Orthodoxy in their Western formulations found any counterpart in the colonial period of Islam.

nent of the Christian civilization of the West spoke of God and God's will for humanity, and what it meant to live in God's image, after God's likeness. So said the Judaism of the dual Torah and so said Christianity in its worship of God made flesh. So that message of humanity in God's image, of a people seeking to conform to God's will, found resonance in the Christian world as well: both components of the world, the Christian dough and the Judaic yeast, bore a single message about humanity.

The powerful religious traditions of the West—the Christian and the Judaic—lost their voice in the nineteenth century and their echo in the twentieth. The twentieth century raised the ineluctable issues of class and nation-state as bases for the bureaucratization of the common life. It did not ask what it meant to form one humanity in the image of one God. Asked to celebrate the image of humanity, the twentieth century created an improbable likeness of humanity: mountains of corpses. The Judaism of the dual Torah fell understandably silent when it confronted the twentieth century's framing of the inexorable question, What is Man? In such a world as this, what was there to say?

THE SECOND AGE OF DIVERSITY

Judaisms on the Modern and Contemporary Scene

from 1789 to the present

The Fall of Judaism and the Rise of Judaisms

In modern times in the West, though not in Muslim countries, the long-established system of Judaism formed in ancient days lost its paramount position. That received Judaic system built on the experience of exile and return, as it had been modified in the oral Torah to encompass the sanctification of the life of the people as the condition of the salvation of the nation at the end of time, now competed with, and even gave way to, a number of new Judaisms. Some of them stood in direct continuation with the received system, revering its canon and repeating its main points. For our theory of the history of Judaism, Reform and Orthodoxy exemplify the Judaisms of continuation. Others utterly rejected the mythic structure and system of the Judaism of the dual Torah. For our examples we take Zionism and American Judaism. These heretical systems outside of the system of the dual Torah amply demonstrate the power of the pattern of the Torah of Moses, for both of them recapitulate the same pattern of exile and return that the original system laid forth, the one explicitly, the other structurally. American Judaism, the single Judaic system most remote from the Judaism of the dual Torah simply replicated the original paradigm, in its categorical structure of "Holocaust and Redemption." And that fact presents its own puzzle, since both categories, Holocaust and Redemption, in no way conformed to the actual events of the lives and social experience of the Jews who found in those categories the meaning of their lives both individually and as an Israel.

That is why the paramount question before us is not why the re-

ceived system underwent modification, restatement, or, in some instances, total rejection in favor of discontinuous and fresh statements
altogether. Our question does not concern the myth and ritual, the
world view, and the way of life of the Judaism of the dual Torah—or
the continuity and change that affected that myth. Rather, our inquiry
addresses the power of the structure of experience and expectation that
sustained the Judaism of the dual Torah. We want to know whether and
how the new Judaisms of modern times recapitulated the experience
and viewpoint of the original Torah.

We shall find that, whether continuous with the Judaism of the dual
Torah or quite distinct from it, the Judaic systems of our age adopted as
their perspective the same pattern: exile and return, alienation and
restoration. I repeat: the single Judaism most remote from the received
tradition in its canon and in its identification of definitive experience,
American Judaism, in its deep structure of Holocaust and Redemption
repeated in acutely contemporary terms the original pattern. What
people expected to happen is what they thought happened—whether it
did or not, and whether what they thought served their interest or
violated it. When we consider religion as an independent variable, a
world-creating power on its own, we may point to American Judaism as
a stunning instance of how a religion defined what was not there and
then led to its formation and realization, not in imagination alone but
also in politics and society.

While I see no such thing as Judaism, but only Judaisms, nonetheless
there is a pattern that has tended to characterize all Judaisms. The
Judaic systems of the nineteenth and twentieth centuries followed a
pattern of suffering and atonement, in theological terms, or a dark age
followed by enlightenment, in secular and political ones, which would
not have surprised the framers of the Torah of Moses, in the aftermath
of the original experience created and recorded in the time of Ezra. But
the details would have astonished the first and founding author and in
the unfolding of Judaism God lives in the details. Orthodoxy and
Reform Judaism were new and interesting, although they made only
slight modifications in the enduring system. Zionism and American
Judaism recapitulated the original pattern in a remarkably faithful but
at the same time fresh and original formulation.

Identifying points of change in modern times presents few problems.
Under some circumstances people simply chose for themselves a set of
questions different from those that had defined the West since the
formation of Christendom in the age of Constantine. They also produced a set of self-evidently true answers. If I want to know what

people find self-evident, I have to uncover the questions they confront and cannot evade. These questions dictate the program of inquiry and the answers follow after the fact. The questions raised by the continuator Judaisms of the nineteenth century—Reform and later Orthodoxy—asked how one could be both Jewish and something else. The Judaism of the dual Torah had answered only the question of how to be Jewish. In making a place for that something else, that corner of life not affected by the labor of sanctification in the here and now aiming at salvation at the end of time, the continuator Judaisms framed in a fresh and striking way the system received from the dual Torah. The questions answered by the new Judaisms of the twentieth century—Zionism and American Judaism—were how one could survive in body and in spirit in an age of total annihilation. The answers had nothing to do with sanctification and salvation. But they conformed in an exact way to the structure of experience that had originated in the imagination of the authors of the Torah of Moses: the pattern of exile and return (Zionism) or suffering and resolution (American Judaism).

Many have speculated on the reasons for the shift in the character of Jewry in modern times from the pattern that persisted from the fourth century through the eighteenth. But an important point of change was in the realm of politics. A political change in the circumstance of the Jews in central and western Europe as well as America demanded the rethinking of the theory of who is Israel and what it means to be Israel. For the original pattern had emerged out of an essentially political problem confronting the author of the Torah of Moses, and it had settled a political question. That pattern served in subsequent settings to create a politics in the form of a powerful and definitive myth of who was Israel. Then a stunning shift in the political circumstance of a Judaism in the West, represented by the American Constitution of 1787 and the French Revolution of 1789, affected Jews' thought about perennial questions.

What happened toward the end of the eighteenth century was the secularization of political life and institutions. Earlier modes of organizing matters had recognized, as political entities, groups and guilds and classes, and the Jews had found a place among them. In the hierarchical scheme, with church and monarchy and aristocracy in their proper alignment, other political entities likewise found their location. When the church was disestablished, the monarchy rejected, and the aristocracy no longer dominant in politics, the political unit (theoretically) became the undifferentiated individual making up the nation-state. Within that theory there was no room for Israel as a political unit,

though (in theory at least) there might be room for the jewish individual, in his rightful place alongside other undifferentiated individuals.
That was the theory that produced a considerable crisis for the Judaism
of the dual Torah.

In the aftermath of the changes in Western politics in the nineteenth
century, Jews asked themselves whether and how they could be something else in addition to being Jewish. That something first invariably
found expression in the name of the locale where they lived: whether
France, Germany, Britain, or America. So could one be both Jewish and
German? The question found its answer in two givens: the received
Judaism of the dual Torah, and certain clearly defined responsibilities
imposed by "being German" or "being French."

The full force of the twentieth-century innovation of totalitarianism,
whether Soviet Communist or German Nazi, also made its imprint
upon the Judaic agenda. Where and how could the Jew endure? That
question predominated. Its self-evident answer was not among Gentiles, but only in the Jewish state. This answer produced one Judaism for
the Jews of the State of Israel and another quite different one for the
Jews of the Western democracies. But at the threshhold of the twenty-
first century it was only in the Jewish state and in the Western democracies that Jews found themselves free to ask questions and answer them
at all.

We see that sweeping changes in the political circumstances of Jews,
as well as in their economic conditions, made urgent issues that had
formerly drawn slight attention, and rendered inconsequential claims
that had for so long demanded a response. The Jews had formerly
constituted a distinct group. Now in the West they formed part of an
undifferentiated mass of citizens, all of them equal before the law and
all of them subject to the same law. The Judaism of the dual Torah had
rested on the political premise that the Jews were governed by God's law
and formed God's people. The two political premises—the one of the
nation-state and the other of the Torah—scarcely permitted a reconciliation. The consequent Judaic systems, Reform Judaism and Orthodox Judaism, had each addressed issues they regarded as acute and not
merely chronic. In the nineteenth century they had alleged that they
formed the natural next step in the unfolding of "the tradition," meaning the Judaic system of the dual Torah. The Judaic systems born in the
twentieth century did not make that claim. But nevertheless they recapitulated the pattern, familiar from the very beginning of the Torah
of Moses, that taught them what to expect and how to explain what
happened.

First was Reform Judaism, which came to expression in the early part of the nineteenth century and made changes in liturgy and then in the doctrine and the way of life of the received Judaism of the dual Torah. Reform Judaism recognized that it was legitimate to make changes and regarded change as reform. Second was the reaction to Reform Judaism called Orthodox Judaism. In many ways it was continuous with the Judaism of the dual Torah, but in some ways it was as selective of elements of that Judaism as was Reform Judaism. Third came Zionism, which to begin with was a theory and a program for responding to the failure of the promise of the nineteenth century and its politics. Finally, in the final third of the twentieth century came American Judaism, a response to the catastrophe of the destruction of the bulk of European Jewry and to the messianic expectations associated with the creation of the Jewish state: hence "Holocaust and Redemption."

Judaisms Within Judaism (1): Reform

If I had to specify the single dominant concern of the framers of Reform Judaism, I should turn to the matter of the Jews' position, beginning in the eighteenth century, in the public polity of the several Christian European countries in which they lived. From the perspective of the political changes taking place from the American and French Revolutions onward, the received system of the Judaism of the dual Torah answered irrelevant questions and did not respond to acute ones. For the issue no longer found definition in the claims of regnant Christianity. A new question, emerging from forces not contained within Christianity, demanded attention from the Jews affected by those forces. For those Jews, the change derived from shifts in political circumstances. The issue confronting the new Judaism derived not from Christianity but from political change brought about by forces of secular nationalism, which conceived of society not as the expression of God's will for the social order under the rule of Christ and his Church or his anointed king, but of the popular will for the social order under the government of the people and their elected representatives. This was a considerable shift. When society was no longer formed of distinct groups, each with its place, definition, language, and religion, but rather was formed of undifferentiated citizens (male, white, and wealthy, to be sure), then Jews in such a society needed to work out a very different sort of Judaism. The Judaism had to frame a theory of who is Israel that was consonant with the social situation of Jews who wanted to be

different, but not so different that they could not also be citizens. Both
Reform and Orthodoxy answered that question. Each rightly claimed
to continue the received tradition, that is, the Judaism of the dual Torah.
But Reform came first and answered forthrightly.

The most dramatic statement of that continuator Judaism emerged
from a meeting of Reform rabbis in 1885 in Pittsburgh. At that meeting
the American Reform rabbinate made a declaration of its definition of
Reform Judaism. To the Reform rabbis in Pittsburgh, Christianity
presented no urgent problems. The open society of America did. The
self-evident definition of the social entity, Israel, therefore had to shift.
The supernatural entity, Israel, now formed no social presence. The
Christian world, in which Christ had ruled through popes and emperors, kings had claimed divine right, and the will of the Church had
born multiform consequences for society, and in which Israel too had
been perceived in a supernatural framework—this world no longer
existed. So the world at large no longer verified that generative social
category of Israel's life, Israel as supernatural entity. And the problem of
the definition of what sort of entity Israel did constitute, of what way of
life should characterize that Israel, and what world view should explain
it—that problem produced a new set of urgent and ineluctable questions and self-evidently true answers, such as the ones stated in
Pittsburgh.

Reform Judaism forthrightly and articulately faced the political
changes that had redefined the conditions of Jews' lives and presented a
Judaism fully responsive to those changes, but still closely tied to the
inherited system of the dual Torah. For Reform Judaism in the nineteenth century, the full and authoritative statement of the system came
to expression not in Europe but in America, in an assembly of Reform
rabbis in Pittsburgh in 1885. At that meeting of the Central Conference
of American Rabbis, the Reform Judaism of the age, by now about a
century old, took up the issues that divided the Judaism and made an
authoritative statement on them that most people could accept.

The very fact that this Judaism could conceive of such a process of
debate and formulation of a kind of creed tells us that this Judaism
found urgent the specification of its systemic structure. It is also testimony to its mature and self-aware frame of mind. In the antecedent
thousand years of the Judaism of the dual Torah we look in vain for
equivalent convocations to set public policy. When statements of the
world view emerged in diverse expressions of the received system, they
did not take the form of a rabbis' platform and did not come about
through democratic debate on pubic issues. The world view percolated
upward and represented a rarely articulated and essentially inchoate

consensus about how things really were and should have been. The contrast tells us not merely that reform Judaism represented a new Judaism but also that the methods and approaches of Reform Judaism enjoyed their own self-evident appropriateness. And from that we learn how the qualities people found self-evidently right had changed over time.

The American Reform rabbis thus issued a clear and accessible statement of their Judaism. We want to know one thing in particular about this Judaism: its formulation of the issue of Israel as political circumstances defined it. For critical to the Judaism of the dual Torah was its view of Israel as God's people, a supernatural polity, living out its social existence under God's Torah. That basic conception engendered the way of life—one of sanctification—and the world view, one of persistent reference to the Torah for both the rules of conduct and the explanation of conduct. The Pittsburgh platform stated:

> We recognize in the Mosaic legislation a system of training the Jewish people for its mission during its national life in Palestine, and today we accept as binding only its moral laws and maintain only such ceremonies as elevate and sanctify our lives, but reject all such as are not adapted to the views and habits of modern civilization. We hold that all such Mosaic and rabbinical laws as regular diet, priestly purity, and dress originated in ages and under the influence of ideas entirely foreign to our present mental and spiritual state . . . Their observance in our days is apt rather to obstruct than to further modern spiritual elevation . . . We recognize in the modern era of universal culture of heart and intellect the approaching of the realization of Israel's great messianic hope for the establishment of the kingdom of truth, justice, and peace among all men. We consider ourselves no longer a nation but a religious community and therefore expect neither a return to Palestine nor a sacrificial worship under the sons of Aaron nor the restoration of any of the laws concerning the Jewish state.

I cannot imagine a more forthright address to the age. The Pittsburgh platform took each component of the system in turn. Who is Israel? What is its way of life? How does it account for its existence as a distinct, and distinctive, group? Israel was once a nation, but today is not a nation. It once had a set of laws to regulate diet, clothing, and the like. These no longer apply, because Israel now is not what it was then. Israel forms an integral part of Western civilization. The reason to persist as a distinctive group was that the group had its work to do, namely, to realize the messianic hope for the establishment of a kingdom of truth, justice, and peace. For that purpose Israel no longer constituted a nation. It now formed a religious community.

What that meant was that individual Jews lived as citizens in other

nations. Difference was acceptable at the level of religion, not nationality, a position that fully accorded with the definition of citizenship for
the Western democracies. The world view laid heavy emphasis on an
as-yet unrealized but coming perfect age. The way of life admitted to no
important traits that distinguished Jews from others, since morality
forms a universal category that is applicable in the same way to everyone. The theory of Israel formed the heart of matters, and what we
learn is that Israel constituted a "we." The Jews continued to form a
group that, by its own indicators, held together and constituted a cogent
social entity. It was also a truth declared rather than discovered, and the
self-evidence of the truth of the statements competed with the self-
awareness characteristic of those who made them. For they recognized
the problem that demanded attention: the reframing of a theory of
Israel. No more urgent question faced the rabbis, because they lived in a
century of opening horizons, in which people could envision perfection.
World War I would change all that, also for Israel. By 1937 the Reform
rabbis, meeting in Columbus, Ohio, would reframe the system, expressing a world view quite different from that of the half century before.

Let us summarize the program of urgent issues and self-evident
responses that constituted the first and most important of the new
Judaisms of the nineteenth century. Questions we find answered fall
into two categories: first, why "we" do not keep certain customs and
ceremonies but do keep others; second, how "we relate to the nations in
which we live." So the system of Reform Judaism explained both why
and why not, the mark of a fully framed and cogent Judaism. The
affirmative side covered why the Jews would persist as a separate group,
and the negative side accounted for the limits of difference. These two
questions deal with the same urgent problem: working out a mode of
Judaic existence compatible with citizenship in America. Jews did not
propose to eat or dress in distinctive ways. They sought a place within
"modern spiritual elevation . . . universal culture of heart and intellect."
They imputed to that culture the realization of "the messianic hope."
And, explicitly the Jews no longer constituted a nation, but belonged to
some other nation(s). If I had to specify a single self-evident proposition
taken fully into account by this Judaism it is that political change had
changed the entirety of "Judaism," but that Judaism had the power to
accommodate to that change. So change formed the method for dealing
with the problem, which was change in the political and social standing
the Jews had enjoyed. So Reform Judaism formed a Judaic system that
confronted immense political change and presented a world view and
way of life to an Israel redefined by the change. The Reformers main-

tained that change was all right because historical precedent had proved that change was all right. But change had long defined the constant in the on-going life of the Judaism of the dual Torah.

The Reformers made much of change in liturgy. And they were right, but for the wrong reasons. The mythic being of the received liturgy had entailed the longing, in the imagination of the nation, for a return to Zion, for the rebuilding of the Temple, and for reconstitution of the bloody rites of animal sacrifice. These political propositions had formed a critical plank in the response to the Christian view that Israel's salvation had occurred in times past and had ended with Israel's rejection of the Christhood of Jesus. In response, the dual Torah had insisted on future salvation, at the end of time. For ages from the original exile in 586 B.C., the Jews had appealed to a Scripture that explained why they had lost their land, their city, their temple, and their cult, and told them what they had to do to get them back. Jews knew who they were. They were a nation in exile. So when the early changes included rewording the liturgy so as to diminish the motifs of the return to Zion and restoration of the cult, they signaled that much else had already undergone revision and that more would have to change as well. Reform ratified change already a generation old, proposed to cope with it, and reframed and revised the received tradition so as to mark out new outlines for self-evident truth.

For the nineteenth-century Jews of the West, the urgent problem was to define Israel in an age in which individual Jews had become something else, in addition to being Israel. Was Israel a nation? No, Israel did not fall into the same category as the nations. Jews were multiple beings: Israel in one dimension, part of France or Germany or America in another. But if Israel was not a nation, then what of the way of life that had made the nation different, and what of the world view that had made sense of the way of life? These now formed the questions people could not avoid. The answers constituted Reform Judaism.

Judaisms Within Judaism (2): Orthodoxy

Orthodox Judaism is the Judaic system that mediates between the received Judaism of the dual Torah and the requirements of living a life integrated in modern circumstances. Orthodoxy maintains the world view of the received dual Torah, constantly citing its sayings and adhering with only trivial variations to the bulk of its norms for everyday life. At the same time Orthodoxy holds that Jews adhering to the dual Torah do not have to wear distinctively Jewish clothing; may live within a

common economy and need not practice distinctively Jewish profes-
sions and may take up a life not readily distinguished from the life lived
by people in general. So for Orthodoxy a portion of Israel's life may
prove secular, in that the Torah does not dictate and so sanctify all
details under all circumstances. Since the Judaism of the dual Torah
presupposed not only the supernatural entity, Israel, but also a way of
life that in important ways distinguished that supernatural entity from
the social world at large, the power of Orthodoxy to find an accommodation for Jews who valued the received way of life and world view
and also planned to make their lives in an essentially integrated social
world proves formidable. The difference between Orthodoxy and the
system of the dual Torah therefore comes to expression in social policy:
integration, however circumscribed, versus the total separation of the
holy people.

Orthodoxy as an articulated system with its own organizations and
social policy came into existence in mid-nineteenth-century Germany
in response to Reform Judaism. It answered the same questions but gave
different answers. Reform maintained that, because the Jews no longer
constituted the holy people living its own distinct existence, but rather a
religious group that was part of a larger nation state, the distinctive way
of life had to go. Orthodoxy held that the Torah made provision for
areas of life in which a Jew could be something other than a Jew. In
education, for example, the institutions of the Judaism of the dual
Torah had commonly held that one should study Torah alone. Orthodoxy in the West included secular sciences in its curriculum as well. The
Judaism of the dual Torah had ordinarily identified particular forms of
dress as Judaic. Orthodoxy did not. In these and in other ways Orthodoxy formed a fresh statement of the Judaism of the dual Torah, and
what made that statement distinctive is that it provided for a life lived
legitimately outside of the Judaic one, as long as it never violated its
norms. Adhering to the received system of the dual Torah differed from
identifying with Orthodox Judaism mainly with respect to indicators
such as clothing, language, and above all, education.

When Jews kept the law of the Torah as it dictated food choices and
keeping the Sabbath, but sent their children to secular schools or in
Jewish schools included in the curriculum subjects outside of the Torah,
they crossed the boundary between the received Judaism and the new
Judaism of Orthodoxy. For the notion that science or German or Latin
or philosophy deserved serious study, while not alien to important
exemplars of the received system of the dual Torah, in the nineteenth
century struck as wrong those for whom the received system remained

self-evidently right. Those Jews did not send their children to Gentile schools, and in Jewish schools they did not include in the curriculum anything other than Torah study.

The Reformers held that Judaism could change, and that Judaism was a product of history. The Orthodox opponents denied that Judaism could change and insisted that Judaism derived from God's will at Sinai and was not historical and man-made but eternal and supernatural. In these two convictions, of course, the Orthodox recapitulated the convictions of the received system. But in their appeal to the traditional, they found some components of that system more persuasive than others. In their articulation of the view that Judaism formed a religion to be seen as distinct and autonomous of politics and society, they entered the same world of self-conscious belief that the Reformers had also explored.

In a sense, Orthodoxy was precipitated by Reform Judaism. The term Orthodoxy itself—though not the organized Judaism—first surfaced in 1795, and covers all Jews who believe that God revealed the dual Torah at Sinai and that Jews must carry out the requirements of Jewish law contained in the Torah as interpreted by the sages through time. Obviously, so long as that position struck Jewry at large as self-evident, Orthodoxy as a distinct and organized Judaism did not exist. It did not have to. Two events took place together: first, the recognition of the received system as Orthodoxy; second, the specification of the received system as religion.

The former of the two events came first: the view that the received system was "traditional" and "Orthodox." The identification of truth as tradition came about when the received system met the challenge of competing Judaisms. Then, in behalf of the received way of life and world view addressed to supernatural Israel, people said that the Judaism of the dual Torah had been established of old, and it was the only way of seeing and doing things, it was how things had been and should be naturally and normally: tradition. But tradition is a category that contains within itself an alternative, namely change, as in "tradition and change."

It is when the system lost its power of self-evidence that it entered the classification of tradition. And that came about when Orthodoxy met head-on the challenge of change become Reform. We understand why the category of tradition became critical to the framers of Orthodoxy when we examine the counterclaim. Just as the Reformers justified change, the Orthodox theologians denied that change was ever possible. Walter Wurzburger says: "Orthodoxy looks upon attempts to adjust Judaism to the 'spirit of the time' as utterly incompatible with the

entire thrust of normative Judaism which holds that the revealed will of
God rather than the values of any given age are the ultimate standard."[1]
The issue important to the Reformers was the value of what was called
"Emancipation," meaning the provision of civil rights to Jews. This
issue defined the debate. Orthodoxy took up the issue precisely as the
other side had framed it. When the Reform Judaic theologians took a
wholly one-sided position of affirming Emancipation, Orthodox theologians adopted the contrary view and denied its importance. If Reform
made minor changes in liturgy and its conduct, Orthodoxy rejected
even these that might have found acceptance under other circumstances. Saying prayers in the vernacular, for example, provoked strong
opposition. But everyone knew that the prayers said in Aramaic were in
the vernacular of the earlier age. The Orthodox thought that these
changes were not reforms at all and represented only the first step of a
process leading Jews out of the Judaic world altogether. As Wurzburger
says, "The slightest tampering with tradition was condemned."

If we ask where the received system of the dual Torah prevailed and
by contrast where Orthodoxy came to full expression, we may follow
the spreading out of railway lines, the growth of new industry, the shifts
in political status accorded to Jews and other citizens the changes in the
educational system and the entire process of change, political, economic
and social, demographic and cultural. Where the changes came first,
Reform Judaism met them in its way and Orthodoxy in its way. Where
change came later in the century, as in the case of Russian Poland, the
eastern provinces of the Austro-Hungarian Empire, and Russia itself,
there, in villages contentedly following the old ways, the received system endured. And in the age of mass migration from Eastern Europe to
America and other Western democracies, those who experienced the
upheaval of leaving home and country met the challenge of change by
either accepting new ways of seeing things or in full self-awareness
reaffirming the familiar ones: Reform or Orthodoxy. We may characterize the received system as a way of life and world view wedded to an
ancient peoples' homelands, the villages and small towns of central and
eastern Europe. Orthodoxy was the heir of the received system as it
came to expression in the towns and cities of central and western
Europe and America. That rule of thumb allows us to distinguish
between the piety of a milieu and the theological conviction of a self-
conscious community.

When, therefore, we explain the beginnings of Reform Judaism, by

1. *Encyclopaedia Judaica,* col. 1487.

reference to political and economic change, we also understand the point of origin of distinct and organized Orthodoxy. The beginnings of Orthodoxy took place in the areas where Reform made its way, hence in Germany and in Hungary. In Germany, where Reform attracted the majority of many Jewish communities, the Orthodox faced a challenge indeed. Critical to the Orthodox theologians' conviction was the notion that Israel, all of the Jews, bore responsibility to carry out the law of the Torah. But in the hands of the Reform the community's institutions did not obey the law of the Torah as the Orthodox understood it. So in the end Orthodoxy took the step that marked it as a self-conscious Judaism. Orthodoxy separated from the established community altogether. The Orthodox set up their own organization and seceded from the community at large. The next step altogether prohibited Orthodox from participating in non-Orthodox organizations. Isaac Breuer, a leading theologian of Orthodoxy, ultimately took the position that "refusal to espouse the cause of separation was interpreted as being equivalent to the rejection of the absolute sovereignty of God."[2]

The matter of accommodating to the world at large did not allow for so easy an answer as mere separation. The specific issue—integration or segregation—concerned preparation for life in the larger politics and economic life of the country. That meant secular education, involving not only language and science, but also history and literature, matters of values. Orthodoxy proved diverse, with two wings to be distinguished. One rejected secular learning as well as all dealing with non-Orthodox Jews. The other cooperated with non-Orthodox and secular Jews and accepted the value of secular education. That position in no way affected loyalty to the law of Judaism—belief in God's revelation of the one whole Torah at Sinai. The point at which the received system and the Orthodox split requires specification. In concrete terms we know the one from the other by their evaluation of secular education. Proponents of the received system never accommodated themselves to secular education, while the Orthodox in Germany and Hungary persistently affirmed it. That represented a remarkable shift, since the study of Torah—Torah, not philosophy—was central to the received system of the dual Torah.

Explaining where we find the one and the other, Katzburg works with the distinction we have already made, between an unbroken system and one that has undergone a serious caesura with the familiar condition of the past. He states:

2. *Encyclopaedia Judaica,* col. 1488.

In Eastern Europe until World War I, Orthodoxy preserved without a break its traditional ways of life and the time-honored educational framework. In general, the mainstream of Jewish life was identified with Orthodoxy, while Haskalah [Jewish Enlightenment, which applied to the Judaic setting the skeptical attitudes of the French Enlightenment] and secularization were regarded as deviations. Hence there was no ground wherein a Western type of Orthodoxy could take root. . . . European Orthodoxy in the 19th and the beginning of the 20th centuries was significantly influenced by the move from small settlements to urban centers . . . as well as by emigration. Within the small German communities there was a kind of popular Orthodoxy, deeply attached to tradition and to local customs, and when it moved to the large cities this element brought with it a vitality and rootedness to Jewish tradition.[3]

Katzburg's observations provide important guidance. He authoritatively defines the difference between Orthodoxy and tradition. So he tells us how to distinguish the received system, accepted as self-evident, from an essentially selective and therefore by definition new system, called Orthodoxy. In particular he tells us how to distinguish the one from the other; he tells us where to find the self-conscious affirmation of tradition that characterizes Orthodoxy but that did not occur in the world of the dual Torah as it glided in its eternal orbit of the seasons and of unchanging time.

I find it difficult to imagine what the urban Orthodox might have done otherwise. They experienced change, they daily encountered Jews unlike themselves, and they no longer lived in that stable Judaic society in which the received Torah had formed the given of life. Pretense that Jews faced no choices scarcely represented a possibility. Nor did the generality of the Jews in the West propose to preserve a separate language or to renounce political rights. So Orthodoxy made its peace with change, no less than did Reform. The educational program that led Jews out of the received culture of the dual Torah, the use of the vernacular, the acceptance of political rights, the renunciation of Jewish garments, education for women, abolition of the power of the community to coerce the individual—these and many other originally Reform positions characterized the Orthodoxy that emerged in the nineteenth century as another new Judaism.[4]

If we ask how new the Orthodox system was we find ambiguous answers. In conviction, in way of life, and in world view, we may hardly call it new at all. For the bulk of its substantive positions found ample

3. Katzburg, *Encyclopaedia Judaica*, "Orthodoxy," col. 1490.
4. Samet, *Encyclopaedia Judaica*, "Neo-Orthodoxy," col. 957.

precedent in the received dual Torah. From its affirmation of God's revelation of a dual Torah to its acceptance of the detailed authority of the law and customs, from its strict observance of the law to its unwillingness to change a detail of public worship, Orthodoxy rightly pointed to its strong links with the chain of tradition. But Orthodoxy constituted a sect within the Jewish group. Its definition of the Israel to whom it wished to speak hardly coincides with the definition characteristic of the dual Torah. The Judaism of the dual Torah addressed all Jews, and Orthodoxy recognized that it could not do so. But Orthodoxy acquiesced in a situation that lay beyond the imagination of the framers of the Judaism of the dual Torah.

To claim that the Orthodox went in search of proof texts for a system formed and defined in advance misrepresents the reality—but not by much. For once the system of a self-conscious and deliberate Orthodoxy took shape, much picking and choosing and assigning of priorities to some things over others would follow naturally. And the result was the same: a new system with a way of life much like the received one but readily differentiated; a world view congruent to the received one, but with its own points of interest and emphasis; and above all a social referent, an Israel quite beyond the limits of the one posited by the dual Torah.

The distinction between religious and secular was lost on the received system of the dual Torah, which legislated for matters we should today regard as entirely secular or neutral, for example the institutions of state (king, priest, army). We have already noted that in the received system as it took shape in eastern and central Europe, Jews wore garments regarded as distinctively Jewish. Some important traits of these garments indeed derived from the Torah. Jews pursued sciences that only Jews studied, for instance, the Talmud and its commentaries. In these and other ways the Torah encompassed all of the life of Israel, the holy people. The recognition that Jews were like others and that the Torah fell into a category into which other and comparable matters fell—that recognition was long in coming.

For Christians in Germany and other Western countries it had become a commonplace to see religion as distinct from other components of the social and political system. While the Church in Russia identified with the Tsarist state, or the church in Poland with the national aspirations of the Polish people, in Germany two churches, Catholic and Protestant, competed. The terrible wars of the Reformation in the sixteenth and seventeenth centuries, which had ruined Germany, had led to the uneasy compromise that the prince might chose the religion of his principality. From that self-aware choice, people understood that "the way of life and world view" in fact constituted a religion, and that one religion might be compared with another. By the nineteenth century, moreover, the separation of church and state ratified the important distinction between religion, where difference would be tolerated, and the secular, where citizens were pretty much the same.

In the West political consciousness reached the Judaic world only in the late eighteenth century for some intellectuals and in the nineteenth century for many others. There was a fundamental shift in the understanding and interpretation of the Torah. Among Orthodox as much as among Reform it was now seen as "Judaism," an -ism along with other -isms. The creative power of the Jews who formed the Orthodox Judaic system was marked by their capacity to shift the fundamental category in which they framed their system. The basic shift in category is what made Orthodoxy a Judaism on its own, and not simply a restatement of the received system of the dual Torah.

The received system, giving expression to the rules of sanctification of the holy people had entailed wearing Jewish clothing, speaking a Jewish language, and learning only, or mainly, Jewish sciences. But clothing, language, and education now fell into the category of the secular, while other equally important aspects of everyday life remained in the category of the sacred. As it came into existence in Germany and other Western countries Orthodox Judaism therefore found it possible to accept the language, clothing, and learning of those countries by recognizing the category of the secular. And these matters serve openly to exemplify a larger acceptance of Gentile ways, not all, but enough to lessen the differences between the Holy People and the nations. Political change of a profound order presented to Orthodox Jews the problem of how to separate and how to integrate. For Orthodox Jews as well as Reform Jews the answers required picking and choosing. Both Judaisms understood that some things were sacred while others were not. That understanding marked off these Judaisms from the system of the dual Torah.

Once the category shift had taken place, the difference was to be measured in degree, not kind. For Orthodox Jews maintained distinctive political beliefs that Reform Jews rejected: in the future coming of the Messiah and the reconstitution of the Jewish nation in its own land. But, by placing these convictions in the distant future, the Orthodox Jews nonetheless prepared for a protracted interim of life within the nation where they lived. Like the Reform they were different from their fellow citizens in religion, not in nationality as represented by citizenship. Orthodoxy, as much as Reform, signaled remarkable changes in the Jews' political situation and—more important—aspirations. They wanted to be different, but not so different as the received system would have made them.

Still, in its nineteenth-century formulation Orthodoxy laid claim to carry forward, in continuous and unbroken relationship the tradition. That claim assuredly demanded a serious hearing, for the things that Orthodoxy taught, the way of life it required, the Israel to whom it spoke, and the doctrines it said had been revealed by God to Moses at Sinai—all of these conformed more or less exactly to the system of the received Judaism of the dual Torah as people then knew. Is it not what it says it is, "just Judaism"? Yes, but "Judaism," Orthodox or otherwise, is not "Torah." Piety selected is by definition piety invented, and the theologians of Orthodoxy were a group of intellectually powerful creators of a Judaism. Their ideal, which they expressed as "Torah and secular learning," defined a new world view, dictated a new way of life, and addressed an Israel different from the Judaism of the dual Torah. To those who receive the dual Torah as self-evident, what the Torah did not accommodate was secular learning. As they received it the Torah did not approve changes in the familiar way of life, and did not know an Israel other than the one at hand. So the perfect faith of Orthodoxy sustained a wonderfully selective piety.

The Twentieth Century and Its Judaisms

Zionism was founded in the World Zionist Organization, created in Basel in 1897. American Judaism in the Zionist formulation came to powerful expression in the aftermath of the 1967 War in the Middle East. Both Judaic systems answered profoundly political questions. Their agendas attended to the status of the Jews as a group (Zionism and American Judaism) and the definition of the Jews in the context of larger political and social change (Zionism). It follows that the urgent questions addressed by the twentieth-century Judaisms differed in kind from those found acute in the nineteenth century. In the twentieth century, powerful forces for social and economic change took political form, in movements meant to shape government to the interests of particular classes or groups—the working classes or racial or ethnic entities, for instance. The Judaic systems of the century responded in kind.

In that same century the definition of citizenship, encompassing ethnic and genealogical traits, presented the Jews with the problem of how they were to find a place in a nation-state that understood itself in an exclusionary, racist way—whether Nazi Germany of nationalist Poland or Hungary or Rumania or revanchist and irredentist France. Zionism declared the Jews "a people, one people," and proposed as its purpose the creation fo the Jewish State. Later on, in the 1960s, shifting currents in American politics—a renewed ethnicism and an emphasis on intrinsic traits of birth rather than ones of ability—called into question Jews' identification with the democratic system of America as that system defined permissible difference. A Jewish ethnicism, counterpart to the search for roots among diverse ethnic groups, responded with a tale of Jewish uniqueness—unique suffering and unique Jewish ethnic salvation and redemption in the Jewish State. These movements addressed political questions and responded with essentially political programs. Zionism wanted to create a Jewish state, but American Judaism wanted the Jews to form an active political community on their own.

These Judaisms are not at all like the ones that were formulated in the nineteenth century. That is for two reasons. First of all, on the surface the Judaic systems of the twentieth century took up political, social, and economic, but not theological questions. Second, while the nineteenth-century Judaisms addressed issues peculiar to Jews, the matters of public policy of the twentieth-century Judaic systems concerned everyone, not only Jews. So none of the Judaisms of the twentieth century proves congruent in each detail of structure to the continuator-Judaisms of the nineteenth. All of the new Judaisms intersected with comparable systems among other Europeans and Americans. American ethnic assertion is the genus and American Judaism the species. Accordingly, we move from a set of Judaisms that form species of a single genus—the Judaism of the dual Torah—to a set of Judaisms that have less in common among themselves than they do between themselves and systems wholly autonomous of Judaic world views and ways of life. The reason is clear. The issues addressed by the Judaisms of the twentieth century and the crises that made those issues urgent did not affect Jews alone or mainly. The common crises derived from the reorganization of political entities, which formed the foundation of nationalism and also Zionism; and from the reconsideration of the theory of American society, which produced, along with the total homogenization of American life, renewed interest in ethnic origins as well as American Judaism. So while the nineteenth-century Judaisms took their perspective from the dual Torah, Jews in the twentieth century had other things on their minds.

It is therefore not surprising that the Judaisms we consider now not only rejected propositions that were important in the Judaism of the dual Torah, as did Karaism and Sabbateanism but they also defined themselves out of relationship with the categories and propositions of the received Judaism. Asking their own questions and answering them out of resources of their own choosing, they took shape more than a century after the initial separation of Reform and Orthodoxy from the received system of the dual Torah. The farther we find ourselves from that original point of departure, the more attenuated become the links to that system. The two twentieth-century systems laid no claim to continue the Judaism of the dual Torah, in no way placed themselves in relationship to it, and implicitly denied all relevance to that Judaism. So in fact they formed heresies that in no way exhibited the claim or the mark of continuity. As a matter of form or convention each claimed antecedents or even precedents, and all adduced proof texts. But we find a new set of questions, a new body of proof texts, and above all a new definition of imperatives confronting the Jews as a group.

The systems of the twentieth century, represented by Zionism and American Judaism, were discontinuous with the received system and found no urgency in such a self-conscious accounting, but treated their several compositions—world views and ways of life, addressed to an identified Israel—as essentially self-evident. Appealing to fully formed systems of their own, the new Judaisms went in search not of the proof texts, whether in literature or in history, which had been so critical to the Reform, Orthodox, and Conservative theologians, but of mere pre-texts: rhetoric to conform to an available program. But the search enjoyed its own justification. Zionism and American Judaism did recapitulate what was essential in the texts in which they searched for validation. For both Judaisms took as the given precisely the pattern of the original Torah: Israel is special, the Land is held on condition, Israel's suffering bears meaning, and its salvation is promised and awaits fulfilment on account of what Israel will do.

The principal difference between the extrasystemic heresies of Zionism and American Judaism (as a system of Holocaust and Redemption) and the continuator Judaisms of Reform and Orthodoxy derives once more from the facts of the Jews' political circumstance. This is a critical point of difference and demands some attention. Reform and Orthodoxy by all definitions fall into the category of religion. Zionism and American Judaism constitute political movements, focused upon political programs. They address an essentially political agenda, although both evoke myths, attitudes and convictions commonly categorized as religious.

The Judaisms of the nineteenth century have a single point of origin in common. All of them take form in the world of intellectuals. All focus upon issues of doctrine and regard as important the specification of why people should do what they do, and how Israel within their several definitions should see the world and live life. The Judaisms of the twentieth century address questions not of intellect but of public policy. They regard as important not ideology, which they identify with propaganda, nor theology, which lies beyond their imagination altogether, but collective action. That action works itself out through large-scale institutions of government, politics, and economics. In the categories of charisma and routine, of individual initiative through intellectual charisma and collective action through bureaucracy, the nineteenth century was the age of Judaisms of intellect, and the twentieth, of bureaucracy. For the Judaisms of the twentieth century all took shape in a world that required the gifts not of intellectuals (though the founders all were persons of substantial intellect and vision) but of organizers, people who could create large-scale institutions and organizations: unions, bureaucracies, and even (in Zionism) entire governments. What mattered to nineteenth-century Judaisms demanded the genius of individual minds: writers, scholars, and theologians. The reason for the shift stands near at hand: the urgent issues of the nineteenth century demanded attention to doctrine and individual deed: What should I think? What should I do? The critical concerns of the twentieth century focused upon public policy: How shall we survive? where should we go? So the Judaisms of an age testified to the character and quality of the age. Jews could evade the intellectual issues of the nineteenth century, but the world forced the political crises of the twentieth on their attention. And that accounts for the difference between the one type of system and the other.

Heresies Outisde of Judaism (1): Zionism

Zionism constituted the Jews' movement of self-emancipation, responding to the failure fo the nations' promises of Jewish emancipation. It framed its world view and way of life for the Israel of its definition, in response to a political crisis, the failure, by the end of the nineteenth century, of the promises of political improvement in the Jews' status and condition. Zionism called the Jews to emancipate themselves by facing the fact that Gentiles in the main hated Jews. Founding a Jewish state where Jews could free themselves of anti-Semitism and build their own destiny, the Zionist system of Judaism declared as its world view this simple proposition: the Jews form a people, one people, and should transform themselves into a political entity and build a Jewish state.

Zionism came into existence at the end of the nineteenth century with the founding of the Zionist Organization in 1897, and reached its fulfilment, and dissolution in its original form, with the founding of the state of Israel in May 1948. Zionism began with the definition of its theory of Israel: a people, one people, in a secular sense. Then came the world view, which composed of the diverse histories of Jews a single, singular history of the Jewish people, leading from the land of Israel in exile back to the land of Israel. This component of the Zionist world view constituted an exact recapitulation of the biblical narrative, even though it derived not from a religious but from a nationalist perspective. The way of life of the elitist or activist required participation in meetings, organizing within the local community, and attendance at national and international conferences—a focus of life's energy on the movement. Later, as settlement in Israel itself became possible, Zionism defined migration to the land of Israel as the most noble way of living life, and for the Socialist wing of Zionism, building a collective community (kibbutz). So Zionism presented a complete and fully articulated Judaism, and prior to its complete success in the creation of the state of Israel in 1948, one of the most powerful and effective of them all.[5]

It is self-evident that in Zionism we deal with a response to an essentially political situation. In modern times the word Zionism came into use in the 1890s, in the sense of a political movement of Jewish self-emancipation. The word "emancipation" had earlier stood for the Jews receiving the political rights of citizens in various nations. This self-emancipation turned on its head the entire political program of nineteenth-century Jewry. That shift alerts us to the relationship between Zionism and the earlier political changes of which Reform Judaism had made so much at the start of the century. What had happened in the course of the nineteenth century to shift discourse from emancipation to self-emancipation was two things: first, the disappointment with the persistence of anti-Semitism in the West; second, the disheartening failure to attain political rights in the East.

Jews therefore began to conclude that they would have to attain emancipation on their own terms and through their own efforts. The stress on Zionism as a political movement, however, came specifically from Theodor Herzl, a Viennese journalist who, in response to the recrudescence of anti-Semitism he witnessed in covering the Dreyfus trial in Paris, discovered the Jewish problem and proposed its solution. To be sure, Herzl had earlier given thought to the problem of anti-

5. The Zionism of the post-1948 period faced a different set of issues and is not under discussion here.

Semitism, and the public anti-Semitism that accompanied the degradation of Dreyfus marked merely another stage in the development of his
ideas. What Herzl contributed in the beginning was the notion that the
Jews all lived in a single situation, wherever they were located. So they
should live in a single country, in their own state. Anti-Semitism
formed the antithesis of Zionism, and anti-Semites, growing in strength
in European politics, would assist the Jews in building their state and
thereby also solve their "Jewish problem."

The solution entailed the founding of a Jewish state. That formed a
wholly new conception, with its quite particular world view, and with
its rather concrete and detailed program for the conduct of the life of
the Jews. For the Jews were now to become something that they had not
been for the two thousand years of which Zionism persistently spoke: a
political entity. The Judaism of the dual Torah had made no provision
for a this-worldly politics, and no political tradition had sustained itself
during the long period in which that Judaism had absorbed within
itself and transformed all other views and modes of life. In founding the
Zionist Organization in Basel in 1897, Herzl said that he had founded
the Jewish state, and that in a half century the world would know it, as
indeed the world did.

Three main streams of theory flowed abundantly and side by side in
the formative decades. One, represented by Ahad HaAm, laid stress on
Zion as a spiritual center, to unite all parts of the Jewish people. Ahad
HaAm and his associates laid emphasis on spiritual preparation, ideological and cultural activities, and the long-term intellectual issues of
persuading the Jews of the Zionist premises.[6] Another stream, the
political one maintained from the beginning that the Jews should provide for the emigration of the masses of their nation from Eastern
Europe, then entering a protracted stage of political disintegration and
already long suffering from economic dislocation, to the land of
Israel—or somewhere, anywhere. Herzl in particular placed the requirement for legal recognition of a Jewish state over the location of the
state, and in doing so he set forth the policy that the practical salvation
of the Jews through political means would form the definition of
Zionism. Herzl stressed that the Jewish state would come into existence
in the forum of international politics.[7] The instruments of state—a
political forum, a bank, a mode of national allegiance, a press, and a

6. S. Ettinger, "Hibbat Zion," in "Zionism," Encyclopaedia Judaica 16:1031–1178.
Ettinger cited in col. 1041.
7. Arthur Hertzberg, "Ideological Evolution," in "Zionism," Encyclopaedia Judaica
16:1044–1045.

central body and leader—came into being in the aftermath of the first
Zionist congress in Basel. Herzl spent the rest of his life—less than a
decade—seeking an international charter and recognition of the Jewish
state. A third stream of theory derived from Socialism and expressed a
Zionist vision of Socialism, or a Socialist vision of Zionism. The Jewish
state was to be socialist, as indeed it was for its first three decades. In its
earlier theoretical formulation (before its near-total bureaucratization),
Social Zionism emphasized that a proletarian Zionism would define the
arena for the class struggle within the Jewish people to be realized. The
Socialist Zionists predominated in the settlement of the land of Israel
and controlled the political institutions for three-quarters of a century.
They founded the labor unions, the large-scale industries, and the
health institutions and organizations. They created the press and the
nascent army—the nation. No wonder that for the first quarter-
century after independence, the Socialist Zionists made all the decisions
and controlled everything.

The Zionism that functioned as a Judaism draws our attention to the
movement. In this regard Ahad HaAm made the explicit claim that
Zionism would succeed Judaism (meaning the Judaism of the dual
Torah). Arthur Hertzberg states:

> The function that revealed religion had performed in talmudic and medi-
> eval Judaism, that of guaranteeing the survival of the Jews as a separate entity
> because of their belief in the divinely ordained importance of the Jewish
> religion and people, it was no longer performing and could not be expected to
> perform. The crucial task facing Jews in the modern era was to devise new
> structures to contain the separate individuality of the Jews and to keep them
> loyal to their own tradition. This analysis of the situation implied . . . a view of
> Jewish history which Ahad HaAm produced as undoubted . . . , that the Jews
> in all ages were essentially a nation and that all other factors profoundly
> important to the life of this people, even religion, were mainly instrumental
> values.[8]

Hertzberg contrasts that statement with one made by Saadiah in the
tenth century: "The Jewish people is a people only for the sake of its
Torah." That statement of the position of the Judaism of the dual Torah
contrasts with the one of Zionism and allows us to set the one against
the other. Each can be classified as a Judaism. For each proposed to
answer the same types of questions, and the answers provided by each
enjoyed the same status of not mere truth but fact, and not mere fact but
the just and right and appropriate fact.

8. Hertzberg, "Ideological Evolution," col. 1046.

As a Judaism entirely out of phase with the received system of the dual Torah, Zionism enunciated a powerful doctrine of Israel. The Jews form a people, one people. What made them one people and validated their claim to a state of their own was the central theme of the Zionist world view. No facts of perceived society validated that view. Except for a common fate the Jews in no way formed one people. True, in Judaic systems they commonly did. But the Judaic system of the dual Torah and its continuators imputed to Israel a supernatural status, a mission, a calling, and a purpose. Zionism did not: the Jews were one people— that was all.

Zionist theory had the task of explaining how the Jews formed one people, and Zionist theory solved that problem in the study of Jewish history, read as a single and unitary story. The Jews all came from one place, had traveled together, and were going back to that same place as one people. Zionist theory therefore derived strength from the study of history, much as had Reform Judaism, and in time generated a great renaissance of Judaic studies as the scholarly community of the nascent Jewish state took up the task at hand. The sort of history that emerged took the form of factual and descriptive narrative. But its selection of facts, its recognition of problems requiring explanation, its choice of what mattered and what did not—all of these questions found answers in the larger program of nationalist ideology. So the form was secular and descriptive, but the substance was ideological in the extreme.

At the same time, Zionist theory explicitly rejected the precedent of the Torah. It selected as its history not the history of the faith (of the Torah), but the history of the nation (Israel construed as a secular entity). Zionism defined episodes as history—linear history, Jewish History—and appealed to those strung-together events as vindication for its program of action. So we find a distinctive world view that explained a particular way of life and defined the Israel to which it wished to speak. Like Reform Judaism, Zionism found the written component of the Torah more interesting than the oral. And in its search for a usable past, it turned to documents formerly neglected or treated as not authoritative, for instance, the book of Maccabees. Zionism went in search of heroes unlike those of the present: warriors, political figures, and others who might provide a model for the movement's future. Instead of rabbis or sages, Zionism chose figures such as David or Judah Maccabee or Samson. David the warrior king, Judah Maccabee who had led the revolt against the Syrian Hellenists, and Samson the powerful fighter—these provided the appropriate heroes for a Zionism that proposed to redefine Jewish consciousness, and to turn storekeepers into soldiers, lawyers into farmers, and corner grocers into builders and administrators of great institutions of state and government. The Judaism of the dual Torah treated David as a rabbi. The Zionist system of Judaism saw David as a hero in a more worldly sense: a courageous nation builder.

Yet the principal components of Zionism's world view fitted comfortably within the pattern of the Torah of a Moses. For that Torah held, for its own reasons based on genealogy, that the Jews form one people and should (when worthy) have the land back and build on it a state. It is not surprising that Zionism found in the writings about the return to Zion ample precedent for its program. It linked today's politics to something very like God's will for Israel in ancient times. Calling the new Jewish city Tel Aviv invoked the memory of Ezekiel's reference to a Tel Aviv, and that symbolized much else. Zionism would reconstitute the age of the Return to Zion in the time of Ezra and Nehemiah, and so carry out the prophetic promises. The mode of thought was reminiscent of that of Reform Judaism, although Reform selected a different perfect world of mythic being, a golden age other than the one that for Zionism glistened so brightly.

Yet the points of continuity should not be overstated. For alongside the search of Scripture, Zionism articulated a very clear perception of what it wished to find there. What Zionism did not find, it deposited on its own. And that is what marked it as a heresy of its own systemic design: the celebration of the nation as a secular rather than a supernatural category, and imposition of the nation and its heroism in place of the heroic works of the supernatural God. A classic shift took the verse of Psalms, "Who will retell the great deeds of God," and produced "Who will retell the great deeds of Israel." And that only typifies the profound revision of Israel's history accomplished by Zionism. The earliest pronouncements of the Zionist movement were received in the Jewish heartland of Eastern Europe like the warning signal of the coming Messiah. But to the sages of the dual Torah, Zionism seemed to be blasphemy. God will do it or it will not be done. Considerable time would elapse before the sages of the dual Torah could make their peace with Zionism, and some of them never did.

The Zionist world view explicitly competed with the religious one. The formidable statement of Jacob Klatzkin (1882–1948) provides a solid basis for comparison:

In the past there have been two criteria of Judaism: the criterion of religion, according to which Judaism is a system of positive and negative commandments, and the criterion of the spirit, which saw Judaism as a complex of ideas, like monotheism, messianism, absolute justice, etc. According to both these criteria, therefore, Judaism rests on a subjective basis, on the acceptance of a creed . . . a religious denomination . . . or a community of individuals who share in a *Weltanschauung*. . . . In opposition to these two criteria, which make of Judaism a matter of creed, a third has now arisen, the criterion of a consistent nationalism. According to it, Judaism rests on an objective basis: to be a Jew means the acceptance of neither a religious nor an ethical creed. We are neither a denomination or a school of thought, but members of one family, bearers of a common history . . . The national definition too requires an act of will. It defines our nationalism by two criteria: partnership in the past and the conscious desire to continue such partnership in the future. There are, therefore, two bases for Jewish nationalism—the compulsion of history and a will expressed in that history.[9]

Klatzkin's stress on "a will expressed in history" of course carries us back to the appeals of Reform and Conservative theologians to facts of history as precedents for faith. The historicism of Zionism fell into the same classification of thought. But for the theologians the facts proved episodic and ad hoc, mere precedents. Zionists found it necessary to reread all the histories of Jews and to compose of them Jewish history, a single and linear system leading inexorably to the formation of the Jewish state. Klatzkin defined being a Jew not as something subjective but something objective: "land and language. These are the basic categories of national being."[10] That definition led directly to calling the Jewish state, "the state of Israel," so making a clear statement of Zionism's doctrine of who is Israel.

As Klatzkin said, in contributing "the territorial-political definition of Jewish nationalism," Zionism offered a genuinely fresh world view:

Either the Jewish people shall redeem the land and thereby continue to live, even if the spiritual content of Judaism changes radically, or we shall remain in exile and rot away, even if the spiritual tradition continues to exist.[11]

It goes without saying that, like Christianity at its original encounter with the task of making sense of history, so Zionism posited that a new era began with its formation: "not only for the purpose of making an end to the Diaspora but also in order to establish a new definition of Jewish identity—a secular definition."[12] In this way Zionism clearly

9. Hertzberg, "Ideological Evolution," p. 317.
10. Hertzberg, "Ideological Evolution," p. 318.
11. Hertzberg, "Ideological Evolution," p. 319.
12. Klatzkin, in Hertzberg, "Ideological Evolution," p. 319.

stated the intention of providing a world view that would replace the world view of the received Judaism of the dual Torah and would compete with all efforts of the continuators of that Judaism. Klatzkin states: "Zionism stands opposed to all this. Its real beginning is *The Jewish State* [italics his], and its basic intention, whether consciously or unconsciously, is to deny any conception of Jewish identity based on spiritual criteria." Obviously, Klatzkin's was not the only voice. But in his appeal to history, in his initiative in positing a linear course of events of a single kind leading to one goal, the Jewish state, Klatzkin expressed the theory of history that would supply Zionism with a principal plank in its platform. What the several appeals to the facts of history meant is that the arena of scholarship as to what had ("really") happened defined the boundaries for debate on matters of faith. Consequently the heightened and intensified discourse of scholars produced judgments not as to secular facts but as to deeply held truths of faith, identifying not correct or erroneous versions of things that had happened but truth and heresy, saints and sinners.

Until the massacre of the Jews of Europe between 1933 and 1945 and the founding of the state of Israel three years later in 1948, Zionism remained very much a minority movement in Jewry. Jewish Socialism and Yiddishism in the new nations of Eastern Europe and the New Deal in American Democratic politics attracted a far larger part of Jewry, and the former, though not the latter, formed a competing Judaic system. Before 1948 the Jewish population of the land of Israel/Palestine had reached scarcely half a million, a small portion of the Jews of the world. In the United States and in Western Europe, Zionist sentiment did not predominate, even though a certain romantic appeal attached to the pioneers in the land of Israel. Indeed down to 1967 Zionism constituted one choice among many for Jews throughout the world. Since, at the present time, Jewry nearly unanimously attaches to the state of Israel the status of the Jewish state, affirms that the Jews form one people, concedes all of the principal propositions of Zionism, and places the achievement of the Zionist program as the highest priority for Jewry throughout the world, we may say that today (but not a great many days before) Zionism forms a system bearing self-evident truth for vast numbers of Jews. Because Zionism alone of the Judaisms of the nineteenth and twentieth centuries possessed the potential of accurately assessing the power of anti-Semitism and its ultimate destiny. Zionism turns out to have selected the right problem and to have given the right solution to that problem.

Heresies Outside of Judaism: American Judaism

By American Judaism I mean the system of Holocaust and Redemption. The "Holocaust" refers to the murder by the Germans of six million Jewish men, women, and children in Europe in 1933 through 1945. The "Redemption" is the creation of the state of Israel. This Judaic system flourishes in America and forms the principal force in the lives of American Jews. The world view stresses the unique character of the murder of European Jews, and the providential and redemptive meaning of the creation of the state of Israel. The way of life requires active work in raising money and political support for the state of Israel. Different from Zionism, which held that Jews should live in a Jewish state, this system serves to give Jews living in America a reason and an explanation for being Jewish. This Judaism lays particular stress on the complementary experiences of mid-twentieth-century Jewry: the mass murder in death factories of six million of the Jews of Europe, and the creation of the state of Israel three years after the end of the massacre. These events, together seen as providential, bear the names Holocaust, for the murders, and Redemption, for the formation of the state of Israel in the aftermath. The system as a whole presents an encompassing myth, linking one event to the other as an instructive pattern, and moves Jews to follow a particular set of actions, as it tells them why they should be Jewish. Diverse Judaic systems flourish in America. But the Judaism of Holocaust and Redemption is the system that took shape here.[13] the distinctively American Judaism is the one that exercises enormous power over the minds and imaginations of Jewish Americans. It tells them who they are, why they should be Jewish Americans, and what they should do because of that identification. It also tells them who the Jewish group is and how that group should relate to the rest of the world and to history.

The urgent questions answered by American Judaism constitute two separate and distinct questions. The first is addressed to the particular world of the Jews, and the second is addressed to the world at large. The first question is, Why should I be different? Why should I be Jewish? The second is, How should I relate to the world at large? The Judaism of Holocaust and Redemption that dominates Jewry in America has

---

13. A counterpart system of Holocaust and Redemption forms an important component of Israeli nationalism, but it serves a different purpose, explains a different set of facts, and answers questions peculiar to the Israeli context. So the corresponding system, while interesting, makes no contribution to systemic description. Comparison among systems will have to consider the two species of the common genus.

made available a powerful and critical experience in answer to the question of why be Jewish: because you have no choice. The same Judaism explained that Israel should relate to the world at large in its own state and nation overseas and in its distinctive and distinct communities at home. So the two questions answered by American Judaism speak to the inner world and to the outer world as well.

But the two questions are not unrelated, for both of them emerge from the special circumstances of the American of Jewish origin whose grandparents or great-grandparents immigrated to this country. For that sort of American Jew there is no common and acknowledged core of religious experience by which "being Jewish" may be explained and interpreted. Because anti-Semitism as a perceived social experience has become less common that it was from the 1920s through the early 1950s, there is also no common core of social alienation to account for the distinctive character of the group and explain why it continues to endure. Indeed, many American Jews, though they continue to affirm their Jewishness, have no clear notion of how they are Jewish, or what their Jewish heritage demands of them. For this critical part of the American Jewish population Judaism is merely a reference point, one fact among many. For ideologists of the Jewish community, the most certain answer to the question of the third generation must be, "There is no real choice." And the Holocaust provides the answer: "Hitler knew you were Jewish." The formative experiences of the Holocaust are now immediately accessible through emotions unmediated by sentiment or sensibility. These Judaizing experiences, take the place of the Torah in nurturing an inner and distinctive consciousness of being Jewish. So the first of the two questions before us, the inner one, is the question of who we are and why we are what we are and not something else. The Holocaust answers that question.

By the late 1960s third–generation American Jews, that is, the grandchildren of the immigrant generation of the period from 1880 to 1920, born between 1920 and 1940, had found in the continuator-Judaisms of the synagogue something conventional and irrelevant. These Judaisms did not address their questions and provide self-evidently valid answers. And how could those Judaisms serve, when they invoked experiences of learning and sensibility that were unavailable to American Jews after the immigrant generation and their children? To make of those Judaisms the model for viable life—an explanation of the world and an account of how to live—Jews found they had to give what they did not have. They either needed memories that few of them possessed, or else they had to try to find a road back, and few were willing. The

world of the everyday did not provide access to so subtle and alien a
world view as that of the Judaism of the dual Torah with its conception
of humanity and of Israel, let alone to the way of life formed within that
world view. How were they to engage the emotions without the media-
tion of learning in the Torah that few possessed or wished to attain?
And how could they define a way of life that imparted distinction
without too much material difference? To state matters in a homely
way, what distinctively Judaic way of life would allow devotees to eat
whatever they wanted? The answer to both questions was that access to
the life of feeling and experience and to the way of life that made one
distinctive without leaving the person terribly different from everybody
else emerged in the Judaic system of Holocaust and Redemption. This
system presented an immediately accessible message cast in extreme
emotions of terror and triumph; its round of endless activity demanded
only spare tme. The system of American Judaism realized in a poignant
way the conflicting demands of Jewish Americans to be intensely Jewish, and to be Jewish without exacting much of a cost in meaningful
differences from others.

The founding, immigrant generation of Judaism in America, 1880–
1920, did not define a system of Judaism, let alone a set of such systems
that it imagined it could transmit to the next generation. It contributed
in rich and important ways to what the coming generation would
inherit and utilize. But it defined nothing, except by negative example.
The second generation, which was born 1900–1920 and was paramount
1920–1950, wanted to be American, not Jewish. As an inherited religious tradition with rich theological perspectives and a demanding,
enduring way of life Judaism bore little relevance to the American
children of the Europeans who had walked on that path to God and had
lived by that mode of sanctification. And the immigrants took that fact
for granted. The second generation accepted more from the founders
than it had planned. For while explicitly opting for America and
against Judaism, it implicitly defined life as a set of contrasts between
the Jewish way of life, on the one side, and everything else, on the other.
Being Jewish was what defined existence for the second generation.
That fact of life was so pervasive as not to demand articulation, let alone
specific and concrete expression. The result was that the second generation organized bowling leagues and athletic clubs rather than prayer
circles and study groups. But everyone in the bowling league was
Jewish, and they were also neighbors and friends. The cultural distinctiveness that had characterized the first generation gave way to a Jewishness by association for the second. Whether political or recreational

or philanthropic, the associations took it for granted that the goal was nonsectarian. Little that was definitively Jewish marked the groups' collective life. But how nonsectarian could an association be when all its members lived in pretty much the same neighborhood, pursued the same lines of work, and came from Yiddish-speaking parents? In fact the community life constructed on the basis of associationism character-istic of the second generation constituted a deeply Jewish mode—if not a Judaic system. It took for granted exactly what the first generation had handed on, the basic and definitive character of being Jewish, whatever that might come to mean for the new generation. The found-ing generation could not articulate what being Jewish meant and rarely tried to. But it imparted exactly the imprint of being Jewish that it had hoped to leave behind. The second generation was American and re-mained Jewish. More than that the first generation could not have imagined.

The second generation did little to found camps, youth programs, or schools. The institutions of the second generation recognized no need to make their Jewish character explicit, through either substantive or symbolic means. There were few Jewish parochial schools. Jewish com-munity centers did not regard themselves as agents of the Jewish com-munity. Jewish philanthropic agencies maintained a high wall of sepa-ration between church (synagogue) and state (Jewish community). The result was that little public Jewish money went into Judaic activities of any kind. A great deal went into fighting anti-Semitism and maintain-ing nonsectarian hospitals. Nearly all of the Judaizing programs and activities of the third generation, now considered the norm and perma-nent, date back only to the decades after World War II. Most of the earliest summer camps of Judaic character come from that period, especially camps under religious auspices (as distinct from Zionist and Hebraist ones). The several youth movements got under way in the late 1940s. In the 1960s the Jewish Federations and Welfare Funds fought the battle for a policy of investment in distinctively Jewish programs and activities. Only from the 1970s did they undertake to treat as stylish anything markedly Judaic. These and equivalent facts point to the passage from the second to the third generation as the age of decisive redefinition.

The second generation remembered things that the third generation could scarcely imagine: genuinely pious parents who believed that God had revealed the Torah to Moses at Mount Sinai. But the second genera-tion had also come to maturity in an age in which America turned against the newest Americans, the children of the immigrant wave of

1880–1920 (as well as against older Americans, the blacks, who from the mid 1890s suffered the wave of bigotry that swept over other Americans a generation afterward). Universities open to Jews before World War I imposed rigid quotas against them afterward. More important, entire industries declared themselves off limits to Jewish employment. The fact that the climate of bigotry and exclusion affected others just as much as Jews, so that a majority of Americans of the age were among the excluded minorities, changed little for the mentality of the excluded Jews. They might have gone to swim among an undifferentiated majority, had the waters been open to them, but they were not welcome on the beaches.

The second generation encountered a hostile and threatening world, while the third experienced an essentially neutral and benign one. For the third generation underwent few of the experiences of anti-Semitism—exclusion, vilification, pariahship—that had defined what being Jewish meant to the second generation. Yet that contrast between a hostile and a neutral or even benign situation is somewhat misleading. For three other factors contributed to the growth of the highly articulated and self-conscious Judaism of Holocaust and Redemption among third-generation Americans of Jewish descent. The first was the rise of the State of Israel. The second was the transformation of the murders of nearly six million Jews in Europe into the symbol, the Holocaust. The third was the acceptance of ethnic difference in American life, that is to say, the resurgence of ethnic identification among the grandchildren of all the immigrant generations, on the one side, and among blacks, on the other. That movement of rediscovery of difference responded to the completion of the work of assimilation to American civilization and its norms.

This brings us to the movement at which the Judaic system of Holocaust and Redemption came into sharp focus, with its answers to the unavoidable questions: who are we? Why should we be Jewish? What does it mean to be Jewish? How do we relate to Jews in other times and places? What is "Israel," meaning the state of Israel, to us, and what are we to it? Who are we in American society? These and other questions form the agenda for American Judaism. In order to understand the power and importance of the system, we have to focus upon American Jews of the third generation (1950–1980). That generation, no less than the first and second, has continued to see themselves as Jews, to regard that fact as central to their very being, and to persist in that choice. They have held very strong convictions about how they will continue to be Jews. Most of them have hoped that their children would

marry within the Jewish community. Most of them have joined synagogues and do so because they wanted their children to grow up as
Jews. Above all, most of them have regarded the fact that they are
Jewish as bearing great significance. So American Jews of the third
generation have continued to see everyday life in terms different from
their Gentile neighbors, beginning with the fact that to them, if not to
their neighbors, their being Jewish seems an immensely important fact
of life. The words they use to explain that fact and the symbols by which
they express it, are quite different from those of the Judaism of the dual
Torah and its continuators. They speak, for example, of Jewishness, not
Torah. They are obsessed with a crisis of identity, rather than with the
tasks and responsibilites of "Israel." They are deeply influenced by the
opinion of Gentiles.

In all, they were eager to be Jewish—but not too much so. They did
not wish to be so Jewish that they could not also take their place within
the undifferentiated humanity of which they fantasized. They confronted a crisis not merely of identity but of commitment, for they did
not choose to resolve the dilemma of separateness within an open
society. In preferring separateness, they seemed entirely within the
archaic realm; in dreaming of an open society they evidently aspired to a
true accomplishment of the early promise of political emancipation
(which accounts for the enormous influence of Reform and Conservative Judaisms). The underlying problem was understanding what the
ambiguous adjective Jewish is supposed to mean when the noun Judaism in its received meanings had been abandoned. It was the system of
Holocaust and Redemption that answered that question: Who are you?
What should you do? What do you make of the other? The questions
before us fall into the category of political issues and their urgency and
the self-evident validity of the answers likewise testify to the political
crisis of America in the 1970s.

American Judaism—shifting to the present—as we know it today is
the creation of the third generation, the result of its conscientious effort
to remember what its parents deliberately forgot. The decision was
made in a free society and represented free choice. So the third generation forms the first generation of Judaism to have the right to decide in
an open society whether to be Jewish. More interesting, it is the first
generation to define for itself what "being Jewish" consists of and how
Judaism, as an inherited and received religious tradition, would be
taken over as part of this definition. Its Judaism is the system of holocaust and Redemption, though to be sure that system exercises an
appeal to Jews in diverse relationships to the unfolding of family history

in America. But the questions to which the Judaic system of Holocaust and Redemption provided self-evidently valid answers proved urgent and ineluctable to the third and fourth generation of American Jews, speaking to the world as they experienced it and answering the questions they could not avoid.

So the question and the answer take multiple forms and dimensions: personal and social, historical and theological. The Holocaust formed the question and Redemption in the form of the creation of the state of Israel, the answer. It is that simple. Nearly all American Jews identify with the state of Israel and regard its welfare as not a secular good, but a metaphysical necessity: the other chapter of the Holocaust. Nearly all American Jews are not only supporters of the state of Israel, but also regard their own being Jewish as inextricably bound up with the meaning they impute to the Jewish state.

But scarcely a single important component of Zionism in its own systemic formulation was critical to the way of life of the system of American Judaism. American Judaism absorbs and reworks for its own systemic purposes the creation of the state of Israel. American Judaism is not a Zionism. For Zionism always insisted, and the state of Israel today maintains, that immigration to the state of Israel forms the highest goal, indeed the necessary condition, for true Zionism. And nearly six million American Jews, including a great many deeply engaged by the Judaic system at hand, presently exhibit not the slightest intention of migrating anywhere, though they gladly pay visits. But that is not Zionism.

At what point did the Judaism of Holocaust and Redemption take a position of paramount importance among the Jews of America and become the self-evident Judaism of the bulk of the organized Jewish community? Three factors reinforced one another among the Jews in turning the Judaism of Holocaust and Redemption into a set of self-evident and descriptive facts, truths beyond all argument: the Six Day War of 1967, the reethnicization of American life, and the transformation of the mass murder of European Jews into an event of mythic and world-destroying proportions. Why date the birth of the Judaism of Holocaust and Redemption so precisely by the 1967 war? People take as routine the importance of the state of Israel in American Jewish consciousness. But in the 1940s and 1950s, American Jewry had yet to translate its deep sympathy for the Jewish state into political activity, on the one side, and the shaping element for local cultural activity and sentiment, on the other. And the memory for the destruction of European Jewry did not right away become the Holocaust as a formative event in contemporary Jewish consciousness. In fact the reethnicization of the Jews could not have taken the form that it did—a powerful identification with the state of Israel as the answer to the question of the Holocaust—without a single, catalytic event.

That event was the 1967 war between the state of Israel and its Arab neighbors. When, after a long period of threat, the dreaded war of "all against one" began on 5 June, American Jews feared the worst. Six days later they witnessed an unimagined outcome: the state of Israel stood on the Jordan River, the Nile, and the outskirts of Damascus. The trauma of the weeks preceding the war, when the Arabs promised to drive the Jews into the sea and no other power intervened or promised help, renewed for the third generation the nightmare of the second. Once more the streets and newspapers became the school for being Jewish. On that account the Judaism in formation took up a program of urgent questions—and answered them. In the trying weeks before 5 June 1967, American Jewry relived the experience of the second generation and the third. In the 1930s and 1940s, the age of Hitler's Germany and the murder of the European Jews in death factories, every day's newspaper brought lessons of Jewish history. Everybody knew that were he or she in Europe, death would be the sentence on account of the crime of Jewish birth. And the world was then indifferent. No avenues of escape were opened to the Jews who wanted to flee, and many roads to life were deliberately blocked by anti-Semitic foreign service officials. The contemporary parallel? In 1967 the Arab states threatened to destroy the State of Israel and murder its citizens. The Israelis turned to the world. The world again ignored Jewish suffering, and a new Holocaust impended. But now the outcome was quite different. The entire history of the century came under a new light. A moment of powerful and salvific weight placed into a fresh perspective everything that had happened from the beginning to the present.

The third generation had now found its memory and its hope, in the same way as Zionism had invented a usable past. It now could confront the murder of the Jews of Europe, along with its parents' and its own experience of exclusion and bigotry. No longer was it necessary to avoid painful, intolerable memories. Now what had happened had to be remembered, because it bore within itself the entire message of the new day in Judaism. That is to say, putting the murder of nearly six million Jews of Europe together with the creation of the state of Israel transformed both events. One became the Holocaust, the purest statement of evil in all of human history. The other became salvation in the form of "the first appearance of our redemption" (as the language of the Jewish prayer for the state of Israel has it). Accordingly, a moment of stark epiphany captured the entire experience of the age and imparted to it the meaning and order that a religious system has the power to express as self-evident. The self-evident system of American Judaism for the third generation encompassed a salvific myth deeply and personally relevant to the devotees. The myth made sense at a single instant equally of both the world and the self of what the newspapers had to say, and of what the individual understood in personal life.

This distinctively American form of Judaism clearly connects to the Judaism of the dual Torah. Its exact recapitulation of the pattern of the original Torah hardly requires specification. The exile has its counterpart in the Holocaust, the return to Zion, in the Redemption represented by the state of Israel. But American Judaism is not continuous with it. American Judaism in fact forms a heresy structurally out of phase with the Judaism of the dual Torah. In its stress upon the realization, in the here and now, of ultimate evil and salvation, and in its mythicization of contemporary history, American Judaism offers a distinctively American reading of the received tradition. For when Jews have spoken of fully realized salvation and an end of history, the result has usually been a new religion, connected to but not continuous with the received religion of Judaism.

From Alienation and Restoration to Holocaust and Redemption

The nineteenth-century Judaisms made constant reference to the received system of the dual Torah—its writings, its values, its requirements, its viewpoints, and its way of life. The twentieth-century Judaisms did not. But the connection of all four Judaisms to the pattern of the Torah is clear in every case. The Judaisms of continuation made constant reference to the Torah of Moses. The extrasystemic heresies of the twentieth century did not. Yet all four rested on the premise of the pattern of experience announced in the time of Ezra: exile and return. The distance from alienation and restoration to Holocaust and Redemption is to be measured not in the twenty-five centuries from the Torah of Sinai produced in the time of Ezra. It is to be traced in the distance between the return to the Land of the seventh century B.C. and the return to the Land of the twentieth century A.D. And I see no difference at all, except that those who participated in the contemporary restoration understood what they did in light of the first one, while those who returned the first time around had to wait until Ezra had caught up with them for the full understanding of what they had done.

There are, of course, important differences between the continuator-Judaisms of the nineteenth century and the Judaic heresies of the twentieth. Each Judaism born in the nineteenth century faced the task of validating change that all of the Judaisms affirmed in one way or another. But all of the new Judaisms articulated a principle of change guiding relationships with the received system, which continued to define the agendas of law and theology alike, and to which in diverse ways all the Judaisms recognized themselves as answerable. We cannot point to a similar relationship between the new Judaisms of the twentieth century and the received Judaism of the dual Torah. For none of them made much use of the intellectual resources of that system, found important urgent issues within that system, or even regarded itself as answerable to the Judaism of the dual Torah.

In the end the difference between the twentieth-century Judaisms and the nineteenth-century ones was much more than a century. It was the difference between the civilization of the west in its Christian form and that same civilization as it took new forms altogether. Of what pertinence was the Judaism formed in response to Christianity, with its interest in Scripture, Messiah and the long trends of history and salvation? The new world imposed its own categories: class and class struggle, the nation-state composed of homogeneous cultural and ethnic units, and the search for ethnic identity among diverse and rootless people. These issues characterized a world that had cast loose the moorings that had long held things firm and whole.

For people out of all relationship with the Judaism of the dual Torah, what was left in the twentieth century was a Judaic experience composed of politics, on the one side, and emotions, on the other. And out of that raw material the two Judaisms we have considered built their tower: "And slime they had for mortar." The several Judaisms issued emotional appeals to the experiences of history, meaning what is happening today. Each framed a grievance for itself, a doctrine of resentment. For Zionism it was statelessness. For American Judaism, a sense of alienation expressed that grievance, bringing to words the underlying feeling of resentment.

The ideologies of the twentieth-century Judaisms were responses to intolerable experience. Zionism formed into a single whole the experiences of remarkably diverse people living in widely separated places, showing that all those experiences formed an experience of a single sort—exclusion, victimization, and anti-Semitism—which Zionism could confront. American Judaism linked to an inchoate past the aspirations of a third and fourth generation of Jews who wanted desperately to be Jewish but in their own experience and intellectual resources could find slight access to anything Jewish. The emotion of resentment formed the road for all: for American Judaism, strong feeling about suffering and redemption, powerful appeal to concrete deed in the here and now by people who thought themselves helpless. And yet in these Judaisms, so remote from system of the Torah of Moses, how far have we moved from the starting point? For contemporary Judaism, alienation, exile, and homecoming are the norm; ineluctable reversion is necessary; and meaning for our lives is what is owing. But by whom? And to whom? And why?

EPILOGUE

"AND THE LORD WAS SORRY THAT THE LORD HAD MADE HUMANITY ON THE EARTH . . . BUT NOAH FOUND FAVOR IN THE EYES OF THE LORD"

The human condition needs a religion that lends dignity to defeat and emphasizes the power of acceptance and the courage of endurance. For the human condition begins with the destiny of death, the ultimate defeat for humanity's frail hope. The enduring circumstance of nations, at least of those that go on and on, ultimately ends in defeat. Judaism framed its vision of humanity "in our image, after our likeness," in the memory of defeat, and found its lesson in surviving. Nourished by that pattern—framed in terms of exile and return, punishment and reconciliation, or holocaust and redemption—Israel, the Jewish people, endured for most of the history of humanity and lives today.

Israel has told its story in many ways, but it has always been the same story. Whatever happened bore a single meaning. It was the tale of exile and homecoming for the nation, suffering but meaning in the suffering for the individual. The story of Israel has been the tale of slaves who overcame degradation, the invented history of a nation that survived one disaster after another. Many identify with that story, not because it tells how things are, but because it gives hope of how things should be. The pattern of death and resurrection for one man conforms to the original pattern of exile and return for a whole nation, and has throughout time and among numerous peoples. So Judaism's claim upon the attention of the world and the reason that it records a religion worth studying is simple. Judaism attends to the human condition, exemplified in the death and life of the ever-dying, always-enduring people, Israel. The Torah's message of survival, endurance, courage, patience, discipline, and hope—that message proves remarkably congruent to the condition of humanity in God's image.

219

What of tomorrow? No one can predict the Judaic systems of the twenty-first century, except in two details. First, there will assuredly be such systems: the Jews have not stopped making up Judaisms. Second, the long history of systemic recapitulation of a single pattern leaves no doubt about the shape of things to come. The original pattern, imposed on the events of 586 to 450 B.C. to make sense of what had happened, will define the pattern of the future. That is so whether or not what happens conforms to what people expect to happen. In the beginning the chaotic experiences of diverse people were made to conform to a simple pattern. It made no difference whether people went into exile or were spared, or whether they came back from exile or stayed behind. The marginal group that returned to Zion made of its rather special experience the model. Why did that experience become the pattern?

The pattern was invented not because it made up facts, but because it found in facts a pattern worth recording and repeating. The persuasive strength of the tale as told in the Torah of Moses, proclaimed as God's will at Sinai by Ezra in 450, flowed from more than the politics of the day. The tale rather conformed to how people wanted things to be and to how they imagined they had experienced them. Everyone could identify with exile, because everyone could locate that moment at which one became a stranger. And certain as was the encounter with alienation, everyone could also frame a vision of a homecoming, whether to a temple in Jerusalem or to a holy place of a more private design. So the pattern worked not because it replicated what had really happened to people, but because it had the power to impart meaning to what had happened—and so to make people want the same thing to happen once again.

That accounts for the power of the immediate perspective of Holocaust and Redemption, only so far as we remember how these things come and go. The century now drawing to a close has marked the most difficult period in the history of the Jewish people and of Judaism. What happened, as is well known, is that six million Jews were murdered in death factories created by the German government for that very purpose. The issue of the Holocaust draws us to reexamine the entire civilization of the West, which produced the Germany that did these things. National Socialist Germany, hostile to Christianity and to Judaism, drew on the hatreds generated by the one to exterminate the life generated by the other. But it was not Christianity and it marked the failure of the Christian perspective of the West. Judaism lives in the West, and so does Christianity: both of them in new forms and con-

fronting a new politics. And that is the source to which we turn for
hope, we who remain faithful to the Torah of Moses at Sinai, as we
contemplate the future of the world: Christianity and Islam do live,
imparting to the face of the world that original visage: God's image of
creation.

If the singular message of the pattern may be stated in a single
sentence, it is this: for a Jew it is a sin to despair. The Jews' assigned task
within humanity has been, despite everything, to endure and abide in
perfect faith and trust: to hope. That is what it has meant to be Israel,
"in our image, after our likeness." The critical Judaic component of the
Christian civilization of the West spoke of God and God's will for
humanity: the living God of Abraham, Isaac, and Jacob, not the God of
the philosophers, and not the construct of the theologians. The issue of
the Torah is the issue of everyday life: what it means to live in God's
image, after God's likeness. So said the Judaism of the dual Torah; so
too said Christianity in its worship of God made flesh. So that message
of humanity in God's image, of a people seeking to conform to God's
will, found resonance in the Christian world as well: both components
of the world, the Christian dough and the Judaic yeast, bore a single
message about humanity. The task at hand demands a gift of grace: the
grace to hope and not despair, to say, even in the twentieth century,
Amen. Your will be done. And by going on with life, the Jewish people
have said just that. That is our gift to the world.

Let me close with the message of the fourth-century sages that in my
judgment imparted to Judaism its final and distinctive definition. It is
that the task of Israel is to hope, that the message of Genesis—there for
the sages to uncover and make explicit—is always to hope.

GENESIS RABBAH XCVIII:XIV.

4.   A. "I hope for your salvation, O Lord" (Gen. 49:18):

          B. Said R. Isaac, "All things depend on hope, suffering de-
pends on hope, the sanctification of God's name depends
on hope, the merit attained by the fathers depends on
hope, the lust for the age to come depends on hope.

          C. "That is in line with this verse: 'Yes, in the way of your
judgments, O Lord, we have hoped for you, to your name,
and to your memorial, is the desire of our soul' (Is. 26:8).
'The way of your judgments' refers to suffering.

          D. "'. . . to your name:' this refers to the sanctification of the
divine name.

E. "'. . . and to your memorial:' this refers to the merit of the fathers.

F. "'. . . is the desire of our soul:' this refers to the lust for the age to come.

G. "Grace depends on hope: 'O Lord, be gracious to us, we have hoped for you' (Is. 33:2).

H. "Forgiveness depends on hope: 'For with you is forgiveness' (Ps. 133:4), then: 'I hope for the Lord' (Ps. 130:5)."

For a Jew it is a sin to despair. This I think defines the iron law of meaning, telling sages what matters and what does not, and guiding their hands to take up those verses that permit expression of hope—that above all. The pattern revealed, if not at Sinai then in the holocaust of 586 and the restoration after it, forms the one statement that Judaism—despite it all—has made to all humanity. Given the definitive event of the day of the sages—the conversion to Christianity of the great empire of Rome in the age of Constantine—the task of hope did not prove an easy assignment. But in our time it is still more difficult and therefore all the more a measure of our humanity in God's image. For the same God who said, "I am sorry I made man," also saved Noah and called Abraham, and shepherds Israel and today watches over humanity for eternity. We know it because, after all, we have survived the twentieth century, all of us who live. We do live.

The power of the experience of exile and redemption, to which all Judaisms appealed, should not spend its force solely within the circle of Israel. For properly interpreted, it is a theory of human existence, an account of meaning in an otherwise senseless existence of accident and happenstance. Indeed, the sages of the Judaism of the dual Torah made explicit the notion that in Israel humanity found its model and its paradigm, and that within the social experience of Israel, the center lay in exile—but also the hope for return. This the sages of the dual Torah stated within their idiom, which still speaks to us, in commenting on verses of Scripture.

XV. Pesiqta deRab Kahana

XV:I.1. A. R. Abbahu in the name of R. Yose bar Haninah commenced discourse by citing this verse: "But they are like a man [Adam], they have transgressed the covenant. There they dealt treacherously against me (Hos. 6:7).

B. "They are like a man, specifically, like the first man. [We shall now compare the story of the first man in Eden with the story of Israel in its land.]

C. "Said the Holy One, blessed be he, 'In the case of the first man, I brought him into the garden of Eden, I commanded him, he violated my commandment, I judged him to be sent away and driven out, but I mourned for him, saying "How . . ."' [which begins the book of Lamentations, hence stands for a lament, but which also is written with the consonants that also yield, Where are you].

D. "I brought him into the garden of Eden, as it is written, And the Lord God took the man and put him into the garden of Eden (Gen. 2:15).

E. "I commanded him, as it is written, And the Lord God commanded . . . (Gen. 2:16).

F. "And he violated my commandment, as it is written, Did you eat from the tree concerning which I commanded you (Gen. 3:11).

G. "I judged him to be sent away, as it is written, And the Lord God sent him from the garden of Eden (Gen. 3:23).

J. "And I judged him to be driven out. And he drove out the man (Gen. 3:24).

I. "But I mourned for him, saying, How. . . . And he said to him, Where are you (Gen. 3:9), and the word for 'where are you' is written, How. . . .

J. "'So too in the case of his descendants, [God continues to speak,] I brought them into the Land of Israel, I commanded them, they violated my commandment, I judged them to be sent out and driven away but I mourned for them, saying, How. . . .'

K. "I brought them into the Land of Israel: And I brought you into the land of Carmel (Jer. 2:7).

L. "I commanded them: And you, command the children of Israel (Ex. 27:20). Command the children of Israel (Lev. 24:2).

M. "They violated my commandment: And all Israel have violated your Torah (Dan. 9:11).

N. "I judged them to be sent out: Send them away, out of my sight and let them go forth (Jer 15:1).

O. ". . . . and driven away: From my house I shall drive them (Hos. 9:15).

P. "But I mourned for them, saying, How . . . :' How lonely sits the city [that was full of people! How like a widow has she become, she that was great among the nations! She that

was a princess among the cities has become a vassal. She
weeps bitterly in the night, tears on her cheeks, among all
her lovers she has none to comfort her; all her friends have
dealt treacherously with her, they have become her ene-
mies] (Lamentations 1 : 1 – 2)."

The evocation of the story of the first man in the Garden of Eden to
interpret the history of Israel in its land produces a matching of details
and a strong message, that after the disaster in Jeremiah's time, Israel
emerged from Eden. They discovered the point-by-point correspondence between the fall of the first man from the grace of Eden and the
fall of Israel from the state of grace represented by the land of Israel.
Working backward, we can uncover the outlines of that same path, as it
leads from Israel to the first man, and from the fall from grace to the
ultimate homecoming of redemption, when time ends and God's rule
commences. Exile and return—these encompass the experience and
existence of suffering of as yet unredeemed humanity, knowing where
it has been, but also where it now heads. To state matters in terms of the
here and now, exile captures what we are, but return, what we can
become.

Abbahu, 222
Agriculture, Mishnaic division of, 76
Aha, messianic hope, 130
Ahad, HaAm, 202–3
Alexander the Great, 32, 59, 63
American Judaism, Holocaust and Re-
    demption, 181–82, 185, 197–99,
    208–18. *See also* Reform Judaism
Anan b. David, 173–75
Ankori, Zvi, 173–74
Anti-Semitism and Zionism, 201–2
Appointed times, 74, 77–78
Aqiba, messianic hope, 126
Arcadius, 114

Babylonian Talmud, explaining Mish-
    nah, 16
Bar Kokhba, 64–65, 72, 75; messianic
    hope, 126–27, 129
Breuer, Isaac, 193
Bun, messianic hope, 125

Canon law and Palestinian Talmud,
    106–7
Canons of Elvira, 114
Central Conference of American Rabbis,
    185–89
Christianity: Judaism in Christendom,
    151–56; Judaism without, 97–98;
    public policy of, and Judaism, 142–47;
    as state religion in ancient Rome,
    113–19
Cleanness and uncleanness, Mishnaic di-
    vision of, 69–72, 85–86
Community Rule (Manual of Discipline),
    50
Conservative Judaism, modern and con-
    temporary diversity in, 14
Constantine, 98, 119, 146; and messianic
    hope, 16–17; state religion in ancient
    Rome, 113–15, 118
Constantinius III, 114
Council at Nicaea, 113
Cyrus, 1, 33, 63

Damages, Mishnaic division of, 75,
    80–84
David, and imperial Israel, 24–27
Dead Sea sect. *See* Essenes
Deuteronomists, model Judaism, 34–35,
    41, 43
Diversity in Judaism: American Juda-
    ism, 208–18; biblical prelude to Juda-
    ism, 20, 22; contemporary Judaism,
    181–218; event and pattern for uncer-
    tain restoration, 32–33; Hasidism,
    169–71; modern and contemporary
    Judaism, 13–15; Orthodox Judaism,
    189–97; Pietism and Judaism,
    164–67; power and pathos of Judaism,
    178–80; Reform Judaism, 182,
    185–94, 196–97, 201; Sabbateanism,
    176–78; sagacity, sanctification, and
    salvation, 43–48; Torah in age of, 12;
    Zionism and twentieth-century Juda-
    ism, 197–202
Dreyfus, Alfred, 201–2

Edict of Milan, 113
Eleazar of Modiin, 128
Elohistic writings: biblical prelude to Ju-
    daism, 22; model Judaism, 34, 43
Esau, ascendancy of, 16
Essenes, 48–49, 59; sanctification and
    salvation, 50–54
Exile and redemption, 1, 22, 31, 221–24;
    biblical prelude to Judaism, 20, 22;
    crisis and resolution, 31; history of
    Judaism, 5; Judaisms to Judaism,
    8–10; redemption as return from, 5, 9
Ezra (viceroy), 2, 22; formation of Pen-
    tateuch, 32–33, 41; sponsorship of
    Torah of Moses, 5–6

Festivals, appointed times for, 74

Gamaliel, 64
Genesis Rabbah, 113; history of Israel,
    133–37

German pietism, Judaism in, 164–67
Gnosticism, 92–95
Green, Arthur, 170

Haninah, teachings of scribes, 102
Hasidism, 165; diversity in Judaism,
   167–71
Heller, Joseph Elijah, 174–75
Heresies outside and within Judaism:
   American Judaism, 208–16; Hasidism
   and Orthodoxy, 167–71; Karaism,
   172–76; Sabbateanism, 176–78;
   Zionism, 200–207
Herod, 63–64
Hertzberg, Arthur, 203
Herzl, Theodor, 201–3
Hilgiah, history of Israel, 136
Hiyya, teachings of scribes, 102
Holocaust and Redemption. See Ameri-
   can Judaism
Holy Things, Mishnaic division of,
   84–85
Humphreys, W. Lee, 24–26, 29

Idi, teachings of scribes, 102
Isaac, 221
Isaac b. R. Eleazar, Israel and Rome
   matched, 123
Ishmael, ascendancy of, 16; teachings of
   scribes, 102
Islam: heresy against Judaism, 176–78;
   Judaism and, 12, 151–56
Israel: age of diversity, 32–61; biblical
   prelude to Judaism, 18–24; Deuteronomistic Judaism for, 27–30; history's meaning and Genesis Rabbah,
   133–37; Rome matched, 123–24; as
   social entity, 7–8; Yahwistic writings
   and imperial Israel, 24–29. See also
   Messianic hope
Israel b. Eliezer Baal Shem Tov, 168

Josephus, 50
Joshua b. Levi, scriptural bases for law,
   104
Judah b. Batera, scriptural bases for law,
   104
Judaism: beginnings of, 15–17; biblical
   prelude to, 18–24; categories in age of

diversity, 43–48; in Christendom,
   151–56; classical period of, 12–13;
   classical system of theology, 147–50;
   common Judaism in age of Restoration, 48–49; contemporary Judaism,
   diversities in, 181–218; Deuteronomistic Judaism for Israel,
   27–30; dual Torah doctrine, 148–49;
   encounter with Christianity, 113–19;
   fourth-century crisis, 119–21;
   Hasidism within, 167–71; history of
   exile, 5; hope for salvation, 221–24; in
   Islam, 12, 151–56; Karaism as heresy,
   172–76; Mishnah in formation of,
   62–98; Mishnah and systemic
   changes, 106–12; modern and contemporary characteristics, 13–15;
   monotheism, 147–48; Palestinian Talmud in formation of, 121–33; Pharisaism, 62–67; power of doctrine of
   virtue, 156–64; power and pathos of,
   178–80; Priestly Code and model Judaism, 34–40; public policy and
   Christianity, 142–47; purposes and
   Palestinian Talmud, 110–12; Reform
   Judaism, 182, 185–94, 196–97, 201;
   restoration, 58–61; Sabbateanism as
   heresy against, 176–78; symbolism,
   10–11; and Palestinian Talmud,
   107–10; theory of history of, 5; Torah
   and salvation, 149–50; Torah as system of retelling of, 10–11; without
   Christianity, 97–98; Zionism and contemporary Judaism, 197–207. See also
   American Judaism; Orthodox Judaism; Reform Judaism
Julian, 98; reconstruction of Temple,
   113–14, 119

Karaism, 199; heresies against Judaism,
   172–76; rejection of dual Torah, 13
Katzburg, 193–94
Klatzkin, Jacob, 205–7

Law code, Deuteronomistic Judaism for
   Israel, 28; Mishnah as, 15
Levi, Israel and Rome matched, 123;
   messianic hope, 130, 132

Leviticus Rabbah, 113; Scripture and deductive logic, 137–43
Lewis, Bernard, 55

Maccabees, 63, 114; diversity of Israel, 32, 59
Maimonides, philosophy and classical age of Judaism, 13
Manual of Discipline (Community Rule), 50
Marcus, Ivan G., 165–67
Mendel, Menahem, 168
Messianic hope, 99–150; in age of diversity, 47; beginning of Judaism, 16; biblical prelude to Judaism, 19; Essenes, 50–54; fourth-century crisis, 119–21; Judaism and Palestinian Talmud, 111–12; Sabbateanism, 172
Midrash, beginning of Judaism, 16
Mishnah, 40; beginning of Judaism, 16; between wars of, 66–70 and 132–35, 71–76; character of as a whole, 86–89; formation of Judaism, 62–98; history of system, 67–86; and Judaism, 89–97; law before 70, 69–71; philosophical law code, 15; systemic changes, 106–12; teachings of scribes, 102–3; tradition of, 99–106; years 140–200, 76–86
Monotheism, Judaic theology of, 147–48
Mysticism, Maimonides, and classical age of Judaism, 13

Nahman of Bratzlav, 170
Nathan of Gaza, 177–78
Nehemiah, formation of Pentateuch, 32–33, 41
Nemoy, Leon, 174–75

Orthodox Judaism, 182–86, 189–97

Palestinian Talmud: canon law, 106–7; formation of Judaism, 121–33; Israel and Rome matched, 123–24; Judaism amplifying Mishnah, 15; purpose in Judaism, 110–12; scriptural bases for Mishnaic law, 102–12; symbolism in Judaism, 107–10
Pharisee, 59; beginning of Judaism, 16;

Judaism and sanctification, 54–58, 62–67
Phineas, history of Israel, 126
Pietism, Judaism in medieval Germany, 164–67
Priestly code, beginning of Judaism, 16; biblical prelude to Judaism, 18, 22–23; and model Judaism, 34–40; sanctification, 40–43
Public policy, Judaism and Christianity, 142–47
Purities, cleanness and uncleanness, Mishnaic division of, 69–72, 85–86

Qumran sect. See Essenes

Redemption. See American Judaism, Holocaust and Redemption; Exile and redemption
Reform Judaism, 182, 185–94, 196–97, 201; modern and contemporary diversity, 14; Pittsburgh Platform, 185–89
Restoration, common Judaism of Age of Restoration, 48–49, 58–61
Rome, Israel matched, 123–24

Sabbateanism, 199; heresy against Judaism, 176–78; and messianic hope, 13, 172
Sabbath, festivals, appointed times, 74
Salvation, in age of diversity, 43–48; Essenes, 50–54; Judaic theology and Torah, 149–50; Judaism and hope for, 221–24
Samuel bar Nahman, scriptural bases for law, 104
Sanctification: Essenes, 50–54; Mishnah and formation of Judaism, 62–98; Pharisees' Judaism, 16, 54–58; Priestly Code, 40–48
Scholem, Gershon G., 176–78
Scribes, beginning of Judaism, 16; teachings of, 102–3
Scripture: beginning of Judaism, 16; Leviticus Rabbah and deductive logic, 137–43
Simeon bar Ba, teachings of scribes, 102
Simeon b. Gamaliel, 64
Simeon b. Yohai, 170; messianic hope, 126

Simon, history of Israel, 136
Smith, Morton, 55, 57
Solomon and imperial Israel, 24–27
Solomon Isaac (Rashi), 1, 3
Spinoza, Baruch, 22

Tanhuma b. R. Hiyya; messianic hope,
   130; teachings of scribes, 102
Theodosius II, 114
Torah: in age of diversity, 12; beginning
   of Judaism, 16; biblical prelude to Judaism, 18–24; dual Torah and Judaic
   doctrine, 148–49; Ezra sponsoring
   Torah of Moses, 5–6; Karaism as
   heresy, 172–76; salvation and Judaic
   theology, 149–50; system of Judaism
   retelling, 10–11

Vermes, Geza, 51–53

Women, Mishnaic division of, 74, 78–79
World Zionist Organization, 197, 201–2
Wurtzburger, Walter, 191–92

Yahwistic writings: biblical prelude to
   Judaism, 22–23, 27–28; Judaism and
   imperial Israel, 24–29; model Juda-
   ism, 34–35, 41, 43
Yohanan: messianic hope, 127; teachings
   of scribes, 102
Yohanan b. Toreta, messianic hope, 126
Yose bar Haninah, 222
Yudan bar Shillum, history of Israel, 135

Zionism, 182; and twentieth-century Judaism, 197–207

INDEX OF BIBLICAL AND TALMUDIC
REFERENCES

Page numbers are given in italics.

Bible

DANIEL
9:11, *223*

DEUTERONOMY
12–26, *29*
13:1, *203*
14:8, *136*
17:11, *203*
28, *21*
33:6, *104*

EXODUS
1–24, *23, 25*
16:25, *131–32*
27:20, *223*
32, *23, 25*
34, *23, 25*
34:10–26, *25*

GENESIS
1:1, *23*
2:5–25, *23*
2–11, *23*
2:15, *223*
2:16, *223*
3:5, *1*
3:9, *223*
3:11, *223*
3:23, *223*
3:24, *223*
12:1, *19*
12:10–20, *23*
12–16, *23*
15:13–14, *39*
18–22, *23*
20, *23*
21:11, *135*
21:12, *135*
23:2, *26*
24–34, *23*
26:1–11, *23*
26:34–35, *136*

27:41, *123*
38, *23*
49, *23*
49:18, *221*

HOSEA
6:7, *222*
9:15, *223*

ISAIAH
11:1, *126*
20:34, *125*
21:11, *130*
21:12, *130*
30:15, *131–32*
33:2, *222*
33:15, *135*

JEREMIAH
2:7, *223*
15:1, *223*

JUDGES
1, *23*

I KINGS
22:47, *124*

II KINGS
22, *29*

LAMENTATIONS
1:1–2, *224*

LEVITICUS
4, *81*
5, *81*
5–6, *81*
6, *81*
11–15, *56*
13, *70, 86*
13–14, *56*

14, *86*
15, *70, 72, 86*
19:1–18, *36*
24:2, *223*
26, *21*
26:3, *38*
26:6, *38*
26:34, *38*

MICAH
2:6, *103*
2:11, *203*

NUMBERS
11–12, *23*
14, *23*
16:33, *104*
20–25, *23*
24:17, *126*

PSALMS
60:10, *128*
80:14, *136*
95 :7, *112, 130*
119:176, *104*
130:5, *222*
133:4, *222*

I SAMUEL
2:6, *104*

II SAMUEL
7:8–13, *26*
7:9, *26*
7:9–16, *26*

SONG OF SONGS
1:2, *102*
7:9, *102*

ZECHARIAH
11:17, *128*

Mishnah

ABOT
1:1, *100*
2:4, *159*
3:10, *159*

MOED QATAN
1:5, *158*
1:7, *158*
3:7–9, *158*

SANHEDRIN
10:4, *104*
11:3, *103*

SUKKAH
5:1–4, *158*

Tosefta

SANHEDRIN
13:9, *104*

Palestinian Talmud

AVODAH ZARAH
1:2, *123*
2:7, *102–3*

BERAKHOT
2:3, *124*
2:4, *125*

SANHEDRIN
10:4, *104*

TAANIT
1:1, *130–32*
4:5, *126–30, 132*

Other Ancient Sources

GENESIS RABBAH
LII:XIL, *135*
LXV:I, *136–37*
XCVIII:XIV, *221–22*

PESIQTA DERAB
KAHANA
XV:I, *222–24*

TANHUMA QEDOSHIN
10, *85*